LETTERS
NOW SENT
VOLUME 1

Compiled by Megan C. Norton-Newbanks

"Dear reader: Letters Now Sent is the book you didn't know you needed. While reading it, get comfy and prepare a tissue box as you will find similarities in the stories to your own life: goodbyes, regrets, happy memories... Each letter will remind you of a fragment from a past life, a life you once lived, a place you once belonged, a place you once visited, a place you once called home, or perhaps you will read about the place you now call home, or about a future home... Regardless, this book is going to leave a mark on you. Despite all the things you encounter in your life and in this book, despite all the differences, you will realize for the -nth time that we all experience the same emotions and that the humaneness, the kindness, the gratitude connects us all."
　　　　　−With love, Tess/Little T; Currently in Bulgaria

"This is a wonderful project that allows people around the world to connect and know that they are not the only ones who feel the way they do about being cross-cultural and not fitting in."
　　　　　−Shakti Hannie, author of Colours of a Cultural Chameleon

"At Velvet Ashes, we hold space for stories that are honest and holy, even when they're messy. That's exactly what you'll find in Letters Now Sent. These letters are honest, sometimes unpolished, and intentionally personal—offering readers a window into experiences that are often hidden or misunderstood. Whether you've lived across cultures or are just beginning to understand that kind of life, these letters will move you. They're an invitation to listen deeply, to honor complexity, and to see others—and maybe yourself—with fresh compassion."
　　　　　−Denise Beck, Executive Director, Velvet Ashes

"I remember my first conversation with Megan about writing a letter to my dad. The idea lingered in my thoughts far longer than it took to write. The letter became a way to revisit our conversations when I would drive him to and from airports: we spoke about the world, history, South Asia and its post-colonial challenges. We spoke about our family, our layered identities, and our interconnectedness. Writing the letter was a way to think, look, feel and to consider how he had always encouraged me to find my own way in the world."
　　　　　−Pradeep Rajendran

"Dear Reader: Submitting a letter for Letters Now Sent was an emotional experience. It brought back memories I do not revisit often, but which have formed an integral part of who I am today. I am forever grateful for the opportunity. I'm sure that every TCK who'll read this book will find in some or all of its pages an experience to which they can relate. I can envision us laughing and crying in turns, as we read these letters written by people whose life experiences are in many ways similar to ours."
　　　　　−Love, Joy Adewumi

"Megan, huge thanks to you for organizing this timely "sequel" and letting so many of us actually "send" our letters. And thank you for your continued work to expand resources and empower TCKs/CCKs with your work!"
　　　　　−Erika G. Bertling

"Working with Megan on this project has been really good. Not only has she done the emotional labor to discern a need within our cross-cultural community, but she has also come up with a unique way to bring people together around the topic of writing, sending, and sharing the letters that have been coming together in our hearts for a long time. Sometimes reflecting on our younger selves learning how to navigate novel challenges, sometimes finding clarity about past transitions for the first time. Megan's project is at once a stunning depiction of our unique experiences and a unifying understanding of our shared commonalities. Thank you for your willingness and courage to bring together so many different cultural perspectives into one work of heart."
     –Rebecca Lesan, PhD; JRL Art & Ecology

"This remarkable collection weaves together letters that capture life stories, upbringings, reflections, and deeply personal insights. I found myself rereading some of these stories, marking passages to share with my husband and daughter, and marveling at how perfectly so many writers expressed feelings I've struggled to articulate. Prepare to be moved, to laugh, to recognize your own experiences in these pages, and to feel compelled to pass this book along to anyone seeking understanding and connection in the TCK world."
     –Andrea Schmitt-Lozano, M. Sc. Psychology; GlobalGirlCoach,
       Life Coach for Teen Girls

"Letters Now Sent is an archive of soul and story, vulnerability and voice. Through letters penned to loved ones, this book captures the raw beauty of growing up as a Third Culture Kid, living in the liminal spaces between cultures, languages, and identities. Each letter invites the reader into deeply personal worlds, where belonging is both searched for and redefined.
     –Mariam Navaid Ottimofiore, author of This Messy Mobile Life
       and The Guilty Can't Say Goodbye

"Reading Letters Now Sent felt like being invited into the most intimate conversations of strangers who somehow became friends. Megan has woven together a tapestry of human experience that transcends borders and generations. As I turned each page, I found myself mentally composing my own letters. Letters to my children, to my grandmother, to the parts of my story I've never fully shared. This collection doesn't just showcase the power of written words; it awakens the letter writer dormant in every reader's heart."
     –Hannah Marie Morris, PhD; International Educator and
       Interculturalist

"Take the time to sit and savour this gift—you hold snippets of other brave people's precious lives in your hands and as you enter into their stories, they invite you to engage with yours. What will you do with this gift?"
     –Hannele Secchia, President, Families in Global Transition

What Ruth Van Reken began many years ago with Letters Never Sent has found a valuable bookend in Letters Now Sent."
     –Michèle Phoenix, author of Pieces of Purple: The Greatness,
       Grit, and Grace of Growing Up MK

Letters Now Sent, Volume 1: A Collection of Letters from the Globally Mobile
Compiled by Megan C. Norton-Newbanks
© 2025 Megan C. Norton-Newbanks; Beyond Borders Publishing; Belonging Beyond Borders, LLC

Beyond Borders Publishing

ISBN 979-8-9872111-2-0
eISBN 979-8-9872111-3-7
Cover illustration by David Isiguzo; Rachel Askew
Interior design by Rachel Askew
Editors: Elizabeth Trotter; Anonymous Editorial Team

Additional Books by Beyond Borders Publishing:
- *A Work of Heart, Volume 1* (2025)
- *Belonging Beyond Borders: How Adult Third Culture Kids Can Cultivate a Sense of Belonging* (2022)

To Ruth Ellen Frame Van Reken—a woman of valor,
grit, grace, creativity, wit, compassion, courage,
wisdom, and endless love for humankind. Thank you
for writing *Letters Never Sent*.

To my Dad, Maman, und Bruder—the Norton core four
is forever rooted in eternal change with eternally fierce
love. Thank you for encouraging me to keep following
my dreams.

To برای جان—my sweet husband whose words
comfort, melt, connect, uplift, affirm, and love. Thank
you for journeying with me through it all. C'est toi
aussi pour toujours و برای همیشه.

To the Contributors to *Letters Now Sent, Volume 1*—
you are brave and kind to share your story with readers.
Thank you for writing your letter and including it in
this book.

And to you, Dear Reader—You are curious and caring.
Thank you for reading with the understanding that
these letters contain parts of stories that we are invited
to tenderly hold and learn from.

TABLE OF CONTENTS

Letter writing is the only device for combining solitude with good company.

–Lord Byron

FOREWORD

*A letter….always arrives from the past. There is a
waiting—a forced patience—built into the
mechanics. You wait for a letter to arrive. You wait
for a reply. In the time it takes for the letter to reach
its destination, anything can happen: minds be
changed, lives lost, loves discovered.*
—Jon McGregor

I grew up writing letters. There were the letters I wrote to parents one
day a week during my boarding school years. There were the letters to
grandparents who existed only in two-dimensional pictures and vivid
stories told to me by my mom and dad. There were letters to friends
during winter break written with the fervor and drama of youth, words
designed to communicate just how much I missed them so that the
friendship would survive distance and time.

Letters were such a common occurrence that I thought little
about them until I realized that I no longer wrote or received letters.
As efficient as the new modes of communication were, I missed the
excitement of seeing a letter in my mailbox. I missed the content,
always a surprise. I missed reading about those moments in the
past and responding as though it was the present. The missing was
nebulous, a vague feeling of something not quite right. Except
for holidays and birthdays, my physical mailbox filled up with
advertisements and bills, while my electronic mailbox drove me crazy
with its constant insistence that I immediately respond.

For many years, letters bridged the distance gap and held the
ticket to connection for those of us who lived between. They were

the lifeblood, the glue, the connective tissue to family and friendship. So, when I first heard about Megan's book idea, I was thrilled. Here was a chance to revive this art; an encouragement to think hard about what we wanted to say, to connect through words to those we love, to express things that are not easily said when face to face or on a video call.

In the book *Letters Never Sent*, Ruth Van Reken offered us a glimpse into her world; a world that she longed to share with those she loved. All of this was communicated through letters that she wished she had sent. In doing so, Ruth gave us an invitation to write our own letters, to put down those thoughts and feelings that are difficult to capture in the spoken word. Instead, they find a place on paper, offering both writer and reader a record of those things felt and perceived during a moment in time. But as Ruth shows, they offer so much more. Letters can mend what is broken, heal what is hurting, and affirm friendships and relationships in profound ways.

In this new book, *Letters Now Sent*, Megan carries on the invitation that Ruth started so long ago through a collection of letters from people across the globe. Indeed, there is no one better to invite us into this process, for anyone who is lucky enough to have a friendship with Megan knows she has kept the art of letter writing alive through letters sent with creativity and love. In short, Megan believes in the healing power of letter writing and asks us to do the same.

The letters you will read in this volume are extraordinary. Written in different languages and forms, some are windows into the thoughts of parents of adult children offering equal measures of the guilt and joy of parenting between worlds. Others invite us into gratitude and poignant reflections as adult TCKs write to their parents. Some are glimpses into memories and events, people and places long past. Others are word pictures into today so that the writer will remember this moment in time tomorrow. There are letters to sons, daughters, siblings, and mentors, letters in French and in Brazilian Portuguese, in German and Chinese. No matter the subject, language, or intended recipient, each letter recounts a narrative of human relationships and what binds us together in this life between worlds.

As you read through these letters, grab a piece of paper or a card, your favorite pen, and write your own letter. Make the almost lost craft of letter writing a sustainable art designed to connect, encourage, and offer moments of rest and healing in a frenzied world.

Write your letters, and as William Wordsworth said so long ago: "Fill your paper with the breathings of your heart."

Marilyn R. Gardner
Author of *"Worlds Apart: A Third Culture Kid's Journey"* and *"Between Worlds: Essays on Culture and Belonging"*

Toivon, että olisimme voineet
viettää enemmän aikaa
yhdessä mukavassa
hiljaisuudessa vain
me kaksi.

I carry you in every country
I've landed in, in every border
I've crossed.

Belonging for me today includes belonging
to the very particular geography where
I now live, it's water and land, birds and
trees, people and commitments.

Você tinha apenas cinco meses
quando nos aventuramos a mudar
para outro país.
Foi a melhor decisão que tomamos

Section 1:
Letters Addressed to the
Reader of This Book

I am so grateful that at an early age you
taught me that a strong sense of belonging can be
planted in a very small gesture of kindness

No one grieves things, places, people,
and cultures that meant nothing to them
So for now, cry, as many tears as you want

We can translate the absurd. We can untangle
the lines. We see the shadow and the light
and live in nuance. We have been on
both sides of the door

Stronger Together
Together forever,
in heart
and spirit,
wide and far

This is one of the best lessons from your moving
around: There are many different ways to
do life, which are all good. You can look in
your own life and know viscerally that
life is beautiful no matter how its done

Hello you, dear reader.

I'm Megan, and I'm the compiler of the letters in this book. It's not as simple and straightforward as that, though. There is a deeper story to share.

As the title indicates, this book is inspired by Ruth Van Reken's book, *Letters Never Sent*. It was the first Third Culture Kid (TCK) book I ever read, and I was undone by her rawness, beauty, and love throughout. The way she intentionally left space for self-reflection and processing opened up my heart to reflect on how my own TCK experiences have shaped parts of my worldview and how I move through the world. If you haven't read it yet, I suggest you do, and also read John Barclay's letter (257), in which he responds to Ruth's book.

Ruth's stories catalyzed my pursuit of researching the TCK profile in graduate school, which ultimately led me to become a TCK consultant. In a very real way, *Letters Never Sent* led me to my vocation and continues to inspire me to do this heart-centered work. I love listening to and learning about cross-cultural experiences families have had in moving both within and outside of the countries they call home.

The book you hold now is a way for more people to listen to and learn from people who have crossed cultures. These letters are precious documents that otherwise would typically be written, read, and kept in private. They are sacred forms of communication between the writer and intended reader and touching keepsakes that can remind us of how the written word can express so much love and affection. I've loved reading them, and I hope you will, too.

Ruth has been my mentor, spiritual director, and friend for several years, and I am so humbled that she has commissioned me multiple times to carry on the work of TCK care. At the 2023 International TCK Care Conference in Chiang Mai, Thailand, she spoke about "passing the baton" of her life's TCK work to the next generation, and I was one of a handful of people she literally gave a baton to. It sits on my desk, and I glance over at it in tears as I write this letter to you.

Two years ago I reread *Letters Never Sent* and began dreaming of a book of letters intentionally sent, not in journal format like hers, but for writers to actually send a letter they would want their intended reader to see. I decided to act on this inspiration and reached out to Ruth for her blessing. On June 30, 2023, at the timestamp 4:50pm I wrote:

Hi Ruth—

I have this idea for a writing project / book that I'd like to share with you. And I would like it released on your birthday: July 31, 2024.

I'd like the book to be called "Letters Now Sent" and it'll be a nod to your book "Letters Never Sent." I would like to invite parents of TCKs, TCKs, Adult TCKs, leaders, etc. to be invited to participate. Their invitation is to write a letter to a TCK and to share in it what they would like to say about an interaction they had with them or what they would like to encourage them on or even what they are seeking forgiveness for. I would really like all the letters to be signed by the letter author; not anonymously. But perhaps the Dear [TCK name] could be anonymous.

I envision this book of letters to be authentic, vulnerable, and transparent. I would really appreciate the letter authors to be able to say what they want to say / to be able to say what they perhaps feel uncomfortable to say aloud. I envision the letters being in different languages—the heart languages of TCKs around the world!

I would like your blessing on the title of the book because it's a nod to your very personal book... and a project that I would love for you to bless as well.

Thank you, Ruth.

Kindly,

Megan

Less than an hour later, Ruth replied: *"I am honored and happy to bless this work of your hands, mind and heart and all you invite to join you. A cool idea! And why you need independence to pursue! Thanks for the honor... Love Ruth."*

I missed my goal to get this book out a year ago for her birthday, but I am so thrilled she'll get it on her 80th birthday in July 2025.

It's been encouraging to have her steadfast support on this project for the past two years. In April 2024 she wrote about the book: *"I know it will be a great blessing and treasure for me but also trust it honors your heart and creativity to even think of this."*

The inspiration behind this project is also rooted deeply in my personal life experiences. Letters have been an integral part of my life almost since I was born. Let me explain.

Letter writing was a beloved part of my global childhood.

As a millennial on the cusp of home internet growing up (with the dial-up noise forever etched in my memory), I had snail mail pen pals throughout my childhood instead of friends' email exchanges or DMs through social media channels. Having lived in six different countries between birth and eighteen, I tried to stay connected with my best friends from each place through letters.

The challenge of keeping up with address changes during my moves—and theirs—made it difficult, and unfortunately, I have lost touch with my dear pen pals. However, I still have the letters I received in one of my childhood boxes and enjoy rereading them from time to time. I often wonder if they've kept the letters I wrote to them.

All my life, I have exchanged snail mail with friends and family, often adding one of my favorite surprises in the card: confetti! My friends affectionately call me the "Confetti Queen" and have learned to open my cards over the trash bin to contain the fluttering glitter. One of my friends who received one of my cards recently wrote back, saying, "No one sparkles quite like Megan." I truly enjoy spreading a little confetti cheer in my mail.

One of the reasons I love writing letters is that it allows me to express, in a personalized way, just how grateful I am to be connected with the recipient. While emails, text messages, phone calls, and DMs are all valuable ways to stay in touch with friends and family long distance, there's something uniquely special about holding a piece of mail that someone has carefully crafted and sent. It's a tangible piece of them—a heartfelt artifact.

I save every letter I receive.

It's hard to imagine now, with all the ways we can stay connected, but there was a time when my only means of communication with my grandparents in the US was through snail mail, even into my twenties. I was living in Europe, and with no email, Skype (the platform before Zoom took over!), or smartphones available to them, letter writing was our only option. I would send them postcards from my travels across Europe. When my grandpa passed away and his belongings were being sorted, I discovered a box containing a stack of those postcards I had sent.

I also have a collection of postcards from my childhood. My dad often traveled for work and made a point of sending postcards from each country he visited. I carried on the tradition, mailing postcards from my own global adventures to both family and friends. One of my favorite mailing memories is sending a postcard from the Burj Khalifa in Dubai, where they have a post box at the top viewing deck. In my office, I have postcards, cards, and letters pinned to my cork board. What treasures they are to me!

 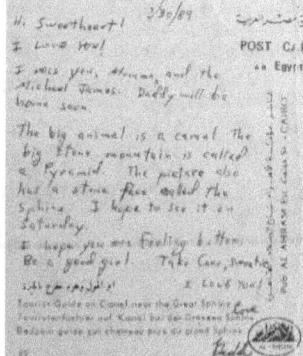

Postcard from my Dad to me when I was a wee baby in 1989.

 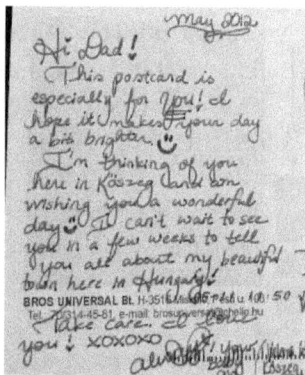

Postcard to my Dad in South Africa from my town in Hungary.

In her book, *Colours of a Cultural Chameleon*, Shakti references these kinds of saved letters. She shares, "I wish I had the other half of these letters, the ones I sent out." She asks, "Have my peers 'Marie Kondoed' away all their memories?" (page 171). I have several boxes of letters, too. And in the process of inviting people to this project, I received numerous photos of boxes of letters showcasing that indeed others have saved their letters.

I think about all the letters tucked away in old boxes now—fragile paper holding fierce emotions, folded memories, silent prayers. We all have our own versions of those boxes, don't we? Those figurative and literal spaces where we've stored our (un)sent words, our (un)read hopes. Quiet corners of the heart, packed full in both figurative and literal places in our lives.

A letter restored my relationship with my own brother.

In my late twenties, I went through a period where I struggled to communicate with my brother. I felt frustrated because he wasn't forthcoming about his life, and it upset me that I didn't know more about both his professional and personal situations, because I knew he was struggling in both areas.

I wanted to support him and be there for him, but it seemed like he had put up emotional barriers—and communication ones, too. Despite my attempts to reach out, I eventually became numb to the lack of response. He changed his phone number, address, and email and wasn't on social media, leaving me without any means to contact him.

This was also the period right after graduate school when I was traveling extensively on a very tight budget. I took US cross-country Greyhound bus trips instead of flying or driving, as I didn't own a car. On one particular trip, a man who had just been released from jail sat right next to me, and he initiated a conversation. At one point he asked if I had any siblings.

I told him about the estrangement between my older brother and me. His tone became urgent and serious. He said, "It was my sister's letters during my incarceration that got me through." Then he added, "Write to your brother. Don't give up on him." I don't remember much about our conversation after that. I just knew I needed to reach out to my brother.

And so, I got his address from my parents and sent a handwritten letter to him.

Letters are also part of my love story.

I married my long-distance boyfriend after dating for two years. While long distance might not seem significant in today's world with various communication methods available, there were unique challenges to our situation. My husband, a man the same age as I am, still uses a flip phone and doesn't own a personal computer. To send a text message, he has to press the numbered buttons multiple times to select each letter. (Gen Z and future generation readers won't even understand what that means.)

Our entire cross-country relationship was maintained through traditional phone calls—no FaceTime or video calls—and letter writing. I felt like an old soul expressing my feelings with pen and paper. He embraced this form of communication, reciprocating with his

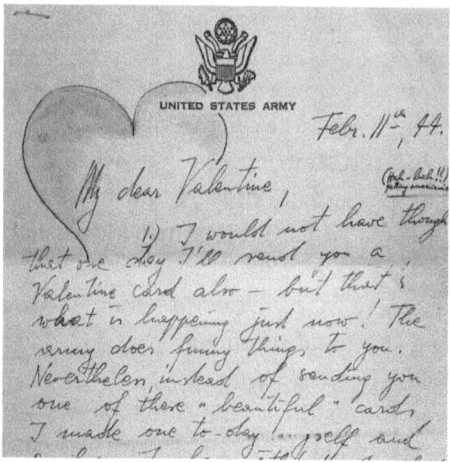
1944 love letter bought at estate sale in 2007.

own handwritten letters.

Our correspondence was a kind of answered prayer to me. Way back in university, one of my best friends visited estate sales and then resold antiques and other treasures she found in those homes. During one of her thrifting adventures, she discovered a handwritten note dated 1944. It was a letter from a US soldier to his "gal" back home, filled with love, concern, and longing. Though some of the words are faded and the cursive handwriting is challenging to read, the heartfelt sentiment shines through. My friend gifted me this beautiful piece, knowing how much handwritten letters mean to me.

This enduring love letter has accompanied me through several countries and homes in adulthood, inspiring me to seek a partner who would write letters like this to me. Although such heartfelt correspondence may seem rare in an age dominated by virtual messages, I believed it was possible to experience this kind of genuine expression of love once more.

During our dating era, my now-husband Bryce wrote me letters on lined paper torn from a notebook, and his romantic gestures made me fall deeply in love with him. On our wedding day, I gave him the tri-folded 1944 love letter that I had cherished for sixteen years, hoping to be cherished in the same way the soldier's beloved was. I told him how I had longed for a partner who would write to me as the soldier had written to his wife. Bryce and I now have our own collection of cards and letters in our couple's box—and yes, there are heart-shaped confetti pieces among them.

I believe in the transformative power of letters.

Certain confessions, affirmations, and celebrations written in letters can have a profound impact on the reader, surpassing other forms of communication. Letters possess a unique ability to touch the heart and be deeply reflective of the author's intentions. Handwritten letters carry a timeless value, offering joy and fostering closer connections.

In a world increasingly dominated by digital communication, which often mirrors the speed at which we process—or fail to process—our emotions, a letter serves as a meaningful gesture to convey depth in our relationships. The enduring power of handwritten communication lies in the special ways people express themselves through this form. Equally moving is the act of reading these words and holding the vulnerability of the writer.

A letter is not just a message; it is a cherished piece of someone's heart. This book contains such pieces of hearts. Handle with care.

A note about the letters you'll find here.

This has been a grand experiment to invite individuals to write letters that will be published. It takes a lot of courage to enter into some of our stories. It takes even more courage to write a public, *published* letter. I am in awe of and have the highest respect for the letter writers. The letters are unfiltered, heart-wrenching, lovely. They show how there are so many different ways of telling our stories and histories.

What remains precious and personal communication between the writer and the intended reader are now cultural artifacts that are compiled for us as a wider audience to have a window into familial worlds that have cross-cultural stories. The personal accounts in this book are lived experiences of people who have complex and interstitial cross-cultural stories to share. In reading these people's letters, we get insight into the nuances of Cross-Cultural Kids' (CCKs) and Third Culture Kids' (TCKs) experiences and some of the impacts of them.

Embodied empathy, compassion, and understanding is what I feel in this collection. I have shed so many tears reading these stories. Tears of understanding, tears of sorrow, tears of wonder, tears of joy. Tears of deep admiration for the writers who have vulnerably and authentically shared their stories, their wisdom, and love with each reader beyond their intended one.

Remember that the authors here are our neighbors, friends, and family. Some of the words you may disagree with, and you may think that certain letters shouldn't have been included for this reason or that reason. Some letters may come across abruptly and some parts of this collection may be triggering to you.

May I suggest you consider what is coming up for you internally that makes you feel discomfort, or sorrow, or hope or ambition, or any range of emotions and reactions when you read a submission. Think about how the letter content aligns or doesn't align with your worldview or life experiences. Think about how the person who wrote the letter is being truthful and vulnerable with theirs and is inviting you into their story. You may want to "label" the writer a certain way. May I ask that you don't, as you don't know their entire story. They've shared only a part of it.

These letters, in their subtle and not-so-subtle content, challenge us to think about our own assumptions, beliefs, and values. They challenge us to step out of our comfort zone and into someone's pain and joy and the complexities of their lived experience. There will be discomfort in reading some of these letters. What we can do as readers is to honor the dignity and self-told truth in them.

One of my mentors recently reminded me, "If it's a real relationship, it's a truth-full one," and I want to stress that these are real people writing from the heart truthfully to us. May we respect the storytellers here and commit to be truthful in our responses. These letters showcase our common humanity and the nuances we need to value. Several times the editorial team and I questioned whether we should include some of the letters as they may be polarizing and misunderstood; but, we decided to include them so that we, collectively, can exercise leaning into stories with respect and curiosity. We are joined here by our passion for stories, not by our passports or self-protection coping mechanisms.

As Marilyn noted in the Foreword, letters sent and received are relics now from the past which we read in the present. In hearing from writers, I've heard updates from them about how their intended reader has responded to their letter included in this book. There has been some re-experienced heartache, pain, and sorrow. Equally, there has been some joy and celebration to know about the impacts of truth-telling. That's the power of letter writing.

I've been witness to how these letters have deepened wounds and/or created stronger bonds. This has been a really unanchoring experience for me; reading through personal mail—at times feeling embarrassed—thinking what right do I have to know these details or what do I do with them? I've had many calls with my therapist, as you can imagine.

I encourage you to read Matilda's letter to you that starts on page 33, as she's a licensed mental health practitioner and I've asked her to write some suggestions about how to navigate feelings that may emerge for you as you read the letters. If you find that reading a letter brings up anything for you that you need additional support in holding, please connect with a licensed mental health provider.

What I find to be true in reading this collection is this: sometimes we need to let things just "be." Let them be messy or magical, unfinished or unhinged. What's true is that the human experience is all of these things, and when we get to witness a tiny sliver of someone's experience, we have the responsibility to respond with care. It's not in our power or control to "fix"; it is within our power and control to consider how we respond.

As you read these letters, please do so with care, respect, curiosity, and love. They hold real emotions from heartache, regret, and pain, but also beauty, hope, joy, and merriment. They reflect the cross-cultural human experience: one that is full of life's deepest paradoxes. I encourage you not to read this book in a traditional, linear fashion. Instead, wander through and between sections. Explore how different paradoxes emerge across the narratives.

Remember, these letters do not contain the whole story from the writer and intended reader. But they do divulge significant parts of whole stories. These are parts of stories that we are invited to tenderly hold and learn from. We get close to people's hearts through them. And in that proximity we see that our humanity is not tidy or clear cut; it's sweet and salty and spicy and at times really sour. It's in this proximity that we may see more likeness than difference. And it's in this proximity that we can learn to build more bridges when the world is building walls. May we send our hearts through post rather than install yet another fence post in self-protection.

We are blessed and honored to read these letters.

May you go gently, dear reader.

always,
Megan

P.S. This is how I recommend to read the letters:

Give yourself time to read. These are words not to be rushed through. Get a box of tissues—tears are going to flow. Maybe make yourself a cup of tea.

With each letter, pause beforehand. Remember that each letter is from a different writer. The letters don't follow any kind of sequence, so treat each letter as its own stand-alone "book" in that the one before and the one after aren't related to the previous one or the successor. Jump around the sections. Read a letter from a parent and then one from a child to a parent, and then one to another family member. The 'letters to younger selves' are powerful to read as a section.

Also, because the letters in this volume have been written by contributors from around the world, punctuation and spelling may vary. These have not been changed to preserve the integrity of each letter.

At the top of each letter, you'll find the location where the writer crafted their letter and the date on which it was submitted to this Volume. At the bottom of each letter, you'll find the writer's full name and a list of cities and/or countries in which they have lived. (Some writers did not include all of the places they have lived.) Reading this geographical information creates additional wonder about the writer's journey. And lastly, you'll notice that some writers have chosen to remain anonymous.

If one of the letters is written in a language you cannot read, you may use Google Lens or Translate with your camera phone to hover over the page. This AI technology will translate content into a language you can read. Please note, however, that any letters translated into English have been done so by the author—not by an automated translation tool. This is intentional, allowing the writer to choose how best to convey their intended meaning. As a result, the grammar, clarity, and flow may differ from a standard English translation. This is a deliberate choice to preserve the writer's original voice and intent.

And finally, a note about the handwritten fonts you'll see on the covers and subsection dividers: the front and back covers, along with the subsection title pages, feature handwritten excerpts chosen by the contributors themselves. Each writer selected a line to handwrite and include in the book. There are also handwritten words I've gotten from family and friends in cards I've personally received. These are from letters actually sent.

Dear Reader,

What a great opportunity Megan has given us all to pause for a moment and reflect on our lives as well as the lives of others with whom we have intersected in countless ways. Thank you, Megan, for inviting us all to join in bringing these sacred offerings of our hearts and souls to you in this collective space.

Why do I believe this type of writing has power and meaning, not only for the reader but particularly for the writer?

Because doing something similar changed the course of my life!

But a word of warning as well. Know that when you write and let the world see it, you have cast your soul to the wind. How people read it, how they respond, can be in completely different ways than you anticipated. That is part of what changed my life.

You see, I grew up as a Cross-Cultural Kid (CCK)—Third Culture Kid/Missionary Kid (TCK/MK) variety specifically. That meant that somewhere I had picked up the idea that if I had enough faith, I should have no pain. If I had pain or grief, somehow that negated my faith.

One day as an adult, in a way I cannot explain, I had an inner vision of Jesus in the Garden of Gethsemane the night before he was crucified. We read in the Bible how he agonized with God, asking if there was another way than the cross for him. That vision changed everything for me. I saw that at his moment of greatest faith, Jesus had his greatest pain. At the moment of his greatest pain, he had his greatest faith.

For the first time, I realized that pain and faith were not antithetical! It gave me the freedom at age thirty-nine to finally look at my life story in a new completeness. Why? Because I didn't need to choose between them. I could look at my story through the lens of both/and rather than either/or.

Why did I need that? Because on one hand I loved my life. Being born and raised in Kano, Nigeria, gave me a deep love for the sound of distant drums beating in the night. Of pounding rain on tin roofs. Of the sandstorm whipping dust and tiny stones onto my face as the Saharan desert landed in our yard at the beginning of each rainy season. Of the smell created as those first drops of rain settled the dusty storm.

So many other things I loved. Climbing the flame of the forest trees where every branch became a different room as I played "house"

Ruth and her sister headed to boarding school in 1952.

there with my friends instead of wherever else other children create their imaginary worlds. Playing soccer each afternoon with the students attending the school my father built literally from scratch— even though the only ball we had was the outside casing of some discarded soccer ball that we stuffed with rags and periodically had to stop the game to put the rags back inside! What now seem like magical moments were normal life to me then.

But then, I lost that world I loved. For me, as for many of you, that particular magic stopped when I repatriated to the USA at age thirteen. No trees to climb, no drums to hear, no wet dust to smell, no soccer to play. (In 1958 most people in the USA didn't seem to know what soccer was!) Snowstorms replaced harmattan at Christmas. Watching American Bandstand on TV each afternoon became the closest I could come to the beating drums of my past.

I sensed the mockery of my eighth grade classmates for my cotton skirts while they wore wool—important to help keep warm in Chicago winters, but what did I know? I, who had felt so confident and secure before, descended into internal confusion. What had happened? Where did I go? Who was I supposed to be now? I only knew through my journaling years later how much I lost when I left the home of my childhood. At the time, I just wondered what was wrong with me and why I was so sad.

When high school started, I reinvented myself. Forget telling these new friends anything about my days in Africa. Try to overlook mentioning that I lived with my aunt and grandma because my parents had returned to Nigeria (except to my closest friends who figured it out when they came to visit me at home!).

Instead, learn to carry my books in the fashionably correct way friends explained to me. Take a bus with them and go to every American football game played by Taft High School Eagles. Learn when to cheer with the rest—even though calling a game football when players mostly used their hands to hold the ball and run didn't make a lot of sense. Join every club that seemed reasonably interesting. Sing with the choir. Stay active with church youth group. When folks asked how it was to have my parents gone for four years, I always said (and believed), "I'm fine. I'm used to it."

Yes, I was the perfect chameleon. And it worked! I had a great time, and I made friends I have kept to this day. Mentally, the African drums had faded to near silence, and the memories felt like a distant dream. By my senior year, I was even voted "Girl Most Likely to Succeed" from my class.

But as I walked up to get that award, a seed of doubt crossed my mind. "Would they have given this to me if they knew who I really was?" And who was I, really?

Roll ahead a few years. By then I was married and working as a nurse, and my husband Dave got a scholarship to do an elective in Africa during his senior year in medical school. How great! We expected to go to Nigeria and work in the city my folks lived in, and I would even have my first baby there!

Shockingly (to me at least!), Nigeria denied us visas to go, and we wound up in Liberia instead. From there we managed to go to Nigeria for Christmas with our new daughter. The oranges were green as they should be, the house I grew up in had shrunk to half-size from my memory, the trees I used to climb had become too tall now, and yet, all seemed quite right with this world. The memories I had hidden resurrected.

When we returned to the USA, David began an internship in St. Louis, often on call every other night. I had a new baby who didn't speak to me, I couldn't stay super busy to numb out any pain as I had my entire life, and I was depressed beyond what I knew possible. I understand it now, but I didn't then. My trip back to Nigeria had lifted the curtain on the world I had so much loved but tucked away in some closed-off space inside. But when the curtain lifted to see that world, with the love came the grief for what I had lost when I got on the airplane to leave at age thirteen.

By grace I survived those years in St. Louis, and we moved on to the U.S. Navy. Dave's schedule was much better, we found a church we liked and made a sense of community with them, and we had our third daughter. Life seemed bright again.

Yet, from time to time this place of silent depression hung over me. I could be quite anxious as well that something terrible was going to happen to my children or others I loved. Mostly, I tried to put it away; others outside of my family didn't see it, and life was again "fine." And in so many ways it was.

We headed back to Liberia with our three children. Open air markets brought back the sights and smells of my childhood. Watching people carry things on their heads felt like home again. I expected to be buried in Africa.

To our shock, one day we woke up to machine guns in our front yard. A coup had taken place. Although we stayed through that, when the new government took over, ultimately they closed both the hospital and government medical school where Dave worked. It seemed time to recalibrate our lives, and we decided we would return to the States for a bit to figure out what was next.

While others in our community were about to go off to boarding school, Dave's parents invited our oldest daughter to come live with them and begin high school in the States so she wouldn't have to change schools a year later. Since I had lived with my grandmother during those years, that seemed better than sending her to boarding school.

Everything made sense—except my old depression returned. My mind and my heart seemed in different places.

One day a woman came to our small study group and talked about inner healing. I asked my friends to pray for that for me. I told them, "I have this perfect life and cannot understand why this kind of depression can hit me so much."

They did, and a few weeks later it occurred to me that I had gone to boarding school at age six, and now our daughter was going to be leaving for school. Could there be any connection?

I had no idea how to pursue that idea, nor were there any therapists around to call. The only idea that came was to try to write to my parents from that moment of first leaving them as a six-year-old.

The rest, as they say, is history. As I began to write, "Dear Mom and Dad..." the feelings of my six-year-old self lying lonely and heartbroken in her bed after the lights were out that first night in boarding school swept over me. The tightness in my chest, the horrible feeling all through my body, my longing for my mommy and daddy... I remembered this was how it felt.

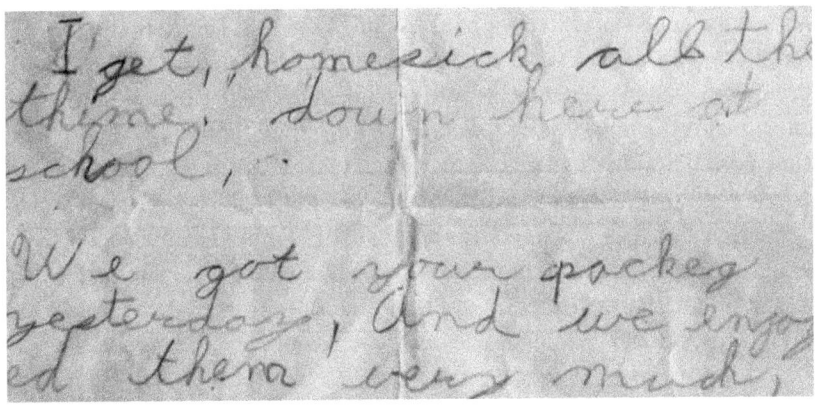
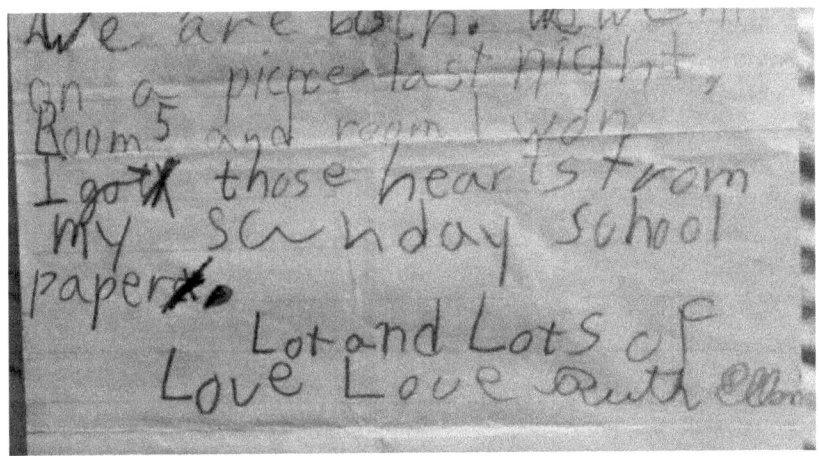

Letters from Ruth to her parents from boarding school. Ruth notes, "Letters to family had to be written every Sunday after Sunday School. No lunch until they were written!"

When it happened at age six, I could only try to push the feeling away. To disconnect. Now, as an adult, I could observe and record those feelings. It was such an odd experience. People asked how I remembered. I always said I didn't remember, I re-experienced it. Someone else corrected me and said, "You didn't re-experience, you let yourself experience it for the first time."

So what did I learn from my journaling? That there was in me an entire layer of grief I had never dared to consciously touch. It was hidden behind all the good of my life... with so much good, how could I say anything was so painful? And yet, if I hadn't loved my family, if I didn't like Nigeria, I wouldn't have grieved so much. We don't grieve what we don't love. Grief was an affirmation of my story, not a denial!

But the next shock was that when I decided to publish it—because I was sure others would love to know they too could have both pain and faith—the response seemed to fit into the either/or categories I thought were past. So many wrote or called and told me their stories, and I heard the pain. Many others, however, thought that because I said I cried at boarding school that I had lost my faith. That I was bitter against my parents and mission.

I was shocked. I wanted to write back to painful reviews and explain I hadn't. My dear mom simply said, "Ruth, you have had your say. Let them have theirs and let it go." That was wise advice, for we do not need to defend our stories. We can simply tell them and be at peace wherever those seeds land.

And so, for many of you, I trust that writing for this project or reading what others have done has unlocked—and will unlock—some deep place within you, perhaps of joy, of sadness, or forgiveness, or celebration. Some of you may want to quit when you get too near the pain, but I'm glad you persevere in writing or reading. There is so much to learn when we move into what we fear or what hurts rather than run from it. And there is much to learn as others respond—or as you respond to the letter that touched you the most!

Thanks again, Megan. Thanks to all who contributed. Thanks to all who are reading. Some things we only learn through writing—or reading what others wrote!

> Ruth E. Van Reken
> Author of *Letters Never Sent: A Global Nomad's Journey from Hurt to Healing* and Co-Author of *Third Culture Kids: Growing Up Among Worlds*

Dear curious reader,

If you've made it here, chances are you are already an inquisitive mind, eager to explore more about what it means to live in constant transition and change. To inhabit the space "in between." To lean into complexity, intersectionality and diversity. That is the most courageous living of all—the quiet, enduring kind of courage. I imagine you are here to not only read about someone else's multicultural experience, but also to delve deeper into your own reflections. To see what resonates, and perhaps, what stirs something new.

While I'd like to think that I have given my own life much contemplation, I recognize that learning how my own experiences as a diplomat's daughter impact me today will forever be a process. One with no true end in sight. Though some memories can feel tender or tangled, I have learned to just be with them, without judgment or resistance. As you read each letter, I encourage you to do the same. I invite you to notice what comes up for you, what you feel both in mind and body, and observe it without judgment, without trying to change or fix it. Sit with whatever comes.

With life in transition, we are often pulled in many directions, cultures, peoples. Our attention is constantly in a myriad of places. I hope you make this read a mindful, intentional one, where you listen to what your emotions and sensations are telling you. Often, listening is the most powerful tool of all. I am sure you already know. In this letter, I hope I can give you some ideas as how to take care of yourself as emotions or reactions come up.

As I've read each letter, I've found myself responding in all kinds of ways, with sorrow, grief, loss, uncertainty, and others of joy, acceptance, humor, nostalgia. At times, I notice myself wanting to avoid or change some of these emotions. Over the years, I've learned processes that help my reactions flow through me, rather than wanting them to change.

I've learned this tool called "RAIN," developed by Tara Brach. It's a process I've taken with me wherever I go that has helped me learn more about my emotions, thoughts, and sensations.

It's important to recognize that sometimes our reactions can be intense and deeply triggering. When that happens, it's completely okay to hold off on practicing the RAIN process—there's no need to rush. For many people, it can be helpful to pause and ground themselves before exploring further. This might mean stepping away for a period of time and taking a few deep breaths or reconnecting with your senses: noticing what you can see, hear, smell, taste, and touch—anything that brings you back to the present moment, to a sense of safety and connection.

Grounding can look different for everyone. It might involve holding a comforting object, focusing on your breath, or taking a familiar walk. Personally, when I feel especially overwhelmed, I turn to a breath practice, wrap myself in my favorite blanket, or take a calming stroll around my neighborhood. These small, grounding rituals help me settle before beginning RAIN with greater presence and care.

I lean into Tara Brach's knowledge as I explain "RAIN" to you now.

R is for Recognize.

Begin by simply noticing. As I read each letter, I notice my reactions, my emotions and the inherent, at times complicated, memories that come up for me. Sometimes, I don't even know what I am truly feeling, but I notice my body reacting—maybe my breath has shifted, my jaw has tightened, or my brow has furrowed. Maybe I'm even distracted and not truly reading anymore. I notice what is happening. I recognize these changes, these emotions, thoughts and sensations that have come up for me, even if I don't really understand them yet. Sometimes, I recognize them by just stating to myself, "Something has shifted."

A is for Allow.

Often, my initial pull is to ignore, dismiss, or push through these feelings, sensations, emotions. Yet, I invite myself to allow. I allow my thoughts, my emotions, my feelings to be there, without judgment, without trying to fix or change them. If I notice judgement, I acknowledge the reaction and allow it to be there without fighting it.

What I find helpful is to create a sense of grounding as I allow. Maybe I set down my book for a while, I put my hand over my heart as I sit with these emotions. I notice my breathing, and slowly begin to breathe deeply, exhale slowly, and allow my emotions to flow through me. I ground myself by noticing my surroundings—a scent, a texture, the weight of my body in a chair. Sometimes, I even speak aloud and state to myself "I'm here," or "It's okay."

I is for Investigate.

I recognize and I allow, and now I gently investigate with care and curiosity. The process in this book is also to engage in your own process and journey. You, curious reader, want to notice what comes up for you with great care and with gentle curiosity. While I investigate, I ask myself questions, such as: "What is coming up for me? How is my body responding? What do I most need right now?" Think of yourself as a gentle, kind caregiver who is trying to understand what needs soothing.

Often, my mind wants to make sense of everything, but often the body knows more. I bring my attention back to the present, to my felt experience in my body right now. I investigate my experience without judgment, with gentleness and safety.

N is for Nurture.

Finally, I nurture. What does this part of me need? I gently, intentionally soothe these reactions with care. I try to sense what this part of me needs right now, whether it be a comforting touch, a hug from me or someone else, a deep breath to let go. I might imagine someone I trust saying to me, "You're safe. I see you. I'm here." And when I can, I say it to myself. I approach that part of me with compassion.

As I step out of my initial nurturing and soothing, I might recognize I need some space and time to process. This journey unfolds at its own pace. I let the emotions settle. I might leave the letters for now. I might take a bath, take a walk, or have a chat with a friend to take care of myself. I encourage you to do the same.

Over the years, I've realized how deeply my TCK experience affects me. These memories — both cherished and complex — can feel overwhelming. Not only because they are the memories I treasure the most, but also because they at times hold me back from fully taking my next leap of faith. This practice has helped me stay present with what is being activated inside of me and respond to it with intention.

I hope it can help you too.

Enjoy your reading,
Matilda Criel, PsyD (she/her)
Clinical Psychologist
Rome; Brussels; Palestine; Washington, D.C.; Los Angeles; Passport Countries: Belgium; Italy; and eventually US

References
RAIN of Self Compassion: Recognize, Acknowledge, Investigate, Nurture (Brach, 2013).
True Refuge (2013) by Tara Brach.

you'll always be my favorite pen-pal. I'm sorry I never got a chance to teach you how to zoom

love THE PEOPLE AROUND YOU

Kaleidoscopes of beautiful colors an ever-changing designs from each place and people who have left their marks on your lives and you on theirs

T'en souviens-tu aujourd'hui, de cet épisode ?

You were not expecting to leave again

Section 2:
A Collection of
Letters Now Sent

A connection to our roots

Those moments opened up worlds within Joe

Each new place can become a piece of home

It's an adventurous thing, isn't it, this life of being a swallow amongst robins?

每一次离别,都是成长的机会

"home" is a constellation rather than a single fixed point

Letters to Children and Grandchildren

Dear Daughter,

I don't know how to start this letter, except to tell you that this is a letter of thanks... and I suppose this is a warning of sorts, that your mother is about to be 'cringe'! But it's heartfelt cringe, my love... so here goes.

When you were born, you blew apart so many of my ideas of how to parent. I'd gathered these ideas from different places around the globe, and together they sounded an incoherent cacophony that your cries shot through with a clarity that saved us. I couldn't do this by simply figuring out the rules, the 'best' way. I had to work with your way. And in doing so, figured out I had a my way too. Thank you.

We were both crying babies. Me in the dust of the Sahara, and you in the green of Staffordshire. But where my cries became the stuff of local legend amongst neighbours, yours were mine to hold behind red brick walls. I often cried with you, often looking for what it was you needed. And so often what you needed was simply me. It's astonishing how often that was my last resort, to simply accept you needed me—to hear you, hold you, and suffer with you. Your cries reminded me of the dignity, the sheer power, of acknowledging need. You were so strident, a righteous knowing that your job was to need, and mine was to be your safety and your comfort. You knew when only hours old of your inherent worth and knowing yours reminded me of mine. Thank you.

Watching you learn how to navigate the world around you has offered me a compassionate gaze on all the maps I have lost, and all the knowings I never knew. We've figured out a lot together; me learning how to parent in a world I didn't know how to be a child in. At every developmental stage we've walked into a new world of cultural norms and expectations, so far from what I knew. Working hard to guide you has gently reminded me of my strength, of all the learnings I had to do on my own. Thank you.

And yet there are some features of the worlds I've walked through that I've tried to bring to our life together—the deep fried fwanke dipped in sugar that you beg me for more often than health would allow, for one. And I've tried to invite openness towards the stranger, especially one in need—though this has been tempered by your instinct for self-preservation, an instinct I had to learn the hard way. You happily dig out the fèves on the 12th day of Christmas, though you avoid the actual Galette des Rois! You have been so tolerant of my attempts to bring my past to your present. Thank you.

The biggest comfort to me though, the connector of worlds I found most precious, was in the fabrics I'd brought with me from Niger. There was a particular cotton print in which I used to carry you, as I had been carried. You would snuggle into my back and sleep and I would breathe a little easier, feeling the bliss of my English child's needs being just as mine had been. Holding you tight helped me hold my story closer. Thank you.

And yet, these shared fragments of story are so few. It's actually very difficult to convey to you the degree of difference in our worlds. For one thing, you enjoy a world of privacy and a lot of free time at home, and with only the people you choose to be with. The individualism of the world we inhabit allows for this, and my own respect for your expressed need backs you up. As an adult now I find myself in need of similarly private spaces—in true 'English' fashion we even recently erected a taller dividing fence in the garden—despite really liking the neighbours! But my childhood was about community—transient community, but community nonetheless. The world of work and leisure overlapped with spiritual community also, and an open home was the default setting.

In contrast, I see you choosing to curate and guard your sense of family with a confidence and sureness that astonishes (and occasionally confuses) me. It's so foreign to me—this confidence you carry that you have 'enough' in terms of your social and emotional world. In the world I lived, where people were always moving and changing, making connections and time together was a way of establishing belonging. And the constant loss meant there was never a sense of 'enough'. Not for me, anyway. You belong simply by knowing this is your place.

I think this is one of the primary differences in our worlds, my love—that you have a sense of territory, and I didn't. Oh, I had the broad view—a sense of the global and where I was supposed to fit into that—but no sense of a corner of my own. Growing up I was routinely admired by adults for my maturity, my 'broad horizons'. But while I was able to see far, my gaze was often squinting to see that which was far from me, the landscapes in the distance. You, on the other hand, taught me the value of a gaze up close. Your chubby child's fist was able to grasp what my TCK heart had been taught to let go of. You taught me the value of the daily, the local, the love of what is here, and now, and mine. Seeing you do it like this has given me confidence to retreat from the crowd when I need to, trusting that being alone is not the same as not belonging. Thank you.

And you continue your lessons, into your teenage years. People used to tell me they could see a sureness in me... that I knew who I was. And to some extent they were right. But with you I'm learning the value of not knowing... not needing to define and defend self, because there is simply enough safety to explore. I didn't feel safe not knowing as a young TCK. The safest thing was to watch and learn quickly, with as much high vigilance as I could muster. There were so many cultural mistakes to make. And the social cost could be high.

I remember critiquing you one day for some minor act of carelessness, and your little face puckered and declared, voice trembling but sure, "But Mummy, I'm a CHILD!" Parenting you has taught me to be kinder to my own child self, who didn't know what you do... that we are allowed to not know. I am learning that I am allowed to not know. Thank you.

And here is the big one... becoming your mother taught me how to stay. My life moving around taught me this, you see... that all love ends. And that was ok, honestly. It was a learning that made me strong in understanding how to survive the loss of love and made me strong too; in knowing it was ok for me to leave too. I padded my heart with the sure and certain sense that no one belongs to me or owes me anything. When friends would fade away I would remember this and feel terribly gracious in not taking their retreat from me personally. And when I saw that I was hurting by staying connected to someone, I knew I would survive the necessary rupture. After all, I had survived so many before. But while my knowing that all love ends protected me from all kinds of pain, it didn't teach me how to stay.

You are relentless in how you love. You have loved me constantly, possessively, persistent in both expectation and your ability to forgive when I fail those expectations. You have taught me about staying-love; a love that doesn't have to choose to stay, staying is instead its default setting. Given that I grew up with a default setting of leaving-love, this is mind-bendingly paradigm shifting. Leaving-love learns to hold love lightly, as a bird in your hand that will choose to fly as soon as it's done with the seeds you bribed it with. This love teaches gratitude, gentleness, and acceptance that as people grow they may evolve needs for new companions.

But here is the magic of staying-love, as I'm learning. Staying-love says, "I will do my growing with you". The staying-love you practise is ever expanding, making space with each new iteration of ourselves. It tells us we are special, unique and irreplaceable. Staying-love says, "I'll leave if I need it, or you ask me to. But I'm going to assume staying until told otherwise." Staying-love audaciously assumes that what was true yesterday remains true today. While leaving-love has me constantly looking for signs we are 'okay', that things are 'good enough', staying-love isn't looking for anything except ways to love better. Staying-love assumes we'll have time to build ever-more beautiful ways of loving. Your love-that-stays insists that there will always be new ways to love and be loved.

Thank you.

I'll stop here now, my lovely girl. There is so much more I could say but I'll stop at 'thank you'.

All my love,
Mummy

———

Rachel Cason
Niger; France; England

Dear Roo,

I watch you across the lines of uniform-clad students at your school's morning assembly. You're easy to pick out: the only blond head in a sea of black and brown and the occasional red hijab. I like coming to your school once a week to coach the new teachers, to encourage them and see them grow. But I especially like seeing your world and catching glimpses of you. I try to avoid visiting your class so I can distinguish my professional role on Tuesdays from being your mom. However, during morning assembly I'm focused on you. What are you thinking and feeling as you sing the words: "My homeland, my love and my heart are for thee?" When your sister graduates to primary school, I picture her belting out the national anthem, fully committed to the statement, but I wonder about you. You've spent most of your life here, yet do you consider this your homeland?

You asked me if you could please dye your hair brown. You assure me no one teases you or gives you extra attention because of your foreignness. But I know you don't like to stand out.

You stopped eating the sandwiches I sent in your lunchbox in kindergarten. When I asked if there was something you would like instead, you replied, "Mom, here's what I really want…you know that rice with the tiny, little makarona? That's what I really want." Local rice, with vermicelli. You were Toula from My Big Fat Greek Wedding eating "moose kaka" surrounded by blond girls eating PB&J, but your "moose kaka" was PB&J.

In second grade you came home wondering why kids kept asking you if you support Issra-eel or Filasteen. People on the street asked us this as well when they found out our nationality, but you as a second grader shouldn't have had to represent your entire passport country and worry about what the correct response was.

You also came home asking if it's true that Christians and Muslims can't marry because that's what some girls in your class scolded you with when they noticed how much you enjoyed playing with Ahmed at recess. I told you about my best friend, Jeremy, when I was in second grade and that it's okay to be friends with a boy and you don't need to worry about marriage when you're seven. I notice you don't talk about Ahmed anymore, and now you have a girl best friend.

Sometimes you word your sentences strangely, and I realize you're translating directly from Arabic. You get "mad from your sister" and things "fall from your hands". At home you speak English with our same accent, but I noticed at school you mirror your classmates' and teachers' English.

I'm proud—and honestly jealous—of you for how flawlessly you speak Arabic to your friends and teachers. I'm especially proud of how easily the words roll off your tongue in an argument. Everyone says you and your sister sound exactly like local children, yet I hear you say you're scared to talk to new people or ask a question in case you don't say it correctly. If only you could see what I see in you, but maybe you wish I could better feel what you feel.

Sometimes you ask me if we can move to the village where our friends live and be homeschooled. And sometimes you long for your passport country, dreaming that life is better there. It's hard to compare a summer filled with cousins and ice cream and playgrounds and no one ever trying to take your picture or touch your hair to your daily life of early mornings to catch the school bus and afternoons filled with homework. In some ways village life and homeschooling would be easier and better. In some ways our passport country and the education system there would be easier and better. Would you more confidently sing that national anthem?

At the end of the day, I find you in your class line. You wave sweetly to your teacher and your friends then run to me. You hug me then we start walking to the car. I'm glad that we live in a physically affectionate culture and that you still like holding my hand. Every time we walk through the school, you seem so comfortable and confident, sharing snippets of your day with me, interrupted by greeting teachers along the way.

I don't know if you consider this your homeland. Maybe some days you do and some you don't. Maybe you won't actually know until you're older or until you live somewhere else. You might never sing the anthem while you live here, and you might long to sing it when you're lying in a dorm room one day on the other side of the world. For now, I can rest, homeland undefined, that you're not trying to hide your hair or disengage from conversations or relationships. You do have a best friend. We've figured out lunches that I'm able to make easily and you're happy to eat. You tell me about funny English phrases your teachers use, and you assure me you don't ever correct them. Isra-eel and Filasteen and Ahmed don't come up anymore, and we can handle new issues when they do.

Love,
Mama

———

Anonymous

46

My dearest Robin,

While I am writing you this letter, you are aged 8. I am not sure whether you're aware of the significance of your current age, but for me it marked a life changing event as I relocated with my amma to India. Can you imagine leaving behind your best friends, and having to start from scratch in a totally new school system on an entirely different continent? Strange isn't it?

Since your birth I have made it a point to travel to India every year. India is my motherland; my amma's land. In the past the two of us travelled together, but this year Papa was able to join. In my loud chaotic Delhi, it was an amazing sensation to notice how at ease both of you were. 'They're making music, amma', you said when I asked you whether the constant sounds of blowing horns didn't disturb your untuned ears. Such diverse worlds, but—like me—you seem to adapt easily to new circumstances and focus on the positive aspects. Is this a trait imprinted in the DNA of cross-cultural kids? I think so.

Robin, we share our country of birth, which is also where we currently live. Unlike you, I have lived in different countries, but you too have parents with different heritages. Do you remember the trip to Delhi where we tried locating my previous homes and we even visited my high school? What you probably don't know is that at the start of my schooling in India I felt alienated. I did my utmost to fit in, to adapt and to be mindful of the Indian etiquettes, but time and again I had the idea that I did not belong. This feeling of not belonging resurfaced often once we moved back to the Netherlands years later. It's tough. In India amma's encouraging words— 'Shakti, be yourself no matter what they say'—helped me through those difficult times. Do you remember the neighbourhood I showed you where in my teens I celebrated festivals from diverse faiths in my own little cross-cultural community with children from all over India? We soaked each other using pitchkaris filled with coloured water during Holi, shared sweets on Eid, and gifted each other presents for Christmas. Now you understand where our family tradition of celebrating the spring equinox, in combination with other festivals originated :-).

During that trip down my memory lane, I came to appreciate that India would always be home. Everything felt so familiar, also the things I disliked didn't take me by surprise. Watching you at ease in a world unlike the Netherlands, it was strange to comprehend that Delhi had never been your home. Do you feel comfortable being immersed in an Indian vibe? You do, right? I feel at home in both, maybe that's why I expect you do too. Having said that, in both countries I sometimes feel odd, misinterpreted or misunderstood. For example, having lived in the Netherlands for the past 25 years, I still find it impossible to describe my experience to family and friends after trips to India. It's the subtleties in the way people behave and the atmosphere which is difficult to describe if you haven't lived in a place. Having lived for a prolonged period during my childhood in both cultures has shaped much of my identity, personality and a desire to create my own little worlds; safe spaces.

While writing this letter I am weighing my words, trying to put my thoughts on paper. It took me a while, and now I wonder why I always find this so tough. I figure it has to do with my fear of 'unwillingly offending others', and also not wanting to be misinterpreted nor perceived as odd and excluded from a group. I have never been discriminated against while living in the UK, US, India and the Netherlands, but still I always had this urge to blend in. I have received my share of hurtful remarks though. My way of dealing with these has always been trying to understand a person's motive or just try to ignore it. Is this fear of being the odd one out a trait that is common in cross-cultural kids?

Seeing the news unfold in the world, I often lose hope and faith in humanity. A feeling of melancholy and world-weariness takes hold of me, which I know is common in many cross-cultural kids. As is our shared love for humanity. So much hurt in this world is inflicted because people don't want to, or are unable to, relate to others and embrace differences. The world is becoming more and more polarized, and parties and presidents are being elected that exclude people based on differences. It breaks my heart to see you grow up in such an inhumane world. I wonder what the world will look like when you come of age. Having watched you interact with adults and children you had never met before has however strengthened me in my belief that I have done something right in your upbringing as a world citizen. You'll be opening this letter when you turn 18. I hope you've held on to your way of approaching the world around you with kindness and curiosity. I feel grateful at the moment that I see this trait in your attitude towards the world at age 8.

Dear Robin, I wish you will grow up in a world without borders, not in one where people are harsh towards others. Discover your true colours—your identity—and be proud of it. 'Be yourself no matter what they say'. Go my dear boy, go and explore the world, meet and interact with people from different cultures and religions, and embrace each other in your differences and your shared humanity. May the cross-cultural spirit stay with you.

> Love you,
> your amma
>
> ─────
>
> *Shakti Hannie*
> *Krommenie, Wageningen, Groningen,*
> *Zwolle, Hengelo, The Netherlands; Delhi,*
> *India; Newcastle, UK; Carhuaz, Peru;*
> *Cambridge, USA*

Dear Grace, minha querida,

I watch as you play with your cousins. One of them uses a word you do not know. Your face scrunches in concentration. You stare. You wait. You absorb the word and work out its meaning. You learn. You adapt and jump right into the circle of giggling, dancing girls again. You amaze me.

I remember the feeling so well, of hearing a word and being unsure what it meant, said in my language, by family, and yet utterly foreign to me. Pronunciation, intonation, definition, all essential to communication and all dependent on location. I notice you correct me if I emphasise the wrong word in a story—"it's always a BEAUTIFUL day for a bear hunt." I wonder how that love for consistency will translate as you grow up in your mobile, transient life. The sweetness of sharing this single sentiment with you eases the pain of not being able to share so much.

You will never see my home in Luanda or the dusty seaside studio where I scuffed up ballet shoes. You will not see the little flat in Malveira and the fresh bread we collected on Sunday. While you splash barefoot in the same garden your father grew up in, there is a life of mine you will never see.

And yet, you will know this displacement and loneliness too. Sharing that with you doesn't feel sweet. It breaks my heart that you will not belong in one place or another. When friends here call you American, in the only country you've ever lived (it's not America) or when family call you English, my heart aches. One day you'll have to answer for yourself "Where are you from?" and you will need to be content when others neither like nor agree with your answer.

You're the third generation of a family of misfits. How do I teach you how wonderful and beautiful it is to be a Third Culture Kid? How do I teach you that not belonging can bring so much freedom and growth and love for the world and the people in it? How do I teach you to be confident in yourself and secure in your identity so that when others ask you that inevitable question, you never waver, you never flinch and retreat as I did over and over again.

I only saw what I lacked—a home, a small town, a life with people who knew me, a house with all my belongings, a simple answer, a single passport, one language. I thought reducing myself to something singular would bring me peace. I thought it would make me fit. I tried to extract myself from the international world. I tried to adopt a new identity, adorned with monocultural influences. Each time someone told me I wasn't quite enough in their eyes; I dug my heels in and tried to be even more.

It didn't work.

The more I exercised the TCK-ness from my heart, the lonelier and more painful life became. The more frustrated I became at myself for not fitting in seamlessly, the more I tried to rid myself of anything odd, anything strange, anything untoward, anything that didn't fit whatever box I was trying to squash into.

I over explained, I underappreciated and hated myself for not fitting. I hated myself for not meeting cultural expectations of friends, family, and community. I wanted out of the box. I wanted a ticket far away from the seemingly impossible task of making myself known and understood.

If I could go back in time, which we never can, I'm afraid, I would shake myself on the floor of my university dorm room, where I lay starving my body and my spirit trying to squeeze into an impossible mould. I would tell myself that being "American enough" is unattainable. I would tell myself that being a patriot is not a requirement for living a life of faith, and that having dual citizenship isn't a flaw.

I would remind myself to practice Portuguese and to read Robert Burns even if no one else understood why. I would tell myself I am a compilation of all and none of the places I have lived.

Because as TCKs, that's true. We're both from everywhere and from nowhere. We're full of lived experiences and void of shared ones. We're a summation of a life others won't understand, one that cannot be retraced but trickles forward in stories, memories, and the ever-present grief for homes left empty.

I want you to know you are so much more than the places you have lived and so much more than the experiences you do not have. You are not limited by not having a hometown and you are not freed by having two passports. It is you, your whole personhood, your compassion, your contagious laugh, your love of games, your thoughtful observations that stack up neatly into Grace, my daughter.

I hope, and pray, that the richness of your international life allows you to throw off the cultural pretences our age is adorned in. I hope you are able to meet people and love them for who they are at their heart, not for what you may or may not have in common.

This is the greatest gift I know as a TCK, to be able to see people unveiled, in their context but not beholden to it, part of a culture but not defined by it. I hope you are able to see yourself in this clarity as well—as an individual, well-travelled, and globally minded yes, and also grounded, secure, known, loved and valued.

I wish all of this, and so much more, for you.

All my love,
Mumma
————

Iona Marcellino
Scotland; United Kingdom; Portugal;
Angola; Middle East; Tennessee,
Mississippi, USA

June 18, 2025
Lisbon, Portugal

Dear Mina, Mikail and Miro,

I don't think I've ever written a letter to all three of you together, but this could be the start of a lovely new tradition. As I watch the three of you frolicking in the waves at our local beach on a sunny weekend, I can't help but think of how incredible your global journeys have been. Mina, your first swim was in the South China Sea when you were born and grew up in Singapore. Mikail, your first swim was in the warm water of the Persian Gulf since you were born and raised in Dubai. And Miro, you first dipped your toes in the icy Atlantic Ocean which is a must being born and raised in Portugal. The three of you were born in three different countries more than 3000 miles apart, but you all share your love for living by the ocean.

That's not all you share, though. You come from a rich and multicultural family. With a TCK mom born in Pakistan and raised in Bahrain, the United States and Pakistan, I often rejoice in the similarity of our TCK experiences of growing up around the world and learning new languages from birth. Of course, you know that Papa grew up cross culturally and bilingually in Germany too, with a German mother and an Italian father from Sicily. When we met in the UK, got engaged in the US, got married in both Germany and Pakistan, and started our married life and careers in Denmark, we knew we were creating something special, but nothing could have prepared us for just how special the three of you would be!

I still remember the day when you came home from school Mina in Dubai, you must've been about five years old and you turned to me and said, "There's a new girl in my class, but guess what Mama? She said she speaks the SAME language to both her parents. How weird is that?" Papa and I chuckled out loud because we loved the fact that we had made multilingualism such a norm for you within our home and through our globally mobile lifestyle, that now it was the opposite that you found strange. Mikail, you were the same, when you were at a playground in Wolfsburg, Germany you struck up a conversation with another kid, but you couldn't believe he had lived in Germany his whole life. You were living in Africa at the time as we had just moved to Accra, Ghana and you couldn't reconcile your childhood with his. "Why do some kids have to move but others don't?" you asked me. I remember telling you how privileged we were to live in so many different countries but agreed that it was often very difficult to move and say goodbye to your friends repeatedly. I'm glad we have always been able to communicate honestly and openly and share with each other how we truly feel and accept all the good, bad, ugly, beautiful and messy emotions that come with constantly creating a life on the move.

Through all our international moves so far, I take so much pride in seeing how you have embraced each culture, each country, each cuisine and made friends from all around the world. Your adaptability, resilience and grit have been incredible. You even moved countries in 2020 in between a global pandemic and went to a new school, in a new country, in a mask on your first day. I'm sorry I couldn't be there for you that day, Mina, and Mikail. Miro's early birth in Portugal at 30 weeks and then his subsequent NICU stay at the hospital was so stressful for us all. Miro, when you were in the NICU, you weighed less than a kilogram and I was worried sick about whether you'd live because you couldn't breathe on your own. But then one day, a nurse saw you kick off your tiny sock inside your incubator. She put it back on you, and you kicked it off again. "This one is a little fighter; he'll be just fine!" she laughed and today I marvel at how true her words ring. You are not only fine, but flourishing. To this day, the sound of Portuguese calms you down.

I know that being part of our multicultural, multilingual and multi-mobile family has not always been easy. Sometimes you struggle to show different parts of your identity. Sometimes you confuse people by speaking German and celebrating Ramadan and Eid. Or by speaking Urdu and Portuguese and celebrating Chinese New Year. But this multiplicity of holidays, traditions and cultures is exactly what Papa and I always hoped you would embrace.

Since October 7, 2023 it has been tough to raise you as Muslims living in the West, because you have felt extra scrutiny on this part of your identity. You have asked me some difficult questions:

"Why do some people not care about Muslim and Arab lives being lost?"

"Why do some people think it's controversial to speak up for Palestinian children?"

"Why do some people value one human life more than another?"

And I have not known what to say to you. The truth is, that it has brought up my own trauma of living in the US post 9/11 as a brown, female, Pakistani, Muslim who often had to hide this part of my identity. It has been troubling to realize that the values that I share and have taught you such as empathy for all, human rights for all, and peace and justice for all are not practiced by everyone. This selective humanity that has been on display since Oct 7th has made me despair. What good is all our international experience and the fact that we have lived and loved in ten countries around the world, when we cannot recognize the humanity in one another?

My wish for the three of you is that you never lose sight of this humanity, that you deliberately reach out to those who are different from you, that you continue to build bridges and not walls, that you remember that people are not their governments, and that you continue to speak up about what you believe in. I have full faith in the three of you to carry this torch forward and pave the way for a better world for us all.

With all my love,
Mama
———

Mariam Navaid Ottimofiore
Bahrain; New York, Massachusetts, Texas,
United States; Pakistan; United Kingdom;
Germany; Denmark; Singapore; UAE;
Ghana; Portugal

April 2, 2025
Auckland, New Zealand

Dear Jessica and Samantha,

As I sit down to write this letter, my heart swells with pride and love for the incredible young women you're becoming. Born in the vibrant cities of Mumbai and Delhi and having spent your early years exploring the diverse landscapes of Chongqing and Taipei, you've truly embodied the spirit of what it means to be Cross-Cultural Kids.

I remember the day we arrived in Chongqing, China. Jessica, you were just five years old, wide-eyed and curious about everything around you. Samantha, barely three, you toddled along, mimicking your sister's excitement. The way you both embraced the new sights, sounds, and smells of the city with such openness still amazes me. That first week, when we visited the local market, you fearlessly tried new fruits and vegetables, giggling at the unfamiliar textures and tastes. Your willingness to dive into new experiences head-first has been a constant source of inspiration for us as your parents.

Moving to Taipei two years later presented its own set of challenges, but your resilience shone through. I recall the day Jessica came home from school, frustrated because she couldn't keep up with her new classmates in class. Instead of giving up, you created your own style of learning, showing an incredible adaptability that would serve you well in the years to come. Samantha, you followed suit, picking up Chinese phrases with an ease that left us all in awe.

Your journey as Cross-Cultural Kids hasn't always been easy. There were tears when we had to say goodbye to friends in each city, moments of confusion about where "home" really was, and times when you felt caught between cultures. But through it all, you've demonstrated a strength of character that goes beyond your years.

The resilience you've developed is a gift that will carry you through life's challenges. You've learned to adapt to new situations with grace, to find common ground with people from all walks of life, and to see change not as a threat, but as an opportunity for growth. Your openness to new experiences has cultivated a curiosity about the world that I hope you'll never lose.

One of the most beautiful things I've witnessed is your willingness to embrace new people. You've formed friendships across cultural and language barriers, showing that connection goes beyond words. Your ability to see the humanity in everyone you meet, regardless of their background, gives me hope for a more understanding and compassionate world.

Your interest in the world around you has blossomed into a deep appreciation for diversity. You've learned to celebrate differences, to ask questions with respect and genuine curiosity, and to see the world through multiple lenses. This global perspective is a superpower in our interconnected world.

As you continue to grow and forge your own paths, I want you to know how proud I am of the Cross-Cultural Kids you are. The experiences you've had and the strengths you've developed are unique and valuable. Embrace your multifaceted identity, for it is what makes you truly special.

My hopes for you are endless. I dream that you'll continue to approach life with the same openness and enthusiasm you've shown since those early days in India. I hope you'll use your experiences to bridge divides, to foster understanding, and to make the world a little bit smaller and a lot more connected.

Remember that your story is one of richness and complexity. There may be times when you feel caught between cultures or unsure of where you belong. In those moments, I want you to know that you belong to the world. Your home is not confined to a single place but exists in the connections you've made and the experiences you carry with you.

Jessica and Samantha, my beautiful girls, you are living proof that home isn't just a place—it's a feeling, a collection of memories, and a tapestry of experiences. Your journey has shaped you into compassionate, adaptable, and globally-minded individuals. As you continue to navigate this complex world, know that your unique perspective is your strength.

You are the bridge-builders, the peace-makers, and the global citizens our world so desperately needs. Your ability to see beyond borders and to find common ground with people from all walks of life is a gift. Use it wisely, share your stories, and never stop exploring.

With all my love and admiration,
Mum

———

Emily Rogers
Clare South, Western Australia; Wellington,
Timaru, Christchurch, Auckland, New
Zealand; Hong Kong; Mumbai (where
Jessica was born), Delhi (where Samantha
was born), India; Chongqing, China; Taipei,
Taiwan

February 23, 2025
Ethiopia

To my TCK valentines,

For us, your parents, the most terrifying part of a big international move to a developing country was wondering how our children would do. A number of people asked us: "But what will you do with your kids?" and they were surprised when the answer was bring them with us!

We have been outside of the American mindset, its beauty of resources but also its child centric society for six months now and we have grown increasingly grateful for your lives here. There are so, so many benefits: outdoor play with many friends, international school, cultural awareness, fresh food... but one of the biggest benefits is the lack of benefits. Your favorite snacks are not always available, sometimes there is cheese and milk in the store and the next week none. Car rides are dusty with no air conditioning. The power will often go out during a favorite movie or football game. You navigate levels of poverty many have never seen, much less even contemplated.

We feared your happiness and your childhood would be taken away with your comforts. But instead of tears and detachment, we have seen flexibility and resilience grow while joy and connection remain. Sure, you can still whine, but you eat with your hands no questions asked, the holes and mud hills in the ground have become your "ninja warrior course", and even you, my two-year-old, know how to quickly kill a big bug in the house (which I am SHOOK by). You are excited when your favorite fruit is available and flexible when it's not. You stop to give a beggar a banana and see the child without shoes. You wait patiently as we go through all the Amharic greetings with a friend. You know how to play with other kids using just body language and a soccer ball.

We know from our own stories that many of the memorable parts of life were when we chose the harder thing. We are thankful you are safe, you belong, you are loved, you have fun, AND you are gaining the often-underrated tool of grit. We hope you are learning how loved you are and who you are, while also realizing that the best life is one that is not all about you anyway.

Cheers to Ethiopia for helping me raise you, my courageous kids.

Proud of you,
Your mom

———

Jenny Browne
USA; Ethiopia

58

January 27, 2025
Madrid, Spain

My Dear Madrileña,

Every sound of your home is foreign to my ears. From the screaming, groaning metro to the nearly silent park swing. The singing in the church is full of people from every country but the one we are in. The crunch of my pan con tomate and the pressured escape of the steam from our cafeteria. To your 7-month-old ears it must be a strange and fascinating symphony. So many sounds swirling together into a beautiful whole.

But by human bias, I filter it all as lesser than my own home. As something subpar. I miss the sounds of steeple bells and open green backyards rustling in the wind. The sound of the car engine starting every day when we left the house. Angry dogs barking and trampoline springs creaking. I miss these sounds because they were the earliest sounds I knew.

The sounds of Madrid will be the sounds of your first home. And I often wonder what this place will feel like to you once you are old enough to understand. Once you can name the things you hear and ponder how they shaped your experiences.

If God allows, we will leave this place when you are two, to be near your grandparents. But I know that someday you will make your way back. Back to your concrete roots. To the raucous sounds of community in the center of Madrid. When you finally make your return, I hope that everything you hear makes you feel like you belong.

Whether or not that hope comes true, there are two beautiful groups of sounds that can come to new homes with you. One is the voices of loved ones. This generation we can talk to our loved ones in many parts of the world any time they are awake. The sweet caress of words of love. The gruff and important correction. The bonding over soft tears. We have brought the sound of loved ones from near and from far into your life and I hope you will choose to seek these sounds as long as you and they are on this Earth.

The other borderless collection of sounds is music. I do not think anyone has fully explored how music streaming has changed our world. We can summon a song for any attitude, any challenge, any celebration from nearly infinite options. Use this blessing with wisdom and it will add immense well-being to your life. Sometimes that means worship songs and sometimes that means NPR Tiny Desk concerts after school. Some days we need violins to reach our full potential and others need brash wailing guitars.

There is one more thing I hope you hear from this day until the day you die. Something you must hear without ears. Something we often disvalue since it is so hard to notice. That is the all powerful voice of God singing over you in whatever land you find yourself. Listen for this inaudible song in the middle of your everyday rush and fears.

Especially when you feel there is no one country that can contain you or you feel you might not have any place to call home. God will answer you:

"I will tell you where your home is. You are my chosen child, and your home is right here with me."

Dad

———

Robert Timlin
Pennsylvania, U.S.A.; Madrid, Spain

Dear Judah,

"Mama, I want to be black or play inside all day," you announced to me when you were five years old and still new to this country called Tanzania. Even at that tender age, you realized you were different. Foreign. And you decided there were two solutions to your predicament: either fit in or hide. And even now, at the age of 13 and entering manhood, I'm sure those same feelings still surface sometimes.

When we first told people that we had decided to move our whole family to Africa, their usual reactions ranged from incredulous to upset about the irresponsibility of taking children to a developing and potentially dangerous country. There was one man, however, whose response will be in my memory forever.

"What a rich life!" he said.

Yes, there is the heat and the bugs and the looming cloud of malaria and other diseases we wouldn't have to worry about somewhere else. Yes, there is the moving around and uprooting and the fact that you have lived in 12 homes in your short life. Yes, there are the many goodbyes and the leaving behind of family and friends. And yes, there is the fact that you will always look different, act differently, and be a foreigner in this country we have chosen to call home, even after years of learning and adapting and growing deeper roots.

But let's not forget how rich such a life can be for you.

It is rich because you experience a world much bigger than your own. A world that goes beyond your Western roots and cultural ideas. A world that pushes you to really explore the nature of Truth and goodness beyond what your culture says.

It is rich because you had to quickly realize that "our way" isn't the "right way." Here, we only use our right hand to eat or pass things. Not wrong, just different. Here, I only wear skirts and dresses and cover my head. Not wrong, just different. Here, you play with soccer balls made out of old plastic bags. Not wrong, just different.

It is rich because you get the prime opportunity to learn another language and culture. It is a gift that we hope will accompany and bless you for the rest of your life.

It is rich because you are learning to respect your elders, a value often lost in Western culture. It has become second nature to you to greet anyone older than you with "Shikamoo," to give up your seat for an elderly person, and to respond respectfully when spoken to.

It is rich because you have met some amazing, I-want-to-be-like-them-when-I-grow-up kind of people from all over the world. You have had dinner with mission organization presidents and marveled at their humility as they sat and read picture books with you on the couch; you have celebrated with us over the amazing generosity of the saints as they support us financially; you have received loving and thoughtful care packages from people you had barely met. What a gift.

It is rich because you experience nature and wildlife in amazing ways. Exploring tidepools by the ocean, catching lizards, sitting on the grass next to zebras, finding stray leopard tortoises, and witnessing a baboon stealing coconut cookies from our kitchen.

It is rich because you learn to love people very different from yourself—different in skin color, different in culture, different in daily habits. May this prepare you as a member of the global church, where people from all tribes and tongues are part of one family.

Remember, my son, through the hardships and the losses, that it is a blessing, truly, to enter another person's world. It is a privilege for you to experience a world so different from your passport countries and find belonging there. It is an honor to be invited into someone's home and someone's life, as a guest and a foreigner. It is incredibly enriching to call someone so very different from you 'friend.'

In those moments when you just want to fit in or hide—may the Lord grant you strength to look up, see his rich blessings, and do the next right thing.

Your Daddy and I are with you, every step of the way.

Love,
Mama

———

Asmara Anyan
Germany; USA; Tanzania

"Buono mamma" dice Lorenzo (12 anni), assaggiando le prime penne alla besciamella che ho preparato per questa cena in Lake View, Milwaukee. La nostra ultima sera di otto lunghi anni in questa casa che ci ha accolto e visto crescere. Claire (10 anni) fa un cenno di approvazione e Thomas (14anni) sorride, per la prima volta in settimane. Più tardi facciamo un giro per le stanze e fissiamo i ricordi che porteremo con noi.

Carissimi figli,
  Avrei voluto trascorrere così la nostra ultima sera a Milwaukee, preparati con questo rito di congedo a partire e continuare. Invece mi sono fatta prendere dagli imperativi della logistica e abbiamo fatto tutto un po' in fretta. Per fortuna papà aveva organizzato la limousine di lusso, con tanto di frigo bar e siamo tornati a sorridere.
  So che tornare in Europa per voi non è stato facile, l'ho sempre saputo. Quello di cui non ero coscente prima di scontrarmi con le vostre incertezze identitarie e di leggere e ascoltare sul tema del dolore irrisolto per perdite piccole e grandi legate all'espatrio, era l'importanza del discorso aperto. E me ne dispiace! Ho avuto paura di attizzare fuochi di tristezza che speravo spenti, non sapendo che dare spazio, normalizzare la situazione e collocare i sentimenti anche quelli negativi fa' bene. Altra generazione? Possibilmente solo impreparazione! Se potessi tornare indientro, vi chiederei senza paura: "come state?". Vi parlerei della mia di nostalgia ad esempio dei brunch domenicali dei miei anni a Quito, che finivano sempre in feste danzanti, o della vista aperta sul lago Michigan che avevamo a Milwaukee, invitandovi a condividere i vostri sentimenti. Ho confuso in passato il dovere che sentivo di prendermi cura di voi con il contenimento della vostra libertà di essere tristi.
  Allo stesso tempo ho notato con gioia—e me ne ricordo nei momenti difficili—che avete sviluppato una grande curiosità verso il nuovo, una profonda capacità di osservare e di accettare comportamenti diversi. Quello che ammiro di più è soprattutto il vostro spirito da protagonista nei confronti della vita che avete conservato dagli anni negli Stati Uniti e la vostra capacità innata di adattarvi, di sfoggiare il registro austriaco se siete in Tirolo, un certo "understatement" se siete circondati da italiani e la comunicazione chiara per il vostro quotidiano in Germania.

"Grazie mamma per averci fatto crescere trilingue" mi è stato detto qualche mese fa. E questa frase mi ha tolto un gran peso dal cuore. Viaggiare è sempre stato importante per me, una seconda natura, sostenuta da letture di ogni tipo. Credo nella ricchezza di uno sguardo decentrato che accoglie altri modi di vedere e vivere la realtà che ci circonda. So che non è ancora facile per voi rispondere alla domanda "di dove sei" ma avete gia la vostra strategia e l'orgoglio di aver avuto un'altra esperienza si fa pian piano sentire.

Io non avrei potuto vivere la mia vita in modo diverso, sono sempre stata nomade anche prima di spostarmi con voi per il lavoro di vostro padre, soprattuto per la mia curiosità verso altre culture, perchè credo nel potere trasformativo del viaggio. Riconosco che ci sono degli svantaggi e che non è sempre facile, soprattutto agli inizi. Anche ora che voi avete cominciato a vivere la vostra vita da giovani adulti in altre città più o meno lontane e che noi ci siamo nuovamente spostati, mi rendo conto che è difficile dire "torno a casa per il weekend". Ma questo ci dà la libertà di scoprire nuovi posti, di incontrarci spesso senza il peso del quotidiano in una città che scopriamo insieme e che ci permette di "ritrovarci". Perché credo che questo sia l'approccio positivo alla nostra esperienze multiculturale: si tratta di continuare e non di ricominciare, di tessere insieme e non di abbandonare, di tener cura con scelta e determinazione (in modo costruttivista si direbbe) di noi stessi e delle nostre radici.

Con l'affetto di sempre,
Mamma

English Translation from Carmela:

"This is so good, mamma" says Lorenzo (12 years old), tasting the first penne with béchamel sauce I made for tonight's dinner in Lake View, Milwaukee. It is our last evening in the house where we've spent eight long years, a house that has welcomed us and watched you grow. Claire (10) gives a small nod of approval, and Thomas (14) smiles for the first time in weeks. Later, we walk slowly through the rooms, fixing memories we are going to carry with us.

My dearest ones,
I had hoped we could spend our last evening in Milwaukee like this, preparing ourselves with this farewell ritual to leave and continue our journey. Instead, I got caught up in the pressing demands of logistics, and we ended up doing everything a bit hurriedly. Luckily,

Dad had arranged a luxury limousine, complete with a minibar, and that's when we found our smiles again.

I know that returning to Europe hasn't been easy for you, I always knew that. Before confronting your identity uncertainties and hearing about the unresolved grief from losses, both big and small, tied to relocating, I didn't realize how important open conversations are. And I'm sorry for that! I was afraid of stirring up sadness I hoped had been put to rest, not knowing that giving space, normalizing the situation, and putting even difficult feelings in their place actually helps. Another generation? Perhaps it was simply a question of being unprepared!

If I could go back, I would ask you without fear, "How are you?" I would tell you about my own nostalgia, for example, the Sunday brunches from my years in Quito that always ended in dancing parties, or the wide-open view of Lake Michigan we had in Milwaukee, inviting you to share your feelings. In the past, I confused the duty I felt to take care of you with setting boundaries to your freedom to be sad.

At the same time, I've noticed with joy—and I remind myself of it in difficult moments—that you've developed a great curiosity for the new, a deep ability to observe and to accept different behaviors. What I admire most is above all your protagonist spirit toward life, which you've carried with you since your years in the United States, and your innate ability to adapt: to bring out your Austrian tone when in Tyrol, a certain understatement when surrounded by Italians, and clear communication for your daily life in Germany.

"Thank you, Mom, for raising us trilingual"—one of you told me a few months ago. And that sentence lifted a great weight off my heart. Traveling has always been important to me, a second nature, nurtured by all kinds of reading. I believe in the richness of a decentered perspective, one that welcomes other ways of seeing and living the reality around us. I know it's still not easy for you to answer the question "Where are you from?", but you already have your own strategy, and the pride of having had a different kind of experience is slowly beginning to show.

I couldn't have lived my life any other way; I've always been a nomad, even before moving around with you for your father's work. What drove me above all was my curiosity for other cultures and my belief in the transformative power of travel. I recognize that there are downsides and that it's not always easy, especially in the beginning. Even now that you've started living your own lives as young adults in cities more or less far, and that we've moved again ourselves, I realize how hard it is to say, "I'm going home for the weekend." But this gives us the freedom to discover new places, to meet up, often without the weight of daily life, in a city we explore together, one that allows us to truly "find each other" again.

Because I believe this is the positive way to look at our multicultural experience: it's not about starting over, but about continuing; not about letting go, but about weaving things together; about caring, choosing with intention and resolve (what one might call a constructivist approach), for ourselves and for our roots.

> With all my love, always,
> Mamma
> ———
>
> *Carmela Masecchia*
> *Naples, Rome, Italy; Brussels, Belgium;*
> *Berlin, Stromberg, Stuttgart, Munich,*
> *Germany; Michigan, Wisconsin, U.S.A;*
> *Schaffhausen, Switzerland*

To Our Boys,

Long before you came into our lives, your dad and I set out on an adventure. We were pulled by a feeling, an instinct that the world had more to offer than what we knew. There was something about living among different people, hearing other languages, trying new foods, being strangers and learners at the same time, that stirred something deep in us.

The longer we stayed out in the world, the more we felt we had stumbled into the journey of a lifetime. We weren't just seeing places; we were changing. The world kept calling and we couldn't imagine turning back.

Then, something incredible happened: we became parents. We became your parents. First Arlo, then Lachlan.

And the world that had once embraced us with wide arms, now embraced you, too. Suddenly, it wasn't just about the food, the languages, or the landscapes. It was about seeing it all through your eyes. Watching you take your first steps in unfamiliar places, seeing how your hearts stretch across countries and cultures, that has been our greatest privilege.

We kept exploring. Not because we were searching for something missing, but because we kept finding more. More beauty. More connections. More of what it means to be human. We built a home base in the U.S. to anchor us, to give us a place to return to, to stay connected to something constant. But we never stopped moving forward. And you came with us, always.

We see what you're learning every day, lessons no classroom could teach. You are becoming humans who understand difference not as something to be feared, but as something to be celebrated.

As you grow up in different parts of the world, you're not just seeing new places—you're experiencing the systems that shape people's lives in ways that aren't always fair. You're witnessing privilege, inequality, and oppression up close, things that are often easier to ignore from the comfort of our own homeland. This awareness isn't always comfortable, and it certainly wasn't something we fully grasped until our own lives expanded beyond what we knew growing up.

We talk about privilege openly in our family, not to incite guilt, but to foster understanding and responsibility. We name it when we see it. For instance, we discuss how your passports grant you access and safety that many don't have, or how the language we speak at home opens doors in various parts of the world. We also point out the unearned advantages that come with being part of a majority culture in one place, and how that can shift when we are the minority in another. We ask questions like, "Who benefits from this system?" or "Who might be excluded here?" during our daily lives, whether it's observing public transportation in a new city or understanding different educational opportunities. We actively seek out diverse perspectives, from the books we read to the people we engage with, making sure to hear voices that challenge our own assumptions. Our goal isn't to have all the answers, but to constantly be learning and evolving our understanding of how power and advantage play out in the world.

We hope you begin to understand that success doesn't only come from working hard, it also comes from a mix of luck, access, and the unearned advantages that some are born into and others are denied. Many of the systems we live in were designed by those in power to keep that power. But awareness is the first step toward change. We hope you carry that awareness with you. We hope it shapes you into individuals who ask better questions, who stand up for others, who challenge the status quo with empathy, and who believe that a better, more just world is worth working for.

We hope you will use your voices to advocate for those who cannot, and that you will share your resources, time, and empathy generously. We hope you seek out opportunities to learn from others' experiences, especially those vastly different from your own, and allow those stories to deepen your compassion.

You are learning that the world is big, and small, and wonderfully complex. You are growing up as Cross-Cultural Kids, navigating borders, building bridges, carrying many homes inside you at once. You demonstrate incredible courage every time you adapt to a new school, make new friends, or navigate unfamiliar social norms. And the connections you forge across continents are truly remarkable, building a network of global citizenship that many will never know.

But we'd be lying if we said it's always easy.

Sometimes, we wonder if we've asked too much of you. If we've taken away more than we've given. We know there are moments you feel the ache of distance, or the confusion of not quite belonging anywhere, and everywhere, all at once. We know that missing people, places, and parts of your identity can be heavy to carry.

Yet still, we believe deeply in the life we're giving you. A life without rigid borders. A life where you can connect, adapt, empathize, and lead. A life where home isn't just a place—it's a feeling, a people, a story you'll always carry with you.

Your ability to adapt, to empathize with diverse perspectives, to communicate across cultural divides, and to see the interconnectedness of humanity gives us immense hope. You are natural bridge-builders, fluent in the language of shared humanity. You understand that "home" can be a mosaic of experiences and relationships, and that this fluidity allows for greater acceptance and less judgment. In a world often fractured by division, your unique upbringing equips you to be agents of unity, understanding, and positive change. We believe these skills will empower you to not only navigate the complexities of life, but to actively shape a future where everyone has the opportunity to thrive.

In fact, this past year, both of you received awards from your schools that speak directly to the kind of humans you are becoming. Arlo, your community recognized you for being principled, demonstrating integrity and a strong sense of fairness. And Lachlan, you were acknowledged as a risk-taker, willing to explore new ideas and approaches with courage. We see these qualities growing in you, and they give us such hope.

And through it all, please know this: You are our greatest adventure. You are our home.

>With all our love,
>Mom and Dad
>———
>
>*Kirsten and Andy Pontius*
>*Tblisi, Georgia; Phnom Penh, Cambodia;*
>*Bucharest, Romania; Abidjan, Cote*
>*d'Ivoire; Lusaka, Zambia; Naktsu, Japan;*
>*Singapore*

Dear boys,

We've talked so many times about change. We've experienced big hard changes, our little family unit. One of the prices we pay with this foreign service vagabond life—a dear, high price—is the stretching of the connection to extended family, resulting in knitting together our nuclear family that much tighter. We have moved and moved and moved how many times; you are stronger for having endured these challenges. Know that the resiliency you create for yourself with these repeated cycles through new-kid-staying-kid-moving-kid helps you to develop your sense of self, and your ability to land well, and reconnect. This is a cycle and skill many FS kids find so familiar; I know that doesn't make it easier just because it is known. But know that I know that, and I acknowledge that it IS hard. I feel that too; having to set up home and life and all the things again and again is part of this life, but it does get tiresome. It is worth it, though. Really.

I think one of the things I learned through this moving moving moving business: creating a clearer definition of what is "home" and what I want for my community. Home is not a place so much as people and a feeling; home is a sense of belonging. Sure, art on the walls, and favorite furnishing contribute to a nice ambiance, but home is people. You are all part of my home. This year, again, our family circle is spreading farther apart. That doesn't make the connections dimmer. We must continue to work to feed into that circle because prioritizing family is how we stay connected. Wherever we are on this globe, we are a unit; we are home. The importance and value of the family unit is one of the most important lessons we have learned through this foreign service adventure.

As you go along, when you try to accomplish something—something difficult, something beautiful, something amazing—surround yourself with people who give you positive energy. Discover people with whom you love doing "nothing" and do nothing with them on a regular basis. The longer you can maintain these relationships, the longer you will live. The cheapest therapy is to spend time with people who make you laugh. Remember: a person is a person because of other people. Your community is important. We humans are meant to be in communities. We are safer together. Invest in relationships because people are more important than devices. Every.single.time. I know I often say that you can never have too many friends, and I 100% stand by that. But. Know, too, you have no obligation to like everyone, and, yes, you are free to intensely dislike a person. You owe everyone— even those you dislike—basic respect. You also owe everyone a second chance, but not a third.

This is going to be a year of change and challenge; it will feel hard and complicated. Take a deep breath, think about what might be, and embrace that with curiosity. Curiosity is the key to staying invested. Putting energy in finding more about a new idea or perspective can help you open doors. Say "I don't know" and then find out more and repeat this practice every single day. I know the workload you have in front of you is very real. I know it is a lot to manage, to chew away at that mountain of must-do to get to the finish line. But I am also 100% certain you've got this. Know that sometimes you try and try but you don't get to the finish line successfully. Don't let that be the end. Failure is not something to be feared. We will fail literally a dozen times to learn the way to succeed. No matter how many times we fail, try new, try different; learn from those mistakes. As long as we keep trying, we are way ahead of everyone who isn't trying. All of your ideas that don't work are simply stepping stones to the one that does. Failure is not falling down. Failure is staying down when you have the choice and the opportunity to get back up. So, fail often. Failing is not a disgrace if you keep failing better. Remember that when you are right, you are learning nothing. When you are wrong, and learn, then you will grow. Also, do not cling to a mistake just because you spent a lot of time making it.

Be kind to yourself, too. Offer yourself compassion. Keep your self-talk encouraging and be your best champion. In the face of so many changes, it can be easy to fall into frustration because things don't flow as well as they did before. Consider how you might offer support to a friend going through the same sort of circumstances and give that same loving care to yourself. You are not too late. You didn't miss anything. Some days will be amazing, and some will be difficult. You will do it well sometimes and you will mess up sometimes. Be kind to yourself because as long as you keep trying, keep doing, keep going, you are doing enough. In fact, forget "should be"; focus on your response. A small part of your life is decided by completely uncontrollable circumstances while the vast majority of your life is decided by your responses. Your response is always more powerful than your present circumstances.

Define what your community is, and actively find ways to contribute to that community, build up those around you, to enhance rather than beat down. Sure, not everyone is going to reciprocate, or be like-minded. Those who do, they will gladly smile back. Those who don't, well, maybe they need your positivity more than anyone else. As the saying goes, "Hurt people hurt people.' It is not your job to fix their hurt, but sometimes, just acknowledge their place in the world, show them that you see them, and do not respond with negative behavior.

Be the one that people go home and talk about around the dinner table because they admire you so; be that example not because you are the coolest, funniest or the smartest. Be that example because you are the kindest. To be known as someone who is kind is one of the greatest compliments a person can garner. Our actions have the power to change the world around us and inspire others in our lives to get up and take action too. Make your actions positive and make them count. Think about what you can do to take personal responsibility. Not just for you, for your own body, but also for your actions and each other.

Embrace a collective mindset: look out for each other. If something happens to one of you, it happens to all of you. This is about finding how much 'us' we can build into the world and including as many people in that 'us' as possible.

It's a privilege to be here, a privilege to be present. The farther you venture from our own little corner in this world, the more you may feel as though you are on your own; know that I always have your back. I am here, even if we are not on the same landmass.

> I love you with all of my heart,
> Mom
>
> ———
>
> *Susie Brown*
> *Iowa, California, Idaho, Colorado, West*
> *Virginia, Maryland, Virginia, USA; Niger;*
> *Tanzania; Cambodia; Burma (Myanmar);*
> *Senegal; Uganda; Sri Lanka; Saudi Arabia*

Dear Hannah,

From your beginnings you've been a keen student of the natural world, taking delight in weird, wonderful critters and their environment; a natural nurturer of both people and animals; a deep thinker pondering questions beyond the obvious. It's been so fun to see you blossom as you explore new interests the past few years, and I know you'll find even more aspects of yourself to explore and develop, yet you'll always keep that core of kindness and care. I'm so very proud of who you are and who you are becoming.

Dad and I worked intentionally on maintaining open conversation with you, and I am so thankful that you talk to us about all sorts of topics. Keep talking to us as you work out your place in the world (my little secret: this may be a never-ending task).

As you stare down "YOUR FUTURE," consider who you want to be when you grow up. Even though you're at a stage of life when everyone's asking, "What do you want to do/study?" I'm less concerned with what you want to do. But rather, who do you want to be? A wise person once advised me to spend time with people I admire because they'd rub off on me. To that end: Surround yourself with people you aspire to be like; intentionally seek them out and spend your time with them. Look for people who will lift you up to the best version of yourself. You have an admirable desire to lift up others; balance that with spending time with people who inspire you and lift you up.

Also, speak up. Your voice is important. Your perspective is unique. People listen to you. Even when you don't see them acting on your suggestions, even when you don't hear them agreeing with your statements, they are listening, and you are changing the world around you by speaking into it. What you have to say matters. And if you're going to speak, make it count by letting people hear you. Be loud and clear and confident; speak up!

Grab hold of your belongingness. Recognize that you may have a tendency to feel like an outsider, even as you move easily between many groups and find commonalities with all of them. But in many situations, you belong every bit as much as everyone else there. Participating in rites of passage (even if the rituals and traditions seem unimportant or boring) help this. I also encourage you to anchor yourself in supportive relationships (such as the Freshman Interest

Group and The Neighborhood) that provide rhythm, consistency and longevity.

As a parent, I sometimes worry that in our moving around I've created a huge problem in your life, by causing so much disruption and loss; that I haven't taught you how to make friends and how to keep relationships; that I've caused you to feel lonely. But... Don't blame everything on being a TCK. While you do have some unique challenges to work through, many of the difficulties you'll encounter in life will be the sorts of frustrations and complexities that all humans struggle with.

University is by nature a transient place where people come and go constantly, and it's bittersweet to see special friends leave even while you cheer their chosen path. Life gets a lot harder when you become an adult and are faced with greater responsibilities; this is a normal developmental stage. Navigating human relationships is hard; it takes practice, and not all relationships work out even when you're a wonderfully kind and good person who gets along with everyone.

I know you to be a strong, adaptable, resilient, capable, engaged, and very interesting person. May everyone around you get to see the same things I can see!

I don't know the state of the world you will inherit after I'm gone. Based on world history, there are recurring patterns of crisis and rebirth among nations and people groups, which means during your lifetime you may experience some societal, multinational, or generational traumas or upheavals.

Remember, you have the tools and skills to heal from all sorts of traumatic events. I think of practical things like tremoring to release stress or trauma, Safety Stories to speak safety into your memories, laughter yoga to help your body let go of stress, prayer to transform your response to situations beyond your imagination.

You also have a deep knowing, because of your life experience. Remember that you have experienced, multiple times, life as you know it being turned upside down, finding that "the way things are done" is definitely not done that way anymore; the daily rhythms and routines are no longer there to comfort you; the sights and sounds and smells and tastes that were your mainstay are no longer there to provide your bearings. And yet, each time, you have found that there are many thousands of people living in this new way, very successfully and happily.

Eventually you come to find these new ways familiar and comforting and you learn how to move through life easily, with satisfaction. This is one of the best lessons from your moving around: There are many different ways to do life, which are all good. You can look in your own life and know viscerally that life is beautiful no matter how it's done. My hope for you is that you hold onto this knowledge and carry it forward no matter what life brings.

I'm excited to see what's next in your journey!

All my love,
Mom

———

Kim Adams
South Carolina, Hawaii, Oregon, Missouri,
USA; Japan; Thailand; Oman

Lieve Ella,

Ik heb getwijfeld of ik deze brief naar je moest schrijven. Ik zeg immers vaak genoeg hoe sterk je bent en hoe trots ik op je ben. Of denk ik het vaker dan dat ik het zeg?

Jij bent tussen jouw 8e en 18e met ons op 'pad' geweest. Van Nederland naar India, Italië en Duitsland. Uiteindelijk heb jij er bewust voor gekozen om in jouw geboorteland, Nederland, te gaan studeren.

Je wilde weer in een land wonen waar je de mensen om je heen kon verstaan zonder weer een nieuwe taal te moeten leren. Het aanpassen aan een nieuwe omgeving was al zwaar genoeg, wist je uit ervaring.

En lieve Ella, wat ben ik er trots op hoe jij jouw leven in Amsterdam hebt opgebouwd. Hoe jij alle lessen geleerd tijdens de verhuizingen toepast om jouw weg naar volwassenheid te vinden zonder jouw normen en waarden en alles wat jouw zo bijzonder maakt, uit het oog te verliezen.

Dat jij altijd zo dicht bij jouw eigen ik ben blijven staan is niet altijd makkelijk geweest.

Je hebt je vaak anders gevoeld, soms buitengesloten door anderen die jouw kracht, eerlijkheid en gevoel van rechtvaardigheid niet konden plaatsen of waarderen. Jij ging en gaat nog steeds de moeilijke situaties die horen bij GROEI niet uit de weg.

Het is zeer menselijk dat je weleens getwijfeld hebt of je er goed aan deed om op jouw eigen koers te blijven. Maar wat er ook gebeurde, en hoe moeilijk het ook was, uiteindelijk keek je wel met een open blik naar de feedback die je kreeg en schroomde je niet om het met mij te bespreken.

Ik heb moeten leren om niet gelijk met een oplossing te komen en om alleen te luisteren. Zoals je ooit tegen mij zei: "Door het voor mij op te willen lossen, geef je mij het gevoel dat ik het niet zelf kan".

Ook al val ik een enkele keer in mijn oude patroon, ik weet dat jij het kunt want dat heb je keer op keer bewezen.

Jouw zelfstandigheid is een eigenschap die jij al heel vroeg had en die door onze verhuizingen versterkt is.

Ik weet nog dat je een jaar of 7 jaar was en heel graag zelf naar school wilde fietsen. Het was niet ver maar je moest wel 2x een doorgaande weg oversteken. Jouw vader en ik hadden al compromis bedacht dat je zelf naar school mocht fietsen als je eenmaal in groep

6 zat. Wij dachten hiermee, 2 jaar uitstel te hebben maar niets was minder waar. Jij versnelde een jaar en kwam als 8-jarige in groep 6 terecht. Tja, wij hadden geen argumenten meer en vol trots fietste jij met de buurjongens naar school.

Op deze jonge leeftijd zagen wij al de eigenschappen die jou zullen blijven kenmerken.

Eigenschappen die door onze jaren in het buitenland versterkt zijn.

Lieve Ella, blijf die slimme, lieve, zelfstandige, eerlijke en loyale dame met een groot rechtvaardigheidsgevoel die oog heeft voor haar medemens. Die open is voor nieuwe ervaringen en die bewust werkt aan het vormen van haar community.

Ik ben ongelofelijk trots op je en kan niet wachten om te zien hoe jouw pad naar volwassenheid vervolgd. En vooral…waar!

Waar je ook terecht zal komen in de toekomst, ik weet zeker dat wij onze hechte familieband ondanks geografische uitdagingen en tijdsverschillen zullen weten te behouden.

Love you to bits,
Mom

English Translation from Arlette:

Dear Ella,

I hesitated about whether I should write you this letter. After all, I often tell you how strong you are and how proud I am of you. Or do I think it more often than I say it?

Between the ages of 8 and 18, you were "on the move" with us. From the Netherlands to India, Italy, and Germany. In the end, you consciously chose to study in your country of birth, the Netherlands.

You wanted to live in a country again where you could understand the people around you without having to learn a new language. Adapting to a new environment was hard enough, as you knew from experience.

And dear Ella, I am so proud of how you have built your life in Amsterdam. How you apply all the lessons learned during our moves to find your way to adulthood without losing sight of your values and everything that makes you so special.

That you have always stayed so true to yourself has not always been easy. You have often felt different, sometimes excluded by others who could not place or appreciate your strength, honesty, and sense of justice. You faced, and still face, the difficult situations that come with GROWTH head-on.

It is very human that you sometimes doubted whether you were right to stay your course. But whatever happened, and however difficult it was, in the end, you always looked openly at the feedback you received and were not afraid to discuss it with me.

I had to learn not to immediately come up with a solution and just to listen. As you once said to me: "By wanting to solve it for me, you make me feel like I can't do it myself."

Even though I sometimes fall back into my old pattern, I know you can do it because you have proven it time and again.

Your independence is a trait you had from a very young age, and it was strengthened by our moves. I remember when you were about 7 years old and really wanted to cycle to school by yourself. It wasn't far, but you did have to cross a main road twice. Your father and I had already come up with a compromise that you could cycle to school by yourself once you were in grade 6. We thought we had bought ourselves two more years, but nothing could be further from the truth.

You skipped a year and ended up in grade 6 at age 8. Well, we had no arguments left, and with great pride, you cycled to school with the neighbor boys. Even at this young age, we already saw the traits that will always characterize you. Traits that have been strengthened by our years abroad.

Dear Ella, stay that smart, sweet, independent, honest, and loyal young woman with a strong sense of justice who cares for others. Who is open to new experiences and consciously works on building her community.

I am incredibly proud of you and can't wait to see how your path to adulthood continues. And especially... where!

Wherever you end up in the future, I am sure that we will be able to maintain our close family bond despite geographical challenges and time differences.

Love you to bits,
Mom

———

Arlette Chatlein
Curaçao; The Netherlands; Nigeria; India;
Italy; Germany; Brazil; Belgium

Dear Lianna, Josiah & Mikayla,

It's hard.
Period.
Full stop.

I never meant for it to be so hard—this heavy, this consuming.
I never meant for your adulthood to be shadowed by the grief that
defined your childhood. The grief that I never anticipated would
become an intimate part of all our lives. The grief that feels elusive,
often unwarranted, but yet simultaneously unrelenting. The grief of the
"stayer".

I'm sorry.
Inadequate words.
A hollow echo.

An apology seems moot and meager, yet I am compelled to offer
it. If I could rewrite your childhood, would I? Would I erase the
rich tapestry of experiences that have shaped who you are? Would
I plant you in a simpler, more familiar world and remove the global
experiences that now define you? No... your life was vibrant and full of
adventure. Yet I want to take away the pain, the hurt and the struggle
that journeyed with us. The endless good-byes followed swiftly by
hesitant hellos, the tears that eventually stopped being shed, the walls
you built to protect yourself from the weight of connection. For that, I
am deeply sorry.

Move. Stay.
Plant. Transplant.
Choices.

Independence is hard and becoming an adult with walls is even
harder. As you navigate and maneuver, please know there is no "right"
way. You can move. You can stay. Both are options, but, as you are
painfully aware, both have associated costs. So, my child, count the
costs you understand, trust yourself and those around you to be able
to thrive amidst those that are unknown. You are capable. You are

equipped and, above all... You are loved.

Grieve, my child, but do not let the pain keep you from the unimaginable opportunities that still await you. Connect, my child. Yes, there may be pain, but on the other side of that hurt is true joy. Choose, my child, and know that change is always possible. Embrace it.

I will love you always and forever,

Mom
———

Linda Bloemberg
Pennsylvania, USA; Amsterdam; Hanoi

Querida filha,

Você tinha apenas cinco meses quando nos aventuramos a mudar para outro país. Como uma típica filha de terceira cultura, você voou antes de aprender a andar e aos três anos você já falava três idiomas antes de ser alfabetizada em alguma delas. Nessas três línguas você estudou em quatro sistemas educacionais diferentes e fez isso com maestria. No entanto, um pensamento equivocado que eu tinha era de que poderia criar você entre culturas como se fosse uma criança local, desconsiderando sua origem, sua história, sua identidade brasileira, suas vivências transculturais e percepção de mundo muito diferentes.

Apesar de você ter lidado de forma brilhante com as línguas e sistemas educacionais diferentes, estar imersa em uma escola local teve um custo emocional muito alto. Isso ficou evidente quando você estava no segundo ano e depois de estar o dia inteiro na escola, imersa em uma cultura bem diferente e sofrendo discriminação, você chegava exausta, chorando por horas sem saber explicar o que tinha acontecido. Isso acontecia quase todo dia. Foi um ano muito difícil, sem saber o que estava acontecendo e como ajudar. Eu fiz o melhor que pude para te ouvir, te acolher e tentar entender o que estava acontecendo, mas você era muito nova para me explicar, apenas percebia e sentia.

Seu pai e eu decidimos transferir você para uma escola internacional. Foi a melhor decisão que tomamos, embora para isso, tivéssemos que usar todas as economias que havíamos reservado desde o seu nascimento. Esta escola foi um verdadeiro oásis para você. Mesmo sendo a única na sua sala e um dos poucos brasileiros na escola, você não era a única expatriada estudando em uma língua diferente da sua língua materna e com experiências transculturais.

Mas quando este ano de refrigério acabou, não podíamos mantê-la na escola no ano seguinte. Você tinha muito medo de ter que voltar para a escola local. Então começamos a orar para que Deus providenciasse sua permanência ou que lhe desse uma experiência diferente se tivesse que retornar para a escola local.

Foi quando recebemos a visita de uma pessoa do Brasil que não apenas se comoveu como se identificou com a sua história por também ter sofrido bullying durante a sua infância na escola por causa da sua origem e crença diferente da maioria. Essa pessoa, então, garantiu a matrícula e a sua permanência na escola para o ano seguinte. Depois ficamos sabendo que, inicialmente, a sua visita não tinha sido planejada e que só tinha passado pela nossa cidade porque o tour do seu grupo tinha sido alterado de última hora para a nossa região.

Sentimos o amor e cuidado de Deus movendo céus e terra, e tours, para prover para as suas necessidades de uma forma surpreendente, que não poderíamos imaginar. Assim, você pôde permanecer na escola onde você não se sentia tão diferente dos outros, embora convivesse com alunos de diversas culturas.

Com amor,
Daniele

English Translation by Daniele:

Dear daughter,

You were only five months old when we ventured to move to another country. As a typical third-culture kid, you flew before you could walk and at the age of three you already spoke three languages before you were literate in any of them. In these three languages you studied in four different educational systems and did so masterfully. However, a misconception I had was that I could raise you between cultures as if you were a local child, disregarding your origin, your history, your Brazilian identity, your cross-cultural experiences and very different perception of the world.

Although you dealt brilliantly with the different languages and educational systems, being immersed in a local school took a very high emotional toll. This became evident when you were in the second grade and after being at school all day, immersed in a very different culture and suffering discrimination, you arrived exhausted, crying for hours without knowing how to explain what had happened. It happened almost every day and it was a very difficult year, without knowing what was happening and how to help. I did my best to listen to you, welcome you and try to understand what was happening, but you were too young to explain it to me, you could only perceive and feel it.

Your father and I decided to transfer you to an international school. It was the best decision we made, although to do so we had to use all the savings we had saved since you were born. This school was a true oasis for you. Even though you were the only one in your class and one of the few Brazilians in the school, you were not the only expat studying in a language other than your mother tongue and having cross-cultural experiences.

But when this year of respite ended, we could not keep you in school the following year. You were very afraid of having to return to the local school. So, we began to pray that God would provide for your stay or that He would give you a different experience if you had to return to the local school.

That was when we received a visit from a person from Brazil who was not only moved but also identified with your story because she had also been bullied during her childhood at school because of her origin and beliefs that were different from the majority. This person then secured your enrollment, and you were able to continue attending the school for the following year.

We later learned that his visit had not been planned initially and that he had only stopped by our city because his group's tour had been changed at the last minute to our region.

We felt God's love and care move heaven and earth, and yours, to provide for your needs in amazing ways we could not have imagined. So, you were able to stay in school where you did not feel so different from others, even though you were living with students from distinct cultures.

Love,
Daniele

———

Daniele Ferreira
Philadelphia, Estados Unidos; Antalya,
Ankara, Turquia; Brasil

April 30, 2025
Kalamazoo, Michigan, USA

Dear Watstein Women,

We are stronger together and together forever. I love you so much. I love our stories and your resilience to persevere through the really hard parts.

You are super troopers.

Sometimes I wonder where along my way a desire to work so far from my "home" came to be. I lived in one place until I was 17. Since then, I have lived in 8 different places. Oziah, you are 15 and have also lived in 8 different places. Frieda you are 12 and have lived in 7 different places. So we don't have similar upbringings in common and I can't say that I can relate to or understand your experience as a third culture kid, but I can give you a BIG hug and I can smile and laugh, and cry sometimes with you and know that wherever we are in the world, we are a family and I love you and will forever do everything I can to make you more comfortable and support you through the hard parts and the fun parts and all the parts.

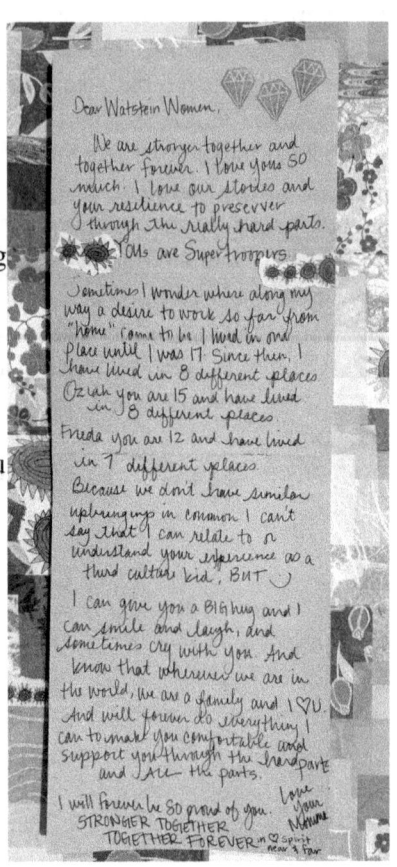

Jemina's handwritten letter to her children.

I have been and will forever be so proud of you. I love you. Stronger together and together forever, in heart and spirit, near and far.

Sincerely,
Your mom
———

Jemina Watstein
Colorado, Montana (Flathead Valley), New
York City, Michigan, USA; Nice, France;
Berlin, Germany; Nonthaburi, Thailand

Aéroport de Zürich, Suisse, en juin, sur le tarmac, en provenance
de Singapour

A ma fille, Tamara,

"Maman, je n'irai pas plus loin. Je ne veux plus partir étudier au Canada, à Toronto."

"Comment ça, ma chérie, tu ne veux plus? Tu es fatiguée du voyage, c'est ça sûrement. Maintenant, on va profiter de nos vacances en Suisse, avant ton nouveau départ de vie là-bas, en août."

"Non, maman, tu n'as pas bien compris. Je n'irai pas plus loin qu'ici; le Canada, c'est trop loin de notre maison de Singapour, où vous restez. Je ne veux plus y aller. Je dois commencer l'université plus près de vous, et aussi, plus près de mes racines." moi : "....." (cela passera, me suis-je dit).

T'en souviens-tu aujourd'hui de cet épisode?

Un peu plus tard, tu m'expliques que cela est clair pour toi; tu veux retrouver tes origines, comprendre d'où tu viens, qui tu es vraiment, après toutes ces années en expatriation, notamment en Asie. Tu ne veux pas être aussi loin de Singapour, notre résidence principale que tu quittes à présent, à l'aube de ton entrée à l'université. Je sais ô combien tu aimes cet endroit par ailleurs; c'est un déchirement pour toi de le quitter. Mais je te vois déterminée, je te sens décidée à renverser le programme, si j'ose dire. Je ne sais donc que te répondre à ce moment précis; ton père est choqué par la nouvelle, ne peut rien dire dans l'immédiat, ni écouter ni entendre—nous n'avons pas passé toutes ces années à l'étranger pour que tu veuilles aller étudier en France, dit-il... cette vieille Europe, te rappelle-t-il! Il n'a pas tort, c'est un non-sens à priori, il est vrai. Ceci dit, je te sais mature, réfléchie; tu ne prends jamais aucune décision à la légère. Tu es indépendante dans tes choix depuis déjà longtemps, malgré tes 18 ans, travailleuse, intelligente, persévérante; je sais que je dois te laisser continuer ton cheminement intérieur et tes réflexions pendant quelques jours.

Je me rappelle aussitôt, dans mon for intérieur, que ce fut notre choix de vie de couple que de commencer à nous expatrier au gré des contrats de travail de ton papa. Tu n'as jamais choisi. A présent, c'est ton tour. Tu es le leader de tes décisions, de tes aspirations, de tes besoins.

Tu passes dès lors un moment à vaquer sur ton ordinateur, depuis l'appartement de tes grands-parents, n'ayant plus de "chez nous" dans notre pays. Je t'observe, sans mot dire. Tu reviens vers moi, nous communiquons: tu as posé tes candidatures en France, à Paris. Tu choisis toujours le droit, cela ne change pas. Mais tu me dis que tu veux redécouvrir ton autre pays, à côté de celui de la Suisse, double nationalité tu as. Passé quelques jours, te voilà prise dans tes deux choix universitaires. Bravo ma fille!

Nous annulons le vol pour Toronto, où nous étions censés partir dans 15 jours pour visiter un peu ce lieu, avec ton frère et ta soeur, avant de te laisser dans ton nouvel environnement. En lieu et place, nous changeons tout; nous sommes adaptables, je dois me le rappeler, cela va avec notre style de vie; je souris donc, je rassure notre petit monde, tout en étant malgré tout je te l'avoue un peu dubitative. Tu m'as prise de court ma chérie, je ne m'y attendais pas du tout, à ce plan-là!

Nous prenons des billets de train—une fois n'est pas coutume, ce ne sera pas l'avion. Direction Paris! Nous allons donc dans la ville où tu as passé quelques années aussi, toute petite tu étais; où ton frère et ta soeur sont nés également. De doux souvenirs reviennent à ma mémoire. Sûrement dans la tienne aussi.

Dans ma tête, j'avertis la ville lumière: prends soin de ma fille, elle m'échappe, si loin, malgré tout.

Je sais que tu vas réussir ton nouveau challenge, nul doute! Je suis très fière de toi. Finalement, les valeurs restent peu importe le lieu de vie: savoir qui l'on est pour avancer, pour respecter son environnement, sa culture et ses traditions. Sans oublier que le monde est beau, qu'il nous fait grandir et évoluer en le découvrant.

À ce jour, je te sais prête à passer à la suite de tes études, ton master, dans un nouveau continent: les États-Unis, as-tu choisi! Attendons encore un peu, pour voir exactement le nom de l'université, et son lieu. Plusieurs t'ont déjà acceptée, sûrement grâce à tout ce que tu as vécu aussi jusqu'à ce jour. Mais une chose reste certaine toutefois: "the sky is your limit and beyond!"

Maman

———

Jeanne Lacroix
Switzerland; Czech Republic; France;
Romania; Japan; Singapore

My Dear Three Musketeers,

Writing this letter wasn't easy. I went through so many drafts on paper, even though we agreed as a family to limit a bit using paper to be more sustainable. Since this letter is dedicated to you, I have made sure that it is short, to the point, and sweet so you can read it one day.

You see, I was raised very differently, and you know that. I did what I was told, worked hard, never questioned my mom, never raised my voice. All schoolwork was done on time. I started working at a young age and my childhood and teen life were boring.

I wished more for the three of you. I wanted you to have more adventures. That's why I decided to raise you differently and expose you to the world.

And here we are, in the UAE, my life and yours have changed forever. And never was the same again. One of you has already left the nest to go to medical school in Ireland, and two more are about to spread their wings this summer to the Netherlands to study sports science and business. Where did the time go?

Now, as I look back, I see that you were an amazing part of a beautiful, diverse, global community. Just look at all the places you've been to all over the world before the age of 18. The languages you speak, the traditions you've kept, the history and cultures you've learned about and embraced. No wonder you did well on your university interviews.

You've built a sense of belonging by understanding organically the power of connecting and engaging wherever you've gone. You never held back, never shied away or shielded yourselves. You were always curious. And eager to learn more. You had the whole experience everywhere. You tried every food, wore every national dress, danced every dance, and respected every tradition.

And oh, goodness gracious, the friendships you made from every corner of the world. The number of kids at your birthday parties every year at my house felt like the United Nations! The local dishes, the etiquette on how to eat, the story behind it all. The musical instruments you picked up and tried to play—from the Duff to the Tabla and more!

What I loved most was how you found joy in the simplest things. Even when it hit 50°C outside in Abu Dhabi, you were frying eggs on the hood of the car, chasing each other with the hose, and making fruit slushies out of local fruits and dates, like it was the best day ever.

Every day was an adventure. Every year, you grow with more awareness and respect for your community. Every success of yours felt like mine.

And now, as you step into this next chapter, just know that I love you, and I couldn't have asked for a better journey or better kids. Keep spreading the joy of embracing the world with open souls, hearts, and minds.

Mumzee

———

Samar Karam
Egypt; USA; Netherlands; UAE

Dear kids,

When I dreamed of a career in the Foreign Service, I wasn't really thinking about the impact of this lifestyle on children. Your dad and I were eager to travel the world, meet people and experience new cultures.

Once you were in the picture, we thought only about the positive aspects that this lifestyle would bring to you: exposure to new cultures, places, languages, and global perspectives. Despite a very timely seminar at the U.S. Embassy in Portugal about the challenges of being a Third Culture Kid, I imagined that you would automatically be resilient—able to leave one place and move to another without regrets and only enthusiasm for the next country. Micaela, I even ignored your daily pleas to move back to Portugal, telling you to just accept our new home. I began to feel twinges of regret when I saw you finally cultivate a best friend in Belgium, only to lose her when her family transferred out after a year.

The regret deepened when you announced you would no longer look for a best friend, since we or they would move and never see each other again. I took comfort in our family's closeness and our active local community, hoping it would help fill some of the heartache, but deep down, I knew that our constant moves were taking some fundamental supports away from you and your development.

Yet I was entirely unprepared for the challenges you faced upon our return to the U.S. For your dad and me, this was a return to a familiar place and routine. But each of you faced a new middle/ elementary/preschool, peers and teachers who did not understand your experience and why you didn't know the Pledge of Allegiance or recognize American currency. We tried to recreate the sense of community we felt overseas, signing you up for sports, dance, catechism, Scouts, which kept us all very busy but didn't cement many bonds. You made some friends but knew these were temporary unless they were other TCKs or kids from families with international experience.

It was heartbreaking when we canceled Micaela's mini-golf birthday party shortly after arrival, because the "D.C. Sniper" was still on the rampage. You cried, "I hate this place! Why did we move here?" and I realized the U.S. was as foreign to us as any other country we had lived in. We participated in Foreign Service Youth Foundation events, aimed at bringing TCKs together. I began to educate myself, beginning with Ruth Van Reken and David Pollack's book *Third Culture Kids: Growing Up Among Worlds*. We attended PTA meetings, volunteered for school advisory committees, and talked to lots of parents to better understand our environment.

A return overseas brought relief when you found peers and a community that understood the challenges of this lifestyle. While you were shocked at the poverty you saw around you, you began to recognize the privileges we enjoyed and developed deep and lasting empathy. We were delighted to see you all become bilingual and enjoy the beauty of South America through family, school and sports trips.

The next transition to Turkey seemed almost predestined after 11-year-old Ben suggested our next post should be in a Muslim country "because we need to understand it better". I worried that the school would be too small for a fulsome educational and social experience, but you embraced your peers from Europe, the Caucasus, Africa and Asia. You played on every sports team and while competition was limited, it felt like a "real" high school experience, especially when Ben's soccer team won the European championship. You relished trips and community service with the tightest knit international community we'd ever experienced.

The move to Spain was bittersweet: with Micaela off to college, our family had a hole, yet we were finally living in your dad's country where you could fully immerse in the culture and see family more often. In some respects, it was as tough as going to the U.S.—it took six months for you to make friends in a rather insular school community; the IB program strictly limited Ben's course options and you didn't even get a chance to play soccer on the school teams. Yet with time, we saw you adapt and make life-long friends. More importantly, it ceiled your bicultural identity.

While each of you entered college with stellar academic and extracurricular resumes, we learned the hard way that the university transition is among the most difficult for TCKs. As 'hidden immigrants', you didn't fit in with the Americans nor the international students. Even for Laura, who did high school in the U.S. and relished her track and cross-country experience, the transition wasn't easy. We didn't recognize the signs of anxiety and depression until later and deeply regret your silent suffering and pain. Your experiences forced us to reflect more seriously about how your sense of identity and belonging made these developmental stages so much harder. I read more books, joined more committees, and attended mental health conferences. I created a resource guide and web page of resources, yet wish I'd learned all of this earlier to provide you with better support.

I am so proud of the adults you have become: intelligent, empathetic, and engaged global citizens working in fields you love that contribute to the improvement of our world. I hope that the unique experiences you enjoyed as TCKs have fueled your passion and success, yet recognize the many sacrifices and losses you endured. I apologize for our failure to better understand the TCK experience, help you process the emotions, and get you more timely help. Let's work together to make sure others are wiser and better prepared to fully exploit the many advantages this lifestyle brings, with support for its challenges.

Most of all, I want to thank you for being so resilient and strong and for YOUR service to the U.S. and the world!

Love always,
Mom

———

Kim DeBlauw
USA; Mexico; Togo; Portugal; Belgium;
Bolivia; Turkey; Spain

Dear Alessandro, Francesca, Nicolas, and Sofia,

I write to you today with my heart full—full of love, pride, and gratitude for each of you. You have navigated life with resilience and grace, made and said goodbye to countless friends, learned and forgotten languages, created homes in places that once felt foreign, and defended and questioned your origins time and time again.

True Third Culture Kids to the core, you have embraced the adult world with the same gusto, bravery, and spirit of adventure that defined your childhood. You have stepped into new chapters fearlessly, building lives in places we never imagined when moving around was both an adventure and a challenge. And yet, no matter where you are, you carry within you the strength, adaptability, and courage that have always defined you.

When I was your age, I never imagined I would raise my children the way I had been raised—always on the move, always adapting. At your age, I was still trying to figure out who I was, where I came from, where I belonged. I know these questions still linger for you, but I also see that you have embraced this life wholeheartedly, turning uncertainty into opportunity, and making the world your own.

I cherish our memories—climbing Mount Takao, collecting ema boards at Tokyo shrines, cheering from the bleachers at Valley Catholic School, and spending rainy days in our cozy home in Bussum, dancing to Stendi Panni, building Legos, playing Brio, solving puzzles, and creating magical worlds with your Sylvanians and Polly Pockets. Those moments are etched in my heart.

I am so proud of the strong, determined individuals you have become.

- Alessandro and Francesca, when we moved to Italy, and you stayed behind in the States, you both took it in your stride, continuing university like the champions you are, finding jobs on your own, carving your own paths.
- Alessandro, I still remember our pride when you got into OSU, ran for State in the 400-meter relay at Hayward Field in Eugene, and got the job at Intel.
- Francesca, when you scored that winning goal for the Soccer State Championship and now, with your incredible work ethic, you pour the same dedication into your career.
- Nicolas, you lead with strength and heart—captain of your high

school football team, excelling in your EU Business School thesis and who knew you would become the linguist that you are with three languages in your pocket. You always rise to the challenge.

- Sofia, from the moment you won your first tennis match and played at State, to coming back from your recent Great Barrier Reef field trip with a passion I knew would shape your future—I could see you had found your calling.

If I could have one superpower for a day, it would be creating portals—to teleport to each of you, even if just for ten minutes, to share a coffee, a meal, a hug, or bring you freshly made pasta al forno. You are spread across the globe, and I miss you so desperately.

Thank you for letting me and your Papa guide you the best way we knew how. We are honored that you choose to spend your precious holidays with us—the six of us, together, twice a year, as we have for so long. Thank you for allowing us to continue creating memories.

I love you all beyond words.

Mummy

———

Sam Frearson-Tubito
Basseterre, St.Kitts & Nevis; Bordeaux,
Angers, France; Kinshasa, Lumbumbashi,
Zaire; Otford Kent, London, England;
Abidjan, Cote D'Ivoire; Hong Kong;
Lusaka, Zambia; Cairo, Egypt; Mauritius;
Marmaris, Turkey; Milan, Bologna,
Modena, Italy; Bussum, Noord Holland;
Tokyo, Japan; Portland, Oregon, USA;
Athens, Greece; Madrid, Spain

Liebste F., A. und L., (Dearest F., A. and L.)

It is the first time that I send a letter to all three of you, so it may feel unusual, but there are a few things I want to share with you all.

Now that you are all adults I can share with you some thoughts that I hope will help you navigate your life—wherever it will take you. You have experienced from a very young age that friends come and go. Not many stayed, but those who did—no matter where they are in the world—are part of our "extended family" that you can count on, always.

From the beginning you have been immersed in a symphony of languages and cultures: that is your normal. You are three unique combinations of a colorful mix of German, Italian, Swiss (German and Italian), Dutch, British—and all the cultures and languages you have been in touch with so far, like French, Spanish, Russian, Thai and counting. You are all the languages you understand and use, the traditions you decide to uphold and the values and beliefs that shape you. You are the bridge between worlds, between past and future, weaving together realities that may seem to clash for the untrained eye, but that, beneath the surface, are deeply connected.

You know my passion about languages and my commitment to meaningful, effective and harmonious communication. In a time when everything seems to be about "fast" and "short" which too often means also "superficial", the ability to slow down, to actively listen, to read between the lines, and to genuinely understand a person or situation is more valuable than ever. So, please, try to switch off and slow down every now and then.

The current world seems, once again, to be at a turning point. We cannot foresee what will happen next, but we learn from history, and we can take action one day at a time.

I hope your future is peaceful. I hope you can live in a space where you can grow without being "othered" for your origins, languages, beliefs, values and opinions. The fear of "foreignness" in today's world is real, and cultural and linguistic biases continue to fuel division. However, you have the skills and strength to prevent walls from being built in the first place. You know that nobody has the right to silence or "other" you. However, stay safe and stand strong in the knowledge that your skills are far more than the sum of their parts. Your languages are your power: they equip you to take informed decisions, to navigate challenges considering multiple perspectives, and to resist narrow-minded, destructive and manipulative thinking.

I have often said that "my languages are my home": your languages create your home—a safe place within you and around you, no matter where you are. You carry them with you.

Our languages don't just shape our surroundings or help us express ourselves; they make our lives multifaceted, inclusive, open to diverse worldviews and flexible. Every single one of our languages carries echoes of all the others—their sounds, meanings, histories.

I see this richness in you that nobody can take away. In the way you effortlessly switch between languages, in your ability to adapt to new environments, in the way you approach people from all walks of life with curiosity and empathy. I am deeply proud of you—proud that you don't judge others based on their accent, their skin color, their clothing, or their lifestyle.

You have already shown resilience and grit in the face of uncertainty. The pandemic tested all of us, but you navigated it with courage. Knowing you are equipped to handle complex situations gives me peace of mind.

We live in a world where unfortunately, simplicity, uniformity, and ignorance often prevail. But you know better. Your multifaceted perspective ensures that you won't blindly follow what others say. You understand the consequences of such thinking, and you have the ability to stand up, speak out, and take action.

Some believe that being multicultural and multilingual means being "not entirely anything". But you are whole, not fragmented. You don't have to choose—one language, one culture, one identity. You are not only... but also... (and more). Every language you use, every story you carry, every choice you make shapes the rich, multi-layered tapestry of you. Don't let anyone reduce you to just one facet.

Many internationals struggle with the concept of home. Home isn't just a place: it is you. Like a snail carrying its shell, you bring it wherever you go. Those who get this navigate change best. Belonging isn't given—it is created, and it comes from within. You decide where, with whom, and how.

We have given you a foundation rooted in unconditional love, curiosity, and flexibility—along with five languages and the memories they hold. Now, it's your turn to build. We will be here, cheering from the sidelines. Take the time, decide who and what you want to be in your life, choose your path, and set your boundaries.

I cherish every moment we share and every memory we create. I love you as you are—and as you will be—always. Like Ungaretti said: m'illumino d'immenso.

> With all my love and admiration,
> Eure Mama
>
> ———
>
> *Ute Limacher-Riebold*
> *Ticino, Zurich, Switzerland; Lombardy,*
> *Tuscany, Italy; Paris, France; The*
> *Netherlands (South Holland)*

5 May 2025
Chiang Mai, Thailand

Dear Tyler, Ian, Joya, Seth, Mercy, Levi, and Gracelyn,
When we left to move overseas, I was so earnest. I threw myself into everything—learning the language, connecting with local culture, and fully immersing myself in where we were living. I wanted to do it right, and I thought that meant going all in.

I often judged those who clung to visiting the US regularly, who made sure to retain not only their home culture but also their love for all things American. I was determined that our family—our children—would do it better. We would learn languages, put down roots, and live deeply, without thoughts of returning to the US.

We really thought we would stay in Sweden forever.

But then life happened. Work became untenable, and we knew it was time to move on. So we did. We threw you into a new culture and a new language without fully understanding that the transition from Sweden to Germany would be too harsh—too much, too painful. You all paid a high price, and we never asked your permission.

Looking back, I sometimes wonder if it would have been better to hang up missionary life and settle in the US back in 2009. I was so focused on making sure you could fly—soar easily around the globe, managing cultures and languages—that I neglected the need for rest, for a home, for a safe place to lay your heads at night.

I raised you to be like swifts—birds that can fly endlessly, even sleep while they fly, and rarely land. Six of you have launched into new lives, but I deeply regret that we never created a true "home base." I regret that you were forced to fly too high, too long, and sometimes in unsafe conditions.

If I could do it over, I would have invested more time, energy, and resources into building a nest for you. We would have chosen a single country to be our home—a place to return to. We would have built deeper connections there, rather than just visiting briefly every few years.

I'm sorry that I worried so much about flying and not enough about nesting and resting. I'm grateful that you have found people to be home for you, and I hope that Dad and I can create a place for you to return to whenever life feels weary.

We are so very proud of you all. You have flown so well, but I

97

know some of the storms left scars—scars we might have prevented. I hope you can build your own nests—places of rest and respite.

I love you,
Mom

P.S. "No Roots" by Alice Merton captures so much of what I've felt while raising you across three cultures.

———

Debbie Kramlich
Lima, Peru; Lancaster, Pennsylvania,
Columbia, South Carolina, USA;
Kathmandu, Nepal; Friedrichshafen,
Riedlingen, Germany; Holsbybrunn,
Sweden; Chiang Mai, Thailand

Dear Hope, Caleb, Sarah, Micah, and Seth,

The five of you are my greatest blessings. I should tell you all more often.

Our lives have been far from 'normal.' I imagine one of you is quietly mumbling, "Understatement of the decade." From your start as military kids, you knew the definition of sacrifice before you could even say the word. Daddy was gone far too much; his bedtime stories were often video recordings. I remember one homecoming when little Sarah kept touching his face as she realized he was the same man from the computer screen. The many places we lived and the tears that fell from goodbyes to dear friends; each move becoming more difficult the older you each became. The first move that seemed hard for you all — leaving Pearl Harbor and our community of friends that became like family left an ache in our hearts. And yet, even today we still cherish and maintain many of those friendships. The military community provided your first connection into the TCK world.

Even after Daddy's retirement, sacrifice was still an unwelcome guest in our family. Life on the ocean, sailing from one country to another to spend a little time with missionaries you've never met, meant sacrificing stability — in more ways than one. And through all the challenges, I wouldn't change our time together on the sea for anything. Night watches with God's never-ending display of stars — always looking for Orion as he traversed the dark sky. Reading time in the cockpit after sunset with red light. Our entrepreneurial plans using forks. Homemade pizza and movie nights squeezed in around the table. Christmases spent at anchor while we decorated cookies and made homemade eggnog since we couldn't buy it. The cherished time all together in a tiny space as we rocked along with the waves. I cling to the memories of laughter, hugs, and even the tears and arguments. This is where we united as a family, sailing thousands of miles across the waves.

At your young ages, you have already seen more people, more cultures, and more places than many will in a lifetime. Sailing along the coastlines of Mexico, El Salvador, Nicaragua, and Costa Rica, and our other travels throughout Europe and Bahrain — each one unique; each one adding new colors and patterns to your lives. You are all like kaleidoscopes of beautiful colors and ever-changing designs from each place and people who have left their marks on your lives and you on theirs. Even the five of you are different. God sees and knows all of you. And He loves every part, color, and design that makes each of you unique.

I've seen how the people and places we encountered have taught you kindness and compassion. I've witnessed your consideration of others, from a small child looking for comfort or a friend to play with to an older adult needing physical assistance or just wanting to share their life experiences. And others see it, too. Your kindness will open doors and build bridges. You have the ability to bring people together.

Through all the ups and downs, highs and lows, I've seen each of you persevere and rise above. You learned from your challenges and used them as opportunities to thrive, viewing them as stepping stones rather than obstacles. But there have also been things that were difficult for each of you that I failed to see at the time. Or maybe I still don't see them, and I am so sorry for that. We don't get everything right as parents, but we trust God will fill in the gaps. Those hard things may be what God uses to shape you into the person He planned all along. I am so thankful God is in the business of redemption.

The colors and designs from your childhood can make it difficult to find where you belong. While one color or design may blend perfectly in certain settings, others may stand out. As a result, you might often feel like you don't fully fit in anywhere. Even if you try to adapt or hide your uniqueness, you will still stand out because you are different from the rest of the world. So embrace it. Shine like stars.

I will always feel like there is more to teach you, tell you, but for now remember these few words. I believe in you. I will always be there for you. Anytime, day or night. While we taught you skills to be strong and independent, you can do so much more as a team. You don't have to always be okay. Or perfect. Let me clear that up now—you will never be perfect. None of us can. We learn from our mistakes. You may fail, but after you rest, get back up, and try again. It's the trying again that makes you stronger. Ask for help when you're not okay. Focus on what you can control. Rest is doing something. And most importantly, love Jesus.

Some days will be like 'Day 2'—the waves are big, the wind is too strong, and you may wonder if you'll make it through. Or the wind may be coming from exactly the direction you're trying to go and tacking slows your progress until it seems you aren't moving forward at all.

On other days, the sun warms your soul, and the wind is refreshing and cool, filling your sails so that it feels like nothing is impossible.

God remains constant on both types of days. He is with you through the good and the bad and in every place you may go, so be strong and courageous. You each will move to new places, physically apart by what feels like galaxies to this mama. However, we will stay connected because we all have the same anchor.

Ankyrios. "We have this hope as an anchor of the soul, firm and secure." Hebrews 6:19

With all my love,
Mommy

———

Brandy Kelly
Alabama, Texas, California, Hawaii,
Colorado, USA; Pacific Ocean along
the coastlines of Mexico, El Salvador,
Honduras, Nicaragua, Costa Rica;
and extended stays in seven additional
countries

May 29, 2025
Melbourne, Australia

Dear Kathryn, Nicholas and Aidan,

I was born in the post-colonial, newly independent India and always knew I was a Mission Kid (MK). You know something of my journey as an MK: boarding school in south India from the age of six to fifteen; home in the remote village of Amp Pipal in Nepal; moving to Melbourne to complete Years 11 and 12 at Carey Grammar School and staying on to attend Monash University when the rest of my family returned to Nepal. I had little say in the decisions that determined the course of my growing up years—I just accepted it, as one did in that era! I have very few regrets and am exceedingly grateful for my loving parents and family and school and the wonderful privilege of 'growing up among worlds'.

Of course that was the 'pre-TCK era'. In 1988 when we embarked as a family on our cross-cultural journey from Melbourne to Nepal, the term Third Culture Kid was just emerging into the world of missions (Ruth Van Reken's book *Letters Never Sent* was published that year). When our family of four (Aidan joined us 8 years later!) settled in Lamachaur village in June 1988, you knew you were MKs. You had little say in the decisions that had brought us to Nepal.

We had not been intentional about coming to Nepal, that was where Interserve had placed us, to serve with the United Mission to Nepal. I was very happy to be 'home' again, but you at the ages of six and four (and Mum aged 30) were faced with the realities of cross-cultural adjustments. I admire you all for the ways each of you did that—including learning Nepali. That came much easier to you than to Mum because you gravitated to and were quickly 'adopted' into village life.

I was amazed at how quickly and deeply you imbibed Nepali village culture. Proof of this came when we had our first annual holiday at Kovalam beach in south India. After dinner we strolled along the beach together admiring the sunset over the waves, Janine and I holding hands as we would have done in Australia (but not in Nepal), when you, Kathryn, came running up from behind us to separate our hands and ensure that we maintained a culturally appropriate space between us. We had not taught you that cultural sensitivity. You would not have reacted like that in Australia. But within 12 months of life in village Nepal you had soaked up the cultural norms of the village where PDAs were inappropriate and tried to ensure that we followed them!

Eight years later we moved to south India. You were part of that decision—at least we asked for your input. We listened to your objections: Nepal was home, and you didn't want to leave (nor did we in fact—Nepal had become our home too!). You didn't want us to become staff at Hebron School which was your space. And worse, your status would change to 'staff kids' which carried much stigma. We moved anyway.

By this time, you were teenagers and major transitions for teens is usually challenging. But the overwhelming bonus for us all was the arrival of Aidan at the end of that first semester (1996). You were born in India Aidan, and into the Hebron School community. For the next six years that became your home and your extended family (of 500!). Significantly, we lived together as a family during your early years—until Kathryn graduated and moved to university in Melbourne.

1996 was a pivotal year for me in another way. I went to a conference in Manila and heard David Pollock speaking about the 'TCK profile'—that was an 'aha' experience for me as I understood that not only was I an MK, but I was a Third Culture Kid: I had spent a significant part of my developmental years outside my parents' culture. I had built relationships with all of the cultures (north India, Nepal, boarding school, south India and Australia…) without having full ownership in any. I had assimilated elements from each into my life's experiences, but my sense of belonging was in relationship to other TCKs (The TCK Experience—*Growing up Among Worlds*, 1999, p. 19). Dave also spoke about the 'Re-entry task', and R.A.F.T. As I returned to Hebron, I thought not only of my transition experiences but of you three—my TCKs in the making, as well as the hundreds of TCKs at Hebron whose welfare was my responsibility.

I became a 'TCK evangelist' within the Hebron community—staff, students and parents were harangued with the 'TCK gospel' and I confess to being over-zealous at times. In 1998 Mum and I and Angie D. launched the Leavers' Program for the graduates of that year. It was a rudimentary effort and met with some resistance from the students ("why do we need to waste our time on this?"). We persisted and by the time you graduated in 2015 Aidan, that program had evolved into a carefully developed and intentional program culminating in a Leavers' weekend retreat. It became an essential part of the Hebron experience—preparing students for closure, transition (R.A.F.T.) and re-entry (although that is a misnomer—for you and many students you were leaving your home and entering your passport culture). The Hebron Leavers' program was amongst the first and was, from my observations, the gold standard amongst international schools. Our commitment to student welfare included preparing leavers for life after Hebron—something that was entirely lacking in my student days.

I share some observations of being MKs/ TCKs and the so-called 're-entry' process. My MK experience growing up was predominantly wonderful. My move to Melbourne in 1969 was horrible—lonely and mystifying; I was a classic 'hidden immigrant' and it took me nearly 18 years to curb my desire to flee Australia and to integrate my worlds and accept my Aussie identity.

Kathryn, when you made the move to Melbourne in 2000, you found it very difficult initially, but there were some lifelines: Mum was with you for a while at the start; your extended family were on hand; you were in a supportive Christian community at the Kew Baptist Res; although you missed the Leavers' Retreat program, you had understanding and supportive parents; and you were able to return to Asia, your happy place, with your new friends to visit us and your old friends.

Nicholas, your move to Melbourne was in 2002 and we moved as a family. Those initial months before university began were tough—we did what we could to support you practically. Your lifelines were hockey, getting a car and a job, and chatting throughout the nights via MSN with your school friends scattered around the world. After six months when we moved to the Bible College to study, you chose to move to the Res where Kathryn had been—a wise decision for that became your community (and your roommate was a TCK!). Transitions take time and there were challenges later, but it seemed that your initial transition was smoother than mine or Kathryn's.

Aidan, we moved to Melbourne together after your graduation. Although you were born in India and had spent most of your 18 years there, your transition seems to have been remarkably smooth (compared to mine and your siblings). Your Leavers' Retreat weekend was fantastic (we were there too as 'leavers'!). You had been visiting Melbourne regularly in the preceding years and had many connections with family and friends. We lived together in Grantville which enabled you to work full-time at the CYC campsite—a wonderfully supportive working environment providing a good income too!

You were surrounded by our growing family (by this time Kathryn had married Mark, and you were an uncle, and Nicholas had married Sarah) and other friends. Connections with your friends around the world were via your phone. Once you started your training as a pilot you were on the other side of Melbourne from us all but cared for by your Christian hosts and your new church friends.

Looking back over our decades as a family in Asia I am overwhelmingly grateful—for the hard times too. The toughest decision we made was for you to attend Hebron School as boarders—3000kms and 4 days train journey away in another country! You were very much a part of that decision. The day before Kathryn left for Hebron Mum was told by a critical colleague that she was a terrible mother—you know how untrue that is! Separation was painful but we did our best to ensure that you knew that we all shared the pain because we believed it was in your best interests. Mum's prolific letter writing was par excellence.

As parents we entrusted you to the Hebron staff and amongst many blessings in that experience was the positive impact of 'significant others' in your lives—especially as teenagers. You know who I mean—the teachers and dorm parents whose love and dedication has affected the course of your lives spiritually and academically. Who would have predicted that you would become a high school Science teacher, Nicholas, despite, or because of, your record 5-hour detention from your beloved and legendary Chemistry teacher? (He is one of my great heroes!)

Yes, there were tears—Mum and I never pretended that it wasn't painful, and that was important. But the flipside was the intense anticipation of meeting again (happy tears!) and enjoying family time—absence does make the heart grow fonder! We still relish and appreciate our frequent family times together.

I conclude. Reflecting is a good exercise. We gain better perspective. We become more objective in how we see the good and the bad, the mistakes and the lessons learnt. I have made mistakes and learnt lessons which I hope have benefitted you and the many other Hebronites with whom you shared your experiences of growing up among worlds.

I am so grateful for our individual and shared journeys. I am so grateful for the love and closeness we enjoy together. I am so grateful for each of you and the wonderful people you are. As G.K. Chesterton noted: 'Nothing taken for granted; everything taken with gratitude.'

With much love,
Dad
_____

John Barclay
Nepal; India; Australia

February 14, 2025
KwaZulu-Natal, South Africa

09/2024

My two dearest toasted marshmallows,

You are eighteen and nineteen now. University carries a steep learning curve for everyone, but especially for the ones like you who left home, country, and friends to be grafted back to the place of your heritage.

As second-generation TCKs, you belong to a tribe that your father and I know well. Your childhood was formed in the womb of the cradle of humankind, in KwaZulu-Natal, and it ended abruptly on the other side of a plane ride to the United States. But the things that formed you there still sing in every crevice of your mind and shape the way you see the world.

Repatriation is a season when the losses of the familiar sink in hard for TCKs. And these are the years when you become aware of your roots, the ones that have been transplanted to new soils and now feel wildly distinct and out of place. The places of your childhood are the places where your formative and deepest roots grow. And the soil of South Africa no longer surrounds or supports you.

You'll remember from working on our farm that a transplanted plant often wilts for a while. It is learning to survive in a new and unfamiliar environment. Its roots aren't sure what to make of its new home. They don't know whether they can unfurl and take new life or whether the newness will be hostile to growth. Repatriating TCKs are the same.

While my roots in South Africa will never be as deeply formative as yours, I am here to co-grieve your losses with you. I did the same as a nineteen-year-old with my Cameroonian roots. And your father did too, at eighteen with his Congolese and Central African roots.

Some losses are obvious. Our imperfectly perfect little farmhouse and the stability of its cracked walls. The foamy blueness of whales flirting between the horizon and the Indian Ocean. The oneness of our multicultural, multi-lingual farm family. The wind-whipped cheeks from four-wheeling wild past giraffes. The saggy eyes after Minecraft all-nighters with friends. The laughter with your non-blood sisters farmsteading in the mountains.

The crispy-edged pancakes hot off the griddle every Saturday morning. The seasonal ebb and flow of subtropical downpours and droughts.

But some losses are hidden. Some, you won't even know you miss

106

until you come across them years later. And you'll be caught off guard by a sudden feeling of home. Hidden losses are the sounds, smells, and invisible things that God sprinkled into the backdrop of your childhood. They are the things that you didn't even know weren't everywhere on planet earth. Until they weren't.

Your hidden losses don't have to make sense to anyone else. They don't even have to be pleasant. But something about these background sounds and smells had a profound impact on developing the unseen part of who you are today. And we honor those gifts by naming them.

The background sound of your childhood is the cry of hadedas filling pink southern skies and beckoning your sleepy eyes open. You didn't even know the sound was missing until that first morning in a Midwest dorm room when the synthetic shock of an alarm clock demanded your attention.

It is the faithful singsong Xhosa greeting "Molweni" on your proud farm stoep. It is the mourning doves telling each other off gently and sternly. It is the inexplicable peace of violent rains threatening to crash right through tôle roofs. It is the baying of hounds, whether to threaten skelems or to give chase to dassies, outside your burglar-barred window.

It is the South African flavor in which people have always said your name. It is the twisted, segregated history healing in real time through the harmony of church songs in English, Afrikaans, and Zulu. It is the comfort of our family's age-old call to meals that reaches back to the recesses of your first independently held spoon, "On va prier."

The background smell embedded in the roots of your childhood is a eucalyptus flame licking Karoo lamb ribs on the braai. It is soft buttermilk vanilla steam from an Ouma rusk dunked in Five Roses tea. How can something be so moorishly crunchy and goopy at the same time? It is the barely-there salt in the air where the Indian Ocean laps at the sky. And yes, it is even the familiar sewage plant every time we try to hold our breath at that bend in the highway by Uvongo.

Your roots will fumble around in this new place of red, white, and blue for a while, figuring out what friendly soil is and what isn't. And this is the time. Dit is tyd to close your eyes, take a breath, and rediscover the power of your one unshakable tap root. It is your deepest root. The most formative one. The most familiar one. The most stabilizing one. It is your one root that pushes far past all the others, past every good and rocky soil, reaching like life depends on it, to the source of life. Water. Living Water.

It is in Living Water that you've always found life and truth and all that is good. When everything around is unfamiliar, this source is the familiar.

You'll find community in the taproots of familiar people planted there too. And you'll come to know new people who are automatically family because their taproot seeks life in the same place where yours does. This is the good stuff, my toasted marshmallows.

While your secondary roots stumble around and try to make sense of star-spangled life, sink all your energy, all your questions, all your everything into your taproot's source of life. It is the one and only thing that will never change no matter where you go, how far you fall, or how unfamiliar everything else seems.

Taprooted to the Source with you,
Mom

———

Anna Danforth
Quebec; Lassin, Yaoundé, Cameroon;
California, Iowa, Texas, Washington State,
Idaho, USA; Lesotho; KwaZulu-Natal,
South Africa

February 23, 2025
Islamabad, Pakistan

My dear sons,
   As I look at the young men you've grown into, I feel a deep sense of pride and love for the unique journeys we've shared. Raising you as cross-cultural kids (CCKs) has been one of the most enriching experiences of my life, and I wanted to share some thoughts and memories with you as you step into adulthood.
   From the beginning, it was important for Dad and me to keep our Lithuanian heritage alive in your lives. Teaching you our language and traditions wasn't just about words and customs; it was about giving you a sense of belonging, a sense of where you come from—a connection to our roots that I hope brings you strength and pride. Speaking multiple languages may have seemed challenging at times, but I hope you've come to see it as a gift, a way to carry different parts of the world within you.
   I remember reading one of your favorite stories "Meškiukas Rudnosiukas" over and over again every night:

Ten miške, kur ėglės ošia,
Po pušim sena, sena
Buvo meškinas Rudnosis,
Rudnosienė—jo žmona.
Ir turėjo jie meškiuką,-
Rudnosiuką, kaip ir jie, -
Buvo jis dar be kelnyčių
Ir bėgiojo tik namie.
Vakare, kai tėtis grįžta,
Kai visa šeima namuos,
Sėdi jis šiltam namely,
Klauso pasakų mamos…

And of course, your favorite song "Du gaideliai":

Du gaideliai, du gaideliai
baltus žirnius kūlė,
dvi vištelės, dvi vištelės
į malūną vežė.

Ožys malė, ožys malė,
ožka pikliavojo,
o ši trečia ožkytėlė
miltus nusijojo.

Musė maišė, musė maišė,
uodas vandens nešė,
saulė virė, saulė virė,
mėnesėlis kepė.

These are stories and songs that were passed on through generations—from our grandparents to our parents, to us, and we hope that you cherish and pass on to your own children one day in the future.

Then there were all the adventures we shared as a family, traveling through Southeast Asia and beyond. We didn't just want to show you beautiful places; we wanted you to experience different lives and cultures up close, to see the world through others' eyes. I know it wasn't always the most exciting for you, especially when we skipped the fancy hotels to explore local streets or visited historical sites like temples, stupas, and ruins. But I believe those moments opened up worlds within you, building curiosity and empathy that I already see reflected in how you approach life and relationships.

What I love most about you both is the strength and character that has emerged from being CCKs. You are resilient and compassionate, with a profound respect for others. You've developed the ability to adapt quickly to new situations and connect with people from various backgrounds. This life has given you so many unique strengths— problem-solving, independence, and a sense of curiosity and adventure that runs deep. These qualities, born out of challenge and change, make you adaptable, understanding, and accepting in ways that aren't always easy to find. And I see in each of you a sense of quiet courage that comes from facing the unknown so many times and realizing that each new place can become a piece of home.

But I know this journey hasn't always been easy. There have been times you may have felt like outsiders or like you didn't quite fit in. There were moments when the sense of home felt scattered, with family and friends living oceans apart. And I felt pangs of guilt when I saw you have to say goodbye too many times or struggle to find continuity in a world constantly shifting. But I'm so proud of how you've managed it. You've learned to create "home" in a new way, gathering pieces of each place you've lived and weaving them into your hearts. That's no small feat!

Being a CCK is a unique privilege that offers a wealth of perspectives and relationships beyond borders. You've experienced firsthand the beauty and diversity of humanity. You've grown up with friends from all over the world, gaining a sense of the global community that most people don't truly understand. Embrace that perspective, because it is powerful and rare.

Looking to the future, I hope you'll always appreciate the value of the experiences you've gathered, even when life feels complicated. I hope you continue to find pride in your multilingualism and multiculturalism and the deep empathy and understanding you carry. My dream for you is to use these experiences to build bridges, create understanding, and make meaningful contributions to the world. Remember—you have a voice that speaks across borders, and that is something the world needs today more than ever.

Thank you for embracing this journey with me. Thank you for your patience and resilience, and for the laughter and love we've shared along the way. I'm so proud of who you are and who you're becoming, and I can't wait to see where your unique paths will lead.

> With all my love,
> Mom
> ———
>
> *Daniela Draugelis*
> *Buenos Aires, Argentina; Erlangen,*
> *Germany; Miami, Washington DC,*
> *Arlington, Virginia, USA; Beijing, China;*
> *Jakarta, Indonesia; Islamabad, Pakistan*

Hagar, Uri, Naama and Amir,

Being a TCK (Third Culture Kid) means constantly questioning your identity—shaping and reshaping it, whether consciously or unconsciously. It's about being molded by your choices or by the choices of others, finding stability in instability, and discovering your voice in a messy collage of places, people, experiences, and projections. Just when you think you've figured out who you are, a wave normally in a shape of a move comes and stirs everything up again. To my surprise without a move that was exactly how I felt after October 7, 2023.

As you know, my journey began in Buenos Aires, where my grandparents fled from Russia and Poland, seeking safety after being persecuted for their Judaism. Moving due to political and social upheaval is a common Jewish story—and it's also mine. My parents had to flee too. We were refugees, first in Europe, and eventually we landed in Israel. I became Israeli, but my Argentinian identity remained a part of me. I was able to keep it alive, and now I see how much it matters how others view your heritage. In the late '70s, being an Argentinian immigrant in Israel was accepted and even valued—we could openly celebrate that part of our story alongside the new. Think about your experience, for the two of you that attended high school in Brookline and not in Brussels there is more room to be connected to the Israeli identity, our surroundings matter, there are places and communities that part of our identities are irrelevant or less welcomed.

For many years, I lived in a relatively stable environment, forming a strong sense of self like most people around me. I felt it was my choice to reveal or emphasize the different parts of my identity—I was in control. From that place of stability, I supported Dad's dream and what I then considered a temporary move abroad. That move birthed a completely new version of my identity—and perhaps more significantly, a new identity for our entire family.

In a single move to Brussels, you became TCKs. The way we each carried the different parts of our identity became unexpectedly revealing. These moves often bring families closer, and that was true for us, but they also highlight our differences. Every train ride in Europe reminded me of your grandpa's Holocaust story. Interestingly not to your father. Meanwhile, some of you began to emphasize my Argentinian background while hiding our Israeli identity. It wasn't straightforward. It was frightening. I longed for the balance I once had—where things made sense, and I didn't have to make so many decisions that will influence your path and identity.

What did it mean to send you to an international school versus a Jewish one? Was I encouraging pride or shame in certain parts of your identity? Should you be afraid to express yourselves? Who should we befriend? What would you grow up to believe about yourselves? About others?

Only recently have I begun to reflect on our moves through a Jewish lens. It's striking to realize that every generation in my family moved due to sociopolitical events tied to our Jewish identity. We eventually found some balance in Brussels, adopting a complex international identity, supported by expat friends whose stories resembled ours. But then, terror attacks occurred in Brussels, and we were once again faced with the difficult question: Can we live openly as Jews here?

We decided to move to Boston. That wasn't the only reason, but it was a major one. We couldn't feel truly safe unless we hid certain parts of ourselves. In Boston, we again had to reshape and readjust. Each of us found a different way to carry their identity. I must admit, being Israeli changed from being irrelevant to something meaningful again. Personally, I finally felt like I was in a place where I could express every part of who I am—without fear, and with pride.

Then October 7th happened. And it caught me off guard. The balance I had worked so hard to achieve was disrupted—not by a physical move, but by a horrific event.

In our weekly conversations, Ruth Van Reken and I often talk about identity. We even presented together at a conference. We usually focused on how the "anchors" and "mirrors" shift with every move, affecting the stability of identity formation. But we rarely spoke about how dramatic changes to the places we come from can also reshape our identities and the way people perceive us.

After October 7th, parts of the TCK community that had been my stabilizer for 15 years began turning against Israel and occasionally against me. I felt misunderstood and rejected. The way we connected to our nomadic roots began to shift too. Up until that day, we had spent every summer in Israel with family and friends. Not anymore. For the first time it was only Dad and I traveling to Israel, even within our family we felt so different.

Over the past year, I've moved from fear and shock to the painful realization that Israel is changing more rapidly than I want to admit.

That realization left me feeling lonely. People started seeing me as someone I'm not. Connections didn't survive. It became difficult to navigate between identities and loyalties.

For the first time, I truly understood what Ruth meant when she spoke about humanness as the foundation of it all. She remains one of the few people with whom I can still speak my truth out loud and explore the complexity of who I am.

And now, once again, we're asking: Can we live safely with our complex identities here?

The answer is still unclear. There is no real balance yet.

My hope for you is that you will stay true to your humanness, to the openness that comes with living the lives you lived, but at the same time own and celebrate in your own way your different elements of your identity, try to find your balance without giving up on any part of you including the ones that are hard to carry like being Jewish.

> With love,
> אמא
>
> ———
>
> *Daniela Tomer*
> *Argentina; Israel; Belgium; USA*

To my stepson Guy (U.K.) and my children Robbie (Chicago) and
Lucy (Atlanta),

Thank you for following your dreams and building lives with your
chosen partners, even though it's meant settling far from home. While
many left-behind parents might struggle to express this, Dad and I are
genuinely happy to embrace the unique dynamic of our global family.

On a scale of one to ten (as I often say!), we're doing remarkably
well as a family spread across time zones, flights, and continents.
We've adapted to challenges like inconvenient time differences, long-
haul flights, homesickness, rigid vacation schedules, school holiday
regulations, and the quirks of the International Dateline. Dad and I
do our best to make it all work, and you, in turn, put in the effort to
connect, communicate, and show understanding.

Each of you has your own way of staying in touch, and over time
we've adjusted our expectations and routines to make the most of
what we have. Are we the perfect long-distance family? Of course not.
Perfection isn't the goal—especially when emotions, age differences,
and geographical logistics can complicate things. But what we have
works, and for that, we're grateful.

Thank you for making time to visit New Zealand when you can.
We know how much you love your birth country, and it's heartening
to see those connections endure. We never feel abandoned, and your
efforts to keep us close—despite the distance—mean everything to us.

Thank you, too, for the warm welcomes when we visit you.
Whether hosting us or accommodating our decision to stay off-site
for a bit of breathing room, your understanding of our needs is always
appreciated. We're mindful of how precious your vacation time is, and
we deeply value the sacrifices you make to spend it with us.

We also understand that having us visit—or visiting us—can be
an adjustment, especially when Dad and I are used to our quiet, two-
person household. Thank you for your patience when the energy and
routines shift during those times.

Thank you for making sure we're a part of your children's lives.
We know our role as grandparents is different from that of the in-law
grandparents who live or have lived closer, but "different" doesn't
mean lesser. We respect your in-laws, past and present, and have
always felt their sensitivity to the unique challenges of our long-
distance connection.

We understand your hope that the grandkids are always proactive in their interactions, but we've learned to cherish what we do receive. Whether near or far, grandparenting is never a one-size-fits-all experience. We're confident there's always a place for us in their lives, even if it's not always front and centre.

Thank you for everything you do to keep our family connected, no matter the miles. We may be separated by geography, but we remain bound by love, acceptance, understanding, and shared efforts.

> With all our love,
> Helen / Mum
> xxx
> ___
>
> *Helen Ellis*
> *Scotland; England; New Zealand*

Dear Manu and Maria,

When I was young I loved to write letters. Open the old leather suitcase PopPop likes to 'tidy away' in the loft and you will find bundles of letters tied up with ribbon, that are relics of my childhood, adolescence and the years before your daddy was born. I always had a wanderlust, which is why I chose to study French, German and Latin at school and university, long before I thought of living abroad as a grown-up. I collected penfriends like stamps—Marie-Laurence and Marie-Pierre from France, Annemari from Finland, Tom from the USA and Tini from Germany. Or maybe it's just because my daddy, the Great Grandpa you never knew, and my mummy, your Great Granny, took Great Uncle Patrick and me away on long summer holidays in the caravan to France.

I expect you know that PopPop and I lived abroad for almost all our married life. Daddy was born in Sharjah, in the United Arab Emirates, just a year and a half after Uncle Sam, and we all lived in Dubai, Oman, Norway and the Netherlands together. Daddy, like me, loves languages and can speak Indonesian, Malay and Dutch as well as English and Spanish. He's learning Valenciano so he can understand what Mama and her family say to you.

You were born in Spain and live there. By the time Daddy was your age he had already moved countries. I watch you both growing up, immersed in a cross-cultural family. You are so young, just one and two. Daddy, PopPop and I talk to you in English but Mama, Yaya, Yayo and Tio Jero speak in Valenciano. People outside speak Spanish. Daddy cooks you roast dinners on Sunday, Mama makes you puchero and Yaya cooks arroz al horno and paella. You have two different types of cooking in your house.

PopPop and I talk you over WhatsApp video. You blow kisses, 'bezitos' Mama calls them and you wave like crazy. Luckily, every few months PopPop and I pack our suitcases, get on a plane and fly over to see you, read you stories in English and play with you. I am happy to have been forced to learn another language so I can talk to Mama and her family and to discover another way of cooking. PopPop and I love coming to the seaside in Javea and to be part of your lives.

Some things make us sad. I moved to Dubai to live with PopPop the day after PopPop and I got married. I knew how sad it made Great

Granny and Great Grandpa but it didn't stop me. In the end we lived all over the world for 36 years. My parents also loved being able to visit us in exciting new places too. Your poor Daddy had to keep changing schools. He had to keep saying goodbye to friends, losing the groups he played music in or the sports teams he played in. He kept having a new bedroom, a new language spoken outside his door. He had to learn to live with a life of constant change. I am sad for him too. But I am also happy he is comfortable in so many places, that he doesn't seem to mind whether he keeps moving or stays in one place. PopPop and I are living back in Stamford where I grew up and our life seems a bit boring after living abroad. That makes us sad too, but then we look at all the wonderful friends we have made from many countries and know we have people we care about and who care about us in many places. And so do you.

We are sad that you don't come and visit us more often. We have a big house and a big garden that are perfect for you both to play in. PopPop and I are always finding exciting places we'd love to take you—down to the river with fishing nets, the muddy creeks of Norfolk where you can sit on rocks and cast thick orange nylon string with hooks on and try to catch crabs, the hills you can roll down, the woods where you can go and kick through crunchy leaves in your welly boots. But we know it's hard for you to visit us and much easier for us to come to visit you at the moment. We can't wait for Daddy to be able to show you all the places he grew up one day.

During the many years we lived abroad we learned that Daddy is what's called a TCK—a Third Culture Kid. That's because he lived in places that neither his mummy nor daddy (PopPop and me) grew up in either. And while we were living abroad my friend, Ruth Van Reken, invented a new term for people like you—not TCK but CCK. That's a Cross-Cultural Kid. In many ways you will experience things a bit like Daddy did. You too are living 'between worlds'. You have three languages, two cuisines and have to choose whether to support a Spanish football team or an English one—or both! Every day you live across and between cultures. This makes you a bit different from lots of the other children in your school. You are very lucky. Do you realise that you have a whole other family in England? Great Uncles, Great Aunts, Second Cousins, even some Great Great Uncles and Aunt! There's a big red fluffy Australian Doodle puppy waiting to be cuddled in a place called Midhurst, and an old black and white spotty Dalmation called Layla by the sea in Selsey. So many people who love you and want to spend time with you and show you their worlds too.

Manu and Maria, life will always be filled with happy things and sad things. You are two of our 'happy things'. Always know your home is 'the world' and exploring it can be very exciting.

With lots of love,
Granny

———

Jo Parfitt
Peterborough; Neufchâtel-en-Bray; Dubai;
Muscat; Stavanger, Stamford; The Hague;
Kuala Belait; Kuala Lumpur

Dear Future Daughter,

As I write I feel uncertain about whether something like this is really necessary. Perhaps this is what your grandmother feels when she is reluctant to answer my questions about her past.

You are my daughter and I am your mother, but you must know that I am also a daughter. What does it mean to be a daughter? There is no right or wrong answer to this question; this is just my answer.

Sometimes, being a daughter means teaching your mother things that the world did not give her time to learn. Like whether or not it is okay to click "I agree" to the terms and conditions on a software update. Or how to use AI to erase the people in the background of her photos. Sometimes, it is not things, but a new way of seeing or thinking or being in the world, (like using AI to erase the people in the background of photos) or like eating the continental breakfast at a hotel in Dubai alone during a long layover and finding the experience enjoyable. Sometimes, being a daughter means learning that it is not always okay to agree to everything without pausing to read, or pausing to think, pausing to question and doubt the process. Or learning that the people in the background also play a part in the memory of that moment.

Sometimes, being a daughter means accepting that life's not fair, that some choices are made for you, that life goes on, at times too quickly and at other times too slowly, and you make the best of it.

It also means challenging life's unfairness: in muted struggles, in wordless prayers, in blunt passive aggressive mumbles "아니야." (No) "몰라." (I don't know) when what you actually mean to say is yes, I know. Sometimes, being a daughter means recognizing that in the times you thought your emotions were hidden, they were seen; and the times you needed to be seen, you were not.

Sometimes, being a daughter means running away to a different continent, a country that is 30+ hours of travel away, but then sending your mom a plane ticket so that she can sleep comfortably with both legs stretched out at night after seeing that you have made this foreign place your home. Sometimes, it means feeling like a foreigner in your own home and pretending that you don't. Sometimes, being a daughter means you can't hide.

Sometimes being a daughter means laughing with your siblings in English because your parents don't need to understand and crying in Korean because you need to be understood. Sometimes being a daughter means giving up on the desire to be understood.

Sometimes being a daughter means leaving home, missing home, going home, missing home, staying home, missing home... Sometimes it means missing all the lost time and memories from when you were "home", but your parents were not.

Sometimes it means finding yourself in a battle that has been waging on before you were born and seems to have no end, and sometimes it means fighting your own battles in what feels like an isolated silo. Sometimes being a daughter means embodying hope for a past generation.

In sum, "Daughtering" (v): Teaching, learning, accepting, challenging, recognizing, running, pretending, hiding, laughing, crying, giving up, leaving, going, staying, missing, finding, fighting, embodying.

Dear Future Daughter, if none of this makes sense, that's okay. Because your mother is also a daughter, and sometimes being a daughter means giving up on the desire to be understood.

Dear Future Daughter, my initial intention was to have this letter be about you and your world, but reading it now, it is all about me, and the limits of my current imagination to think beyond my world.

But don't worry, I won't ask you to understand.

Love,
Your Future Umma

———

Youngjae Chang
Seoul; California; Yanji; Daejeon;
Massachusetts; Accra; Jeju

Dear Future Child,

Writing to you at this moment in time is an exercise in humility and hubris all at once. Humility, because I am currently not a mother, and I do not know all the details of my biological and social future. Hubris, because I am currently not a mother, and I do not know all the details of my biological and social future—yet I choose to pen this letter, an act that boldly affirms that, yes, you will exist.

Your father will be a man born in Queens, New York. Half of his childhood was spent there and the other half, in Mandeville, Jamaica. Your mother, the writer of this letter, will be a woman born in Ilorin, Nigeria. Her childhood was split between Ilorin, Nigeria; Calabar, Nigeria; Victoria, Canada; Bowling Green, Kentucky, USA; and Southern California, USA. The soundtrack to your life will be an eclectic mix of your favorite genres, reggae, and Afrobeats. Your memories will include your attempts to eat fufu and Afang soup with your hands while your dad and your uncles, his brothers, banter in Patois.

Your father's confident command of his mother tongue is in stark contrast to my lingua blanca. My mother tongue, the language of my ancestors, is practically nonexistent on my lips; I am linguistically orphaned. My late mother was Igbo and my father is Efik. I was born in Yorubaland, and English was the language with which I was raised. When my Efik stepmother entered the picture, I heard Efik every day. Despite hearing it so often, my mind was and currently is only familiar with the basics of the language. I won't lie; I do envy that your father knows his family's language. Despite this, I smile at the thought of you joining in on Patois-laden banter.

Being the product of Jamaica, Nigeria, and the US, you will turn out to be (among other things) a multidimensional being. If your cross-cultural experience is anything like mine, you will love it some days and be frustrated by it on others. While the Nigerian culture you inherit from me will be the kind that is more in harmony with my Americanness, I fear that this could backfire. That despite the conversations we will have regarding cultural expectations, you will run into an uncomfortable intercultural situation or two that I didn't properly prepare you for. Should this happen, I hope you forgive me.

I know our intercultural conversations will give you an opportunity to express yourself in ways that I never could. I will relish the bittersweet freedom of your expression. Of you, in a number of ways, living the childhood I wish I had. I will delight in some of your thought processes, and I absolutely plan on giving you that look that I hope makes you laugh when your thoughts are "out there." Deep down, I know that your zany musings will only confirm that you are indeed my child.

I also hope I will figure out how to navigate the tensions that will inevitably arise in our relationship. Both directly and indirectly, I was taught that children are to be seen and not heard, but I vehemently disagree with that perspective. That said, I also know that as your mother, there is a high level of responsibility I bear in raising you to be the best daughter or son you can be. And I know that you won't always appreciate the choices that I make with your best interests at heart. I also know that even with my sincerest intentions, I won't always get it right. And I am genuinely sorry.

I won't lie. There's a certain level of envy I have for you, baby. Oh, to be a child that receives reasonable apologies before their birth. And here I am, the future mother who gives those apologies freely to a child who doesn't exist yet. If I am honest, the fear from my childhood still has somewhat of a grip on me: I am an adult woman who still feels seen and not heard.

But enough about me. This is about you. I am excited for you, kid! I smile at the possibilities of what you will be. With the parents you'll have and the community you'll be surrounded by, I look forward to what will come of you, both in the mountain top victories and in the low valley moments. Come what may, I will be there for you.

Here's to you, kid.

Sincerely,
Mom
———

Mary Bassey
Nigeria; Canada; USA

Letters to Parents and Grandparents

Dear Mom,

I never meant to leave you.

More accurately, I never meant to stay away. It started as a dream—when I'd stand in Granny's hallway at the farm, staring at photos of the places she'd travelled to, and imagine myself there. We could blame her and the wanderlust that skipped a generation to find its way into my bloodstream, or we could blame Greg for whisking me away a year after we were married, but in truth: it was me. I was the one who pushed our fledgling marriage out of the nest and onto a plane bound for London. I chose to leave the open grasslands of South Africa, as they waved their goodbye in the wind, and at first, I had no regrets.

London welcomed us with the arms of an ancient ancestor. She put flesh on my British heritage and made me stand proud as I swore allegiance to the Crown. She gave me an exhilarating career as a physical therapist in the hospital where Florence Nightingale once stalked the halls with her lamp, making rounds of wounded soldiers at night. Big Ben watched over me as Megan was born, and Kingston hospital delivered Katie into my arms three years later. We became a family in London, and whilst manicured gardens replaced the smell of freshly mowed lawns, I had very few regrets.

America came calling with her promise of a grand adventure, and Greg and I fell for her siren song. We plucked up our family and dropped it into very unfamiliar buffalo grass territory. I had no map for this country, bar the memory of a Texas-shaped magnet on Granny's fridge, so when we landed in Austin, I comforted myself with the idea that at least she was watching over us. America made me work hard to find new friends, establish schools for the girls, and get my license to continue working. Just as I was finding my feet, God seemed to have other plans. I was visiting you in South Africa when I discovered I was pregnant with Eliza, and within nine months she became the first American citizen in our family. Now we all carry the blue passports that mock me about our "unintentional immigration"... would you believe me if I said we never meant to stay? Because now I do have regrets.

In the 25 years we've been abroad, so much has changed. Grandparents died, cousins married, and nieces and nephews were born who are now grown and off to university. The farm and the beach house where Julie and I made our childhood memories have been sold. But my biggest regret, Mom, is time not spent with you. You've been gone for 11 years now, but grief still ambushes me—hence my letter to you today.

Last weekend I went to visit a friend who'd recently had a baby. As I stepped into her home, I noticed it had the same earthy kikuyu-grass smell as the farm. I immediately felt both at home and desperately homesick. I experienced the most vivid flashback of Granny's house, where we'd spend weekends and summers with our cousins romping carefree around the farm while you and Dad worked. My reverie was interrupted by the arrival of my friend's mother who had come to visit the "grandbaby". As I watched her coo and cuddle, I found myself fighting back tears. With fresh nostalgia in my nose, memories were evoked of the times you came to visit me in London, and later, Austin to meet your granddaughters and help me adjust to my new role as a mother.

I drove home in silence mingled with regret and felt like I owed you an apology: Mom, please will you forgive me for leaving? For keeping your grandchildren a continent away from you and Dad? I know we made trips to see each other regularly, and for that I am grateful, but as I think of all the little moments we didn't have—I can't help but wonder what it would've been like had we stayed. It's in moments like these that I hear your voice, like in the last days of your cancer as you tried to reassure me in my distress. This time you say, "There, there, dear. No use crying. It's nothing more than a monkey's wedding," and I know exactly what you mean. Life is bittersweet, a mystery of paradox, a tightrope of loss and gain.

The sun can shine, even as it's raining.

Our life in America with three teenage daughters is good AND hard without the loving presence and support of family. This is what we unwittingly chose all those years ago. Thank you for having the courage to set us free and the grace to keep encouraging us—even when I know it broke your heart as much as it breaks mine.

I love you, Mom.

Your daughter, in this life and the next,
Carolyn

———

Carolyn Grant
Pretoria, Durban, South Africa; London,
England, UK; Austin, Texas, USA

22 May 2025
Manchester, United Kingdom

Dear Mom,

"If you hate it, you can come home tomorrow..."

Those were the last words you said to me as I stood at the edge of the unknown, hesitating before the security gate at the Regina airport on that icy January morning. I was 21, bundled in layers, full of nerves, clutching a boarding pass to a future I wasn't sure I was ready for. The stars hadn't aligned that day—my first flight was canceled due to freezing fog; I had no idea how I'd make my connection to Paris. Red canceled banners flashed across the departures screen and my mind. I was convinced it was a sign I shouldn't go. Maybe I wasn't cut out for this after all.

And yet, your words gave me just enough courage to move forward.

You were inexperienced yourself, but you were so encouraging for me to take this chance. Helping me pack until 2am the night before (and multiple times that followed...). You didn't promise it would be easy, but you gave me permission to try. I had the safety net of knowing that if it all went wrong, I could come home.

What followed was more than just a semester abroad. It was the start of a life shaped by curiosity, courage, and so many beautiful connections across the world. From that first leap, so many more followed—moving to London, then Australia, then Sweden, starting a family in Canada, and now here we are in Manchester.

And all those places that I lived, you showed up.

I remember stocking our tiny apartment fridge with wine and cheese from the market for your first arrival in France, determined to show you how grown up and well cultured I was. Only we arrived back to the apartment a couple of hours later to the most pungent smell we had ever smelled. I managed to buy the strongest, stinkiest cheese known to man (clearly trying to impress dad here). It took days to air the smell out!

Through it all, you've never tried to hold me back and you've always eased my guilt or fears of missing out at home. You've only ever been a cheerleader.

Now, as a mother myself, I understand a little more about what that meant. Letting go. Watching your child walk into the unknown. The pride, the ache, the weight of what's unsaid. You told me later how small I looked walking through those security gates and watching until you couldn't see me anymore and my flight finally took off. I can only imagine how hard it must have been in those early days, when technology wasn't what it is now. When you couldn't track my flight online or get instant confirmation that I'd landed safely.

You trusted me. You trusted the world. And that trust gave me wings.

As I write this, I'm sitting at my dining table in Manchester. My children are at their cozy, neighbourhood school. You're in Saskatchewan, across an ocean and at least 7 time zones away... but talking can be tricky when you live so far away, in some places it is night, in others it is day... Yet somehow, it doesn't feel that far. We're always connected — by love, by memory, by everything you taught me about finding adventure and returning home again.

Worlds apart but connected forever, faraway together.

> With love,
> Jocelyn

———

Jocelyn Tochor
Saskatchewan, Calgary, Canada;
Rouen, France; London, Manchester,
United Kingdom; Melbourne, Australia;
Stockholm, Sweden

Dear Daddy,

It's been three years since you died, and every day I miss you and our conversations so much. Today, I'm writing to tell you something I'm not sure I ever fully expressed: thank you for making me a TCK.

I was only five years old when you and Mommy made the decision to uproot our family from that little suburban house with the literal white picket fence in the USA. I couldn't possibly have understood then what you were giving up—that carefully constructed American dream with its predictable comforts and familiar landmarks. At five, I couldn't comprehend what it meant for you, a tall white man from upstate New York, to navigate a world not built for you.

Now I can see it—how uncomfortable you must've been whenever you folded your lanky frame into those tiny bus seats meant for much smaller bodies. How well you hid your frustration every time you had to ask me or my sister to read a sign for you. How it must have stung each time a well-meaning server automatically handed you a fork when you'd been eating with chopsticks for years, thanks to having married into a Chinese American family. These weren't just inconveniences; they were daily reminders that you were the other, the gaijin, forever the visible foreigner.

Yet I never once heard you complain. Instead, you showed me how to move through the world with that particular grace that comes from being simultaneously humble and curious. I watched you speak with equal warmth and respect to everyone—from the school's custodian who barely understood your broken Japanese to high-ranking military commanders you had to meet with as head of an international school. You never pulled rank, never leaned on your white American privilege as a crutch. You communicated your deeply-held faith by treating everyone as equally beloved by their Creator.

Remember those adventures in our tiny Subaru van? How you'd turn down unmarked roads, zigzag through random villages, pull over in some seaside neighbourhood, and somehow—despite the language barrier—end up getting us invited into someone's home or treated to a cold drink. You embodied the Okinawan saying Ichariba chōdē—"once we meet, we become family"—long before you ever heard the words. You never treated these encounters as anthropological studies or tourist experiences; instead, these were connections waiting to happen, transcending language and nationality. I didn't realize then that I was learning one of my life's most important lessons: how to be a guest in someone else's world with both delight and respect, how to find family wherever I went.

Daddy, my passport still says I'm American. My face and name reflect my Chinese and German heritage. But Okinawa—that's the home of my heart. You gave me that. Not just a childhood in Japan, but a life where borders feel permeable, where "home" is a constellation rather than a single fixed point. I'll be honest; this gift hasn't always felt like one. There have been times I've ached with the peculiar loneliness of belonging nowhere completely. I've envied people who can answer "where are you from?" without hesitation or qualification. My friendships stretch across time zones, making casual connection complicated. I still question who I am when my identities feel fragmented across continents.

But oh, the richness! I've explored over 40 countries now, lived in several. Each new place feels simultaneously foreign and familiar— that paradox only TCKs truly understand. The languages I speak, the global perspective I hold, my career in intercultural education—these all grew from those seeds you planted when you decided our family belonged not in one culture but between and among many.

Sometimes I wonder if you knew what you were doing—if you understood that you were raising children who would never quite fit anywhere but could make themselves at home everywhere. Did you realize that your example of cultural humility would become my blueprint for moving through the world? That watching you navigate difference with curiosity rather than judgment would shape not just my professional life but the very core of who I am?

I find myself now passing these gifts to others, explaining to those who've never left home that the world is both vastly larger and significantly smaller than they imagine. I recognize your legacy in my reflexive discomfort with nationalism, in my instinctive questioning of any singular narrative. I see you in my own willingness to be the outsider, to stand comfortably at the margins rather than insisting on being centered.

What I couldn't see as a child—what I perhaps couldn't fully appreciate until now—is that your expansive love for the world was not naïve or accidental. It was a daily choice made again and again in faith, sometimes at great personal cost. You chose to live with perpetual discomfort so that the thousands of people you trained and taught over your lifetime might know comfort anywhere. You accepted the vulnerability of being perpetually misunderstood so that others might develop the capacity to understand across difference.

I carry your lessons with me everywhere I go. In every new culture, in every unfamiliar situation, I hear your voice reminding me to approach with humility, to listen before speaking, to find the humanity in each person I meet. This inheritance—this way of being in the world—is worth more than any material legacy could ever be.

So, thank you, Daddy. Thank you for making me a TCK. Thank you for showing me that home isn't a place but a capacity. Thank you for teaching me that identity isn't something to protect but something to share. Thank you for giving me a heart that feels at home in the spaces between cultures, in the beautiful complexity of a multilayered life.

With love and gratitude across whatever distance separates us now,
Your daughter Erika

———

Erika G. Bertling
New York (and multiple states), USA;
Japan; U.K.; Germany; Austria

Dear parents,

Thank you for the wealth of cultures you've given me, deeply ingrained in the fabric of my being. While I am forever grateful for the cultures, languages, and exposure, I wish you understood the struggles I faced to juggle the many expectations that came with them.

I know you will not believe me when I say this, but I never wanted to disappoint you. However, I quickly learned it was inevitable. I would have to disappoint one, if not both, of you. Because my principles are an amalgamation of all the cultures and experiences that make me, me. And in a family as mixed as ours, some of those cultures will always remain foreign to you.

It was hard to navigate the waters at home. We each spoke different mother tongues, were shaped by different societies, and carried different values—how could we ever see eye to eye? We didn't. That was as true then as it is today. Things could have worked out differently though, but I think you were both set in your ways. "My way or the highway". It always confused me how people who touched so many different cultures could still believe there was only one 'right' way. How could that be?

When you both chose to leave your home countries behind to seek the European dream, there was an inner rejection of your roots; both Latina and Arab identities were cast aside. Even though I didn't quite have the words for it at the time, today I understand that I inherited this rejection from you in my early childhood. My teen years into adulthood were a chaotic frenzy of 'where do I fit in', 'I am not enough', and 'something must be wrong with me'.

Somehow, despite that, it took me 28 years to understand why you both rejected your cultures of origin. Each of you for deeply personal reasons. In truth, it wasn't the cultures you were rejecting at all. It was the people within them who hurt you. The ones you ran away from. The ones you left behind.

I've come to believe that cultural belonging is inseparable from the people we love—and the people we can't forgive—from that culture.

It's so ironic, looking back now, that part of your anger towards me was really anger towards yourself. The part of you that you tried to cast aside but never fully let go. Because culture isn't just in the languages we speak. It lives in the unseen layers: the habits, the values, the silences. Even when we try to shut our eyes to it and shine a light in another direction, it remains, quietly present.

In our household, making space for the other was inconceivable. If I could go back I would have asked you for patience, for curiosity, and for a listening ear, instead of that commanding voice. I wish you had taken the time to get to know me. But expressing disappointment seemed a more urgent matter. Disappointment to shape me, to scare me into something I am not, to morph me into you. Like I said, I never wanted to disappoint you, but disappointment was inevitable.

Over the years, I've had to shed layers and understand who I am away from the cultural, family conditioning. And I'm still finding my path. Becoming is an action in the present tense. I am still, and will always be, becoming me.

I'll leave you with this passage I shared with you so many years ago from one of my favorite poems: On Children by Khalil Gibran.

"Your children are not your children.
They are the sons and daughters of Life's longing for itself.
They come through you but not from you,
And though they are with you yet they belong not to you."

In the end, there's so much left unsaid, and so many needs that will remain unmet.

Your daughter,
B.N.
———

Anonymous

Rakas isä,

Vaikka aika on kulunut, kaipaus sinua kohtaan ei ole hälvennyt. Yhä mietin, kuinka paljon olisin halunnut jakaa kanssasi — en vain aikaa, vaan myös kokemuksia, joita olen saanut aikuisena.

Olen kasvanut, valmistunut lukiosta ja suorittanut sekä kandidaatin että maisterin tutkinnot. Olen asunut useissa eri maissa ja oppinut puhumaan ranskaa. Minulla oli kissa, Maki, mutta hän kuoli, ja nyt minulla on kissanpentu, Sora. Olen varma, että olisit pitänyt heistä.

Sinun kuolemasi jälkeen erosin poikaystävästä, jonka tapasit. Olit oikeassa — hän oli todellakin ääliö. Nyt olen ollut uuden kumppanini kanssa jo lähes kahdeksan vuotta. On sääli, ettei hän voinut tavata sinua, mutta olen varma, että olisit pitänyt hänestä.

Kun kuolit niin nuorena, suren sitä, kuinka paljon elämääsi jäi elämättä. Tiedän, että sinulla oli unelmia ja toiveita matkustaa eläkkeellä, ehkä muuttaa pieneen kaupunkiin, saada iso puutarha ja viettää päivät ulkona. Ehkä olisit rakentanut oman saunan, ehkä suorittanut tohtorin tutkintosi loppuun. Ehkä olisit kirjoittanut kirjan — olithan niin taitava ja hauska kirjoittaja. Ehkä olisit hankkinut uuden koiran ja lähtenyt sen kanssa mahtaville seikkailuille. Olisin juhlinut saavutuksiasi kymmenkertaisesti.

Olit hyväsydäminen ja kiltti niin ihmisille kuin eläimille. Meillä ei koskaan tapettu hyönteisiä, koska uskoit, että kaikilla on oikeus elämään. Hyväksyit minut sellaisena kuin olin. Ymmärsit, että oli hyväksi kehitykselleni asua eri maissa, mutta samalla tiesit, kuinka vaikeaa minun oli ymmärtää kotimaatamme. Kannustit minua oppimaan uusia kieliä ja tutustumaan ihmisiin eri puolilta maailmaa. Olit myös hauska ja viisas. Sinulla oli parhaat iltasadut, ja musiikilliset taitosi lumosivat minut. Kun kuulin laulusi kantautuvan talon ja puutarhan läpi, tunsin lämpöä ja turvaa.

Joskus yöllä, kun uni ei tule, ajattelen sinua. Toivon, että voisin lähettää sinulle viestin ja saada vastauksesi. Toivon, että voisin soittaa sinulle ja kuulla äänesi. Toivon, että voisin hypätä lentokoneeseen ja nähdä sinut. Toivon, että voisin laittaa ruokaa sinulle, kuten sinä aina laitoit minulle. Toivon, että olisimme voineet viettää enemmän aikaa yhdessä mukavassa hiljaisuudessa, vain me kaksi. Toivon, että voisin jakaa kanssasi vielä yhden automatkan, jossa laulaisimme mukana radiosta soivia kappaleita. Toivon, että olisimme voineet nähdä Shakiran konsertissa. Haluaisin antaa sinulle suuren halauksen.

Haluaisin kertoa sinulle vielä kerran, että rakastan sinua.

Ajattelen sinua joka päivä, ja aina kun elän jotain suurta tai pientä, mietin, mitä olisit sanonut tai ajatellut.

On niin paljon asioita, joita olisin halunnut jakaa kanssasi.

Kiitos kaikesta, mitä olit minulle.

Sinun,
Na

English Translation from Nora

Dearest Dad,

Though time has passed, the longing for you has never faded. I still find myself wishing I could have shared so much more with you—not just time, but the moments and experiences that have shaped me in adulthood.

I've grown up.

I completed high school and earned both my bachelor's and master's degrees. I've lived in different countries, and I've learned to speak French. I had a cat, Maki—she's gone now—and now I have a kitten named Sora. I'm sure you would have loved them both.

After you died, I broke up with the boyfriend you knew. You were right—he wasn't exactly a gem. Now I've been with someone for over eight years. It saddens me that he never got to meet you, but I'm sure you would have liked him.

You left so young, and I grieve all the life you never got to live. I know you had dreams—to travel in retirement, maybe move to a small town, build a big garden, spend your days outside. Maybe you would have built your own sauna. Maybe you would have finished your doctorate. Maybe you would have written a book—you were such a brilliant and funny writer. Maybe you'd have gotten a new dog and gone on grand adventures.

I would have celebrated your every achievement tenfold.

You were kind-hearted and gentle with people and animals alike. In our home, no insect was ever killed—you believed every life had its right to exist.

You accepted me just as I was. You understood that living abroad would help me grow, even as you knew how hard it was for me to make sense of our homeland. You encouraged me to learn new languages, to connect with people from all walks of life.

You were also funny and wise.

You told the best bedtime stories.

Your music enchanted me. When your voice drifted through the house and garden, it made everything feel warm and safe.

Sometimes at night, when sleep won't come, I think of you. I wish I could send you a message and get your reply. I wish I could call and hear your voice. I wish I could board a plane and see you again. I wish I could cook for you, the way you always cooked for me. I wish we could spend more time together in quiet comfort—just the two of us. I wish we could share one more road trip, singing along to the radio. I wish we could have gone to a Shakira concert together. I wish I could give you the biggest hug. I wish I could tell you one more time: I love you.

I think of you every single day. With every small or great thing I experience, I wonder what you would have said—what you would have thought. There is so much I still wish I could share with you.

I carry your love with me into every new chapter. You are still here—in the way I laugh, in the way I care, in the quiet moments I hold most dear. Thank you for all that you were to me.

Yours always,
Na

———

Nora Sundberg
Thailand; Finland; Vietnam; Egypt;
France; Italy; United Kingdom;
Switzerland; Central African Republic

Dear Mum,

I'm feeling rather emotional writing this letter to you. We live so far away, and I know that you're finding it hard to be alone without dad. You moved there so dad could end his years in the country he loved so much. And now you can't go to yours. I can't quite imagine what it must feel like to have a grown son and grown daughters who live across the world in different directions. Although I'll probably be living that myself. When our boys are adults, I'm not sure we'll all be living in the same country.

I suppose I should tell you that you started it, seeing as you left your home at 19, lived in Lebanon and then met dad. You know what it's like living miles away from your own mum and sisters. I think when I left home as a young adult, I wasn't really thinking about the fact that now my medical insurance is tied into one country. You and I are in similar situations in that regard wanting to live in one country but also circumstances leading us to live in another. I didn't realise that we wouldn't be involved in our nieces and nephews' lives, that we'd wonder where to go back 'home' to. I am grateful though that we are close as a family, although we are not close if we count in distance. I probably talk to my brother and sister more than other siblings do, and we know we love each other. And you and I—we talk often, maybe even more than if I was living close by.

I'm sorry for telling you that you needed to change your attitude when I was growing up in France and you were finding it so hard to be far from family, not speaking the language and not being able to go home as often as you would have liked. Now that I'm in the same situation, I'm realising it's not so easy to change your attitude. Sorry I'm crying a bit, and tears are wetting the paper.

I heard somewhere that once you start living in another country, it's like taking the toothpaste out of the tube. It is impossible to put it back in again, and I suppose your life and my life and our boys' lives prove that we've irreversibly mixed the culture pot. Life is a mosaic of all that your parents have included with their own mixed heritage, then you and dad and now us. I'm not sure I like the term 'citizens of the world'. In one way I see what people mean when they say that. It is, in fact, one world and we are all human, but will there ever be a corner of the world where I feel I belong? That I am not planning to leave? Where people have known me for years and whose faces are familiar? I can't believe I am still struggling with this at 49 years of age.

In a way our toothpaste is out of the tube and wanting something different might be a fantasy. You'd think I would feel settled by now. In myself at least, even if not settled in one place. Sorry I have to laugh. I am not sure we will ever settle in one place. I told N. the other day that they would probably live far from us when they are grown up and he laughed and said we'd likely be the ones still moving around.

It's funny how, out of the three of us siblings, I am the one who has embraced the moving around. Maybe it's because I like the unknown, the adventure of getting to know new people, new places and new ways of doing things. Although it stresses me at the beginning and tires me to do it all over again a few years later, I still love it and do it over and over again.

Every time we go to Switzerland, I can see the boys and even myself have a little bit of envy towards those who have lived in the same neighbourhood their whole life whose parents live around the corner and whose best friend is down the road. They know all the best spots for swimming, they have their favourite restaurant and don't have to worry about what to ask the hairdresser and if they are going to have a weird haircut or not. I keep telling the boys that if they are unsure, it is not because they are dumber than everyone else but that second guessing oneself is part of living in an unknown country.

There's no point in wishing life had been a different way. These are the cards we've been dealt. You and dad have shown us what it means to be hospitable to friends, strangers, foreigners and those who are lonely. Just by being who you are, you have shown us different ways of doing things. Now that I understand how culture works a little bit more, I can see how it is incredibly enriching. Yes, sometimes I do things that shock people where we now live, but I've also been told it's refreshing for them to see someone go against the status quo and do something unconventional from their point of view. It shows them they can also do things differently.

I want to say thank you mum for raising us with amazing Middle Eastern food, different languages, never hesitating to go to places you didn't know and figuring it out with dad. You've taught us the world.

Rhoda
——

Rhoda Bangerter
Lebanon; France; Scotland; England;
Nyon, Bern, Switzerland; New York, USA;
Kyrgyzstan

31 July, 2013

Dear Mom,

Last week, I had the opportunity to visit a village with a long-term expat volunteer and three visiting American high-school students. During our visit we were served chai (tea) and later, a simple but generous lunch of rice and beans. I watched with some embarrassment as one of the teenagers said she could only take a little bit of chai. The hostess laughed nervously, not knowing how to respond to the rejection. During lunch I cringed as the same girl said she didn't want any beans on her rice. The hostess was visibly ashamed about the meal and felt responsible to find something suitable for her guest. She frantically looked around for something to offer to moisten her rice—bean broth? Milk? Chai? The girl refused; she was happy with just rice, oblivious to any discomfort for our hostess. I wanted to tell her to just eat her beans, that her personal preferences weren't important in this situation.

I saw myself at nine years old joining you on an Eid visit to an elderly woman in Muscat. Do you remember how, as we sat on the floor, leaning against cushions along the wall, she came around offering helwa, the rose-flavored goop that always made me gag? I looked at you, silently asking if I had to eat any. You whispered to me to just take a little bit. So I did. But then our hostess exclaimed, "La!" and scooped up a big handful, plopping it into the palm of my hand. I stared at it, mortified. I silently pleaded with you to make it go away, and you said very sympathetically, "I'm sorry, but you have to eat it." Because showing respect and honor to our hostess was more important than my physical comfort or personal preferences. Thank you for teaching me that.

As I settle into another foreign country and reflect on what it takes to adapt to a new culture, I'm reminded again and again that so much of what is helping me adjust is what you taught me as a child growing up overseas.

Thank you for all the times you made me eat things I didn't want to eat in other people's homes—the strange, the spicy, the goopy, the gag-inducing. And drinking Arabic kahwa from little thimble cups. I see how it honors my Kenyan friends and neighbors when I'm able to joyfully accept what they offer, especially when I'm willing to try "delicacies" that they know most wazungu (Western foreigners) don't like.

Thank you for teaching me how to pop a squat! Who knew that this would be the most useful skill to have when traveling anywhere in Africa? I don't remember if you first taught me how to squat in Egypt or camping in Oman, but I know that a hole in the ground, which I'm finding a lot these days, doesn't scare me. Nor does using the bushes.

Thank you for modeling sensitivity to cultural expectations, for teaching me to sit with my feet tucked under me so that I didn't expose my soles to anyone, for making sure I wore modest clothing, for knowing to shake hands with people I met, and never touch food with my left hand, for teaching me how to eat with my fingers. Did you know you were secretly preparing me to one day eat spaghetti with my fingers in Mali?

Thank you for taking me into other nationalities' homes, for including us as children in adult conversation. At the time it was often painfully boring to sit through what felt like hours of meaningless discussion. But it taught me conversation skills and how to interact with people of different ages. It also taught me patience for my current African culture where waiting patiently (and cheerfully!) is a daily activity, where church services last hours, and where meetings are filled with endless speeches. I admit I don't always have the cheerful part down, but I do know what's required of me to show respect, which, once again, is more important than my comfort.

Thank you for always opening our home to others, for modeling what hospitality looks like, for showing me that holidays are about taking in those who are far away from their families during a potentially lonely time. Thank you for demonstrating that a home should be filled with people, to host music nights and game nights and Bible studies and to share meals. Now that I'm in a location where the only entertainment is socializing in homes, I find myself enjoying planning meals and cooking and having people around our table.

Thank you for taking me on budget vacations to 'exotic' countries instead of back to the US every summer. I know it was out of necessity based on our financial situation; the US was just too far away and too expensive. Because of it, you exposed me to the world in a way that just staying in one country never would have. I'm also thankful that we always stayed in budget accommodation, took public transportation, and ate street food.

Thank you for putting me in British school. I know it wasn't a choice, but it gave me a much broader education than if I had been in American schools my whole life. Even though I didn't like being teased for being a Yank, I appreciate that my classmates growing up were from all over the world. Knowing British English has helped me communicate better in other countries, especially in Kenya.

There are a lot of formal cross-cultural orientations and trainings out there, covering many valuable topics. I wonder if they're able to teach in a seminar format what you've modeled to me throughout my life. My guess is not. My desire is that one day if I have kids that I will be able to model these things well to them. I just hope there's no helwa where we live.

Love,
Jennifer

_____

Jennifer Lavery
USA; Egypt; Oman; Bahrain; Honduras;
England; Mozambique; Kenya

April 1, 2025
South Africa

Dear Aderemi,

So much has happened since I last saw you, wasted, struggling to catch your breath, as you sat hunched over in that old armchair. It is crazy to think, isn't it, how quickly the years fly overhead? The years are like swallows hastening north in the springtime, driven by that mysterious ancient rhythm that moves the sea to dance as well. They do not stop for rain or shine, storm or calm. There is an ardency of life in their passing, as they hurry through their directionless path in the sky.

I remember the first time you left for Canada, and my little black fingers itched to touch the snow you touched. I saw pictures of the snow instead. And of the horses. And the white faces, gleaming with joy. I saw you hunched over beside a snowman, clothed in a thick, blue jacket, your hands covered with woolen black gloves. A bright smile crowned your beautiful face.

Perhaps this was the first time that itch came to me; that strong desire to travel as you had done, and as the swallows do. To escape the boring rhythm of normality and to fly north. To touch snow. To ride horses. To see those foreign, European faces for myself. I wanted to go too. And when the call came, I flew.

But I didn't head north, as I would have liked. The strong hands of providence that beats out that mysterious ancient rhythm, pulled me south instead. And I flew with you. You guided us as we entered the plane—that great, rumbling bird, the delight of little wanderers like you and I. Was it twelve hours we spent in its belly, my stomach plummeting at every sudden burst of its temper? Perhaps that was the time I first realised, in my own small way, that to fly wasn't all that better than staying grounded.

But it was too late.

When that giant bird landed, and our sauntering feet hit the floor, I looked around in awe at the sea of faces, some in tones I had seen before in those precious pictures. I said something to you, and I think you smiled. About four years later, I rode a horse for a short while. But after all these years, a decade and a half, I still haven't seen snow. I haven't even touched it.

You struggled to spread our wings and bring us here, to this place in the South. To this greener pasture away from the dying African West. You worked hard and had ambition for us. I remember those times you slept in your office, and drove a beatdown red Volkswagen. The struggle hasn't ended.

It is a constant war, isn't it? Being in this in-between place in the South? Perhaps it was more of a struggle for you than it is for me. You felt it as you climbed your way to the top, battling hostile forces. And you felt it one last time when, after reaching the top, your body began to give way under it all.

If you were still here with me, I'd call you and tell you all that has happened since that time you sat hunched over in the old armchair.

I am much wiser now, perhaps. But I still struggle with the same, old things. Would it still hurt you to see how hard I still find it, after all these years? A decade and a half is a longtime to still be pining for flight.

Could I fly back west? Would those I've left behind still recognise me for who I have become? Would they scorn at me, as many do here in the South? Labeling me as different and outlandish, a dichotomy. Neither here nor there. An alien.

Or should I head north to see the snow?

I wish I could go back to being a little child, sleeping under your office table after school. That was a safe space. There are not many safe spaces out there for wanderers like you and I. Not at school, nor at work. Sometimes—would it hurt you if I say this?—not even at church.

But I think you would understand. They tell me I am very much like you were. It wasn't too long ago when I was in highschool, my spirit bruised beyond words with the daily onslaught of words that told me I was not like them. I spoke to you and you understood. You told me to go speak to my greater Father, the author of that mysterious rhythm, and to ask him 'why?'

Why had he made me such as I am? Different and unique. A swallow in a land of robins. Why had he given me wings to fly?

I am ashamed to say that I sometimes forget. I more readily wish that all the things that link me to my land in the West would be changed. My skin, my accent, my culture, my tongue, my laughter, my physique. But those are the very things that link me to you. If I were to change, I would be less like you, and less of what my greater Father has called me to be.

I still get anxious, you know. Still don't really belong anywhere. Not in the South, and I think maybe, no longer in the West.

Maybe I should head north? See the snow and touch it. But I know that wouldn't change a thing.

It is an adventurous thing, isn't it, this life of being a swallow amongst robins? I know what you would say; that my home isn't here in the South, neither is it in the North, East, or the West. And perhaps that is true.

My home is in the sky with my greater Father.

When I get there, I will ask Him 'why?' And perhaps I will understand better than I can now. But until then, I am learning to fly again.

Your little swallow,
Joy

———

Joy Adewumi
West Africa; Nigeria; South Africa

Dear Mom and Dad,

Several years ago, we had a conversation in which you expressed to me some of your sorrow and misgivings about taking us halfway across the world to raise us in a foreign country. You were especially broken-hearted about the decision to send us off to boarding school. I would imagine that the decisions made within the culture of our mission family seemed sound at the time. But when you got back to the States, and started sharing with those of this culture why you had made these choices, they sounded completely different. I have seen the look on the faces of friends as I tell them how wonderful my childhood was—and all they hear is "boarding school".

When we had that discussion, I was able to offer some absolution. I wish I had gone further than that. I did forgive you, years ago, for any perceived wrongdoing towards me. What's important to note is that none of that forgiveness had anything to do with being raised in East Africa. There is no need to apologize for giving me the glorious experience of growing up in a beautiful part of the world, among a beautiful people. In fact, what I should have said is I thank you from the bottom of my heart.

I thank you for showing me that making other people's lives better happens on an individual basis so much more efficiently than it does on a governmental or organizational basis. You went with an organization, but you approached your work one person at a time. As I look at your letters and remember bits and pieces of conversations we had over the years, I believe you really saw the people you were teaching and preaching to as equals who had the potential to be anything they wanted. You didn't coddle them like children, or dismiss their ignorance as stupidity. You truly believed that their best hope (beyond Christ), was to be given the intellectual and spiritual tools to navigate their own lives. This has helped shape my thinking as I view the world today.

I thank you for giving me the experience of seeing how other people live. Learning about other cultures taught me that there is more than one way of "skinning a cat", as you used to say. And their approach may be better than mine. This has developed in me a sense of trying to see what the "other side" might be thinking or feeling. Knowing how culture and family influences the way we see the world makes me less likely to assume the worst possible motive when someone does something I don't like.

I thank you for all the amazing adventures. I have memories of hunting trips where we rode on the top of the Land Rover with our feet up in the air to push the thorn tree branches away from our bodies. Of our hunted meat hanging from a rope in a tree to keep the scavengers from getting it while we slept in our tents. (Slept? Did anyone really sleep with the prospect of scavengers sneaking into camp at night?) Of a picnic in a place called "World's End View" which lived up to its name. Or another picnic in the bottom of Ngorongoro Crater, where the hawks swooped down to steal sandwiches out of our hands. Of glorious waterfalls and peaks and forests with moss covered ground underneath. And beaches of white sand and high waves; of glorious wildlife with various colors, prints and shapes.

I thank you for making me taste the food. You proved to me that there was a whole world of tastes and textures to be experienced, that may be better than they look. My comfort foods range from a southern fried chicken to a spicy meat samosa.

Thank you for exposing me not only to various African cultures, but to British, Australian, Indian, Swedish, Norwegian, and German, to name a few. Learning even the smallest details about these cultures has broadened my horizons. To this day, I am always drawn to the most foreign person in the room. And if their skin is darker than mine, that's a bonus!

I don't mean to say that there wasn't anything hard about my upbringing. I remember face to face encounters with puff adders, taking refuge on the car to avoid the scorpions that were attracted by our lantern light. I remember an angry man above me in the doorway of a bus who spit into my face as he rode away. There were nights at boarding school where I couldn't sleep because of untreated asthma. There was deep loneliness. Wherever I was, there was somewhere I was missing. There are scars, and coping mechanisms that have their roots in those days. There are fears and insecurities that still haunt me.

But I have lived long enough to know that these things are, in some form, a part of every person. If I had been raised in my birth country, there are other beauties and adventures that would be in my memories. If we had stayed here always, I would have a different set of sorrows to bear, but they would still be there. So, if you had given me the choice I didn't have, I would choose the life I was given. All of it. It has made me who I am today. I am not perfect, by any means. But I have grown accustomed to the person I am. And I am deeply grateful for the intricate threads of the tapestry of me.

I believe that you are now in a place where there is no sorrow or tears or pain. But as I think about your time passing from this life to the next, where you were so grieved by those perceived failures, I find myself drawn to that old saying: Rest in peace, my dear parents. This child has had a good life.

With love and gratitude,
Deanna
————

Deanna Brown
Arkansas, West Virginia, Texas, USA;
Tanzania; Kenya

お母さん

ここ数年、辛かったね。

「辛かったね」と書くだけで涙がこぼれる。

お母さんと過ごした子どもの頃の思いでを辿ると、いろんな想いが込み上がってきて、整理がつかず、涙が流れる。

どれを思い浮かべても、そこには母さんが落ち着いてうちらと一緒にすごしている光景ばかり。妹と二人で、「ママー、ママー」って聞くくだらない質問に対して答えてくれる母さんは、はたから見ると何も特別なようすはない。だけど今思うと、うちらといるだけで嬉しそうだった。子どもたちと同じ空間で時をすごすことが母さんにとってこんなに嬉しいことだったんだ、と初めて感じた。

「なんでママのお手手って血のこの線が見えるの？」と、聞く私。

「あんたたちのお手手も太陽にあてれば血管が見えるよ」と、思い返せばお母さんは微笑んでいるように映る。常夏の日向があるあの二階のリビングで畳がわりに敷いた tiker の上で寝そべりながら答えてくれていた。

「ほんとだ！」

あのリビングでよくカンフー映画も観たね。[1]

We watched so many kung fu series on our Betamax video player. I remember going to the makeshift video shop down the street, walking with a skip, to rent the films. I never questioned it back then but I later learnt that these films were originally shot in Cantonese in Hong Kong before being dubbed in English (perhaps in Singapore), and then subtitled in Indonesian. When I think of it now, I don't know how you managed, Mom, to understand the movies since you don't really speak English and you never learnt to read or write in Indonesian. Was it your way to spend time with us?

私が一番に操れて、使える言葉は英語だけど、お母さんに心を伝えようとすると、やはり英語では物足りない気持ちが山々だ。下手な日本語だけど、母さんとはやっぱり日本語だよね。こう思うと、お母さんは一生のほとんど、数えれば五十年、自分の母語でない世界で生きてきたね。大変だったね。あらめて痛感する。お母さん、ありがとう。[2]

When I was young, I loved hearing you tell me stories about the day I was born. We'd lie down on the tiker. I'd beg you to tell the same story I had already heard so many times. It didn't take much begging for you to tell it again. I can now hear in your voice in my memories how much you enjoyed telling it as I hung on to every word.

Mama, one of the stories you told often was about Dagu, your dog that you named after a girl named Dagmar from one of your favorite movies. Dagu would run alongside you as you rode on the bicycle to Raikoji Station to get to your high school in Nagaoka city. When you reached the railway crossing, you'd tell Dagu to go home for her own safety and forbid her from crossing the tracks. She didn't want to, so you'd have to stop your bike and wait for her to turn around. Then you'd cross the tracks and park your bike next to the station. But you would then say, with some amount of pleasure, that when you got back in the afternoon, Dagu would always be sitting next to your bicycle waiting for you and the only way she could have gotten there was by crossing those tracks that she wasn't supposed to. Then you'd ride the bike back home with her running next to you.

One afternoon, she wasn't there. You wondered why and rode back alone. Once home, you found Grandma, who you called お母さん、

nervously pacing and stuttering when you asked about Dagu. By the time she managed to tell you that Dagu had been hit by a truck, you couldn't bear to show your grief to her. So you told your mother that you were okay.

Ma, three years ago, I came to live in Japan to build my own relationship with your country so it would be my country too. That summer, I visited your hometown without you for the first time in my life. I went to Raikoji Station on my own in the scorching heat of Nagaoka's climate-changed-40-degree, humid 盆地 summer. I used Google Maps to walk to where your old home was. Just as I set out from the station while dripping with sweat, I found the railway crossing that you had told me about over 40 years ago. It was just two tracks, with a simple crossing like any other in the rest of Japan. I reached for my smartphone and took a picture, as you do, for keepsake. But I was disappointed at how anticlimactic it was.

Having heard the story so many times, I thought I'd feel a rush of nostalgia if ever I saw the crossing. But I didn't. I guess the beauty of it wasn't in the railway crossing itself. It's not even in the stories. Instead, it's in the telling of the stories. The stories mattered because I heard them from you, Ma. In those moments that you spent with us to tell us those stories—I think you left behind precious stones on the breastplate of my heart. And I imagine on 小妹妹 / Mei-mei's heart too.

When I was young, my favorite story of all was about how I was born. You told of spending your difficult pregnancy at home sitting by the apartment window—so you wouldn't bleed and lose me—counting the Canadian maple leaves that fell from the tree to the ground. You also told of drinking a jug of milk a day; of how great your appetite was the day I was born; and of how the chilli plant sprouted the day you and Dad took me home from the hospital. You'd tell me as we looked through the albums and the photo of Dad half squatting on the ground next to the chilli plant with a newborn in one arm.

Now, as an adult, I wonder whether 妹妹 also heard stories of the day she was born? I know that that pregnancy was far more difficult for you, both during and after. But did she also get to hear stories of how much joy she brought to you and Dad? Did she get to hear those stories too? Or did she only hear the difficult stories?

I was three years old when we moved to Indonesia while you were pregnant with her. We weren't meant to stay there. The move was not chosen. When I was doing research about people who move in childhood, someone interviewed by Naomi Horoiwa (1987) said of moving in childhood: 'It is like a natural disaster. It comes when it comes, you have no control over it, but you have to deal with the consequences.' Mom, even though you were an adult, I wonder if that is what it felt like to you?

母さん、大変だったね。

ありがとう。

愛^{あい}するお母さんへ
ダナウ

¹ Ma, it's been hard these past few years.
I can feel the tears flood my eyes when I write, 'it's been hard'.
When I think back to my childhood memories with you, so many emotions well up inside me that I can't seem to sort through them, and then the tears flow.
Whenever I think of any of those memories, I see you calmly spending time with us. Ma, I can see you answering each of our silly questions as Sis and I say, 'Mommy, Mommy'. At a glance, there's nothing particularly special about those moments. But as I sit with the memories that come back to me, I notice that you seemed so happy just being with us. For the first time, I realize that those moments that you spent with us kids were precious to you—they made you so happy.
'Mommy, how come we can see the blood lines on your hands?'
'You can see the veins on your hands too if you hold them up to the sun. See?' You'd respond with an amused smile, as we rolled around on the tiker, laid out like a tatami mat, on the floor of the upstairs living room, where the tropical sun shined.
'Oh! Yeah, I can see it!'
We also often watched kung fu movies in that living room, didn't we?
² English is the language I am most fluent in but when I try to express my feelings to you, Ma, English just doesn't feel right, you know? My Japanese is not great, but with you, Japanese feels right.
When I think about it, Ma, you have lived most of your life—more than fifty years—in a world that isn't your native language. It must have been hard. I can feel it painfully for the first time. Okaa-san, thank you.

———

Danau Tanu
多伦多; Lampung, Tangerang, Jakarta;
東京; Singapura

May 23, 2023
Johannesburg, SA
5:27 AM (SAST)/11:27 PM (EST)
Dear Mom,

James will be retiring in a few days, and I'm excited to return home. The thought of being in one place and never moving again sounds like heaven to me. As I pack these last few boxes, I can't help but reflect on the wonderful life we've lived abroad. We've had so many adventures. Living in Africa was definitely the best place to raise the boys. I love the people they've become by learning from their friends at their international schools. Most of all, their lives were shaped by the caring individuals who supported us in each location. Our cooks, gardeners, and guards taught them the beauty of our African heritage in terms of culture, kindness, ingenuity, friendship, and practical skills.

But Mom, I'm seventeen years older and wiser now. There's one aspect of our journey that brings me sadness. It's how I treated you—not out of spite, but out of self-centeredness. I remember your farewell visit before we left the States for our first family adventure in Cameroon, Central Africa. We shared our final hug in the parking lot. I didn't shed a tear, while you, on the other hand, cried more than I'd seen since Daddy passed away.

I remember thinking, "Why is she sad? I'm so excited." I sincerely apologize for my insensitivity. Looking back, I can't imagine the sadness you felt—your child was leaving for a foreign land, taking your grandbabies with her. Babies whom you loved, and I can only imagine you wondered how long it would be before you saw them again.

It's ironic that my eyes didn't water when we were in the parking lot of my apartment, but they are flowing down my face as I write you this letter. I'm sorry for only thinking about myself. I never felt your anger; you simply loved all of us from afar with all you had. You showered the kids with gifts from their Gee Gee throughout the years. Whenever we returned to the States for summer break, we came to your home with ten suitcases and a calendar full of tasks, visits, and entertainment we had planned, treating your home as if it were a depot.

Oh God, how I wish I had done things differently. I would have been more sensitive to what you wanted to do with us. I would have prioritized your wishes because you deserved to be at the top of our list.

Mom, I'm forever grateful for the love and grace you showed us over the years, and I look forward to spoiling you when we return.

With All My Love,
Your Baby Girl

———

Sharoya Ham
Guinea; Cameroon; Ivory Coast; Zambia;
Uganda; South Africa; New Jersey,
Washington DC, Georgia, USA

Oh Dear Dad,

I wish you could see me now. I'm on a motorcycle riding through Southeast Asia with Mickey, and we're headed for a Chinese village on the border between Thailand and Myanmar. We had heard of the exodus of people fleeing China during the various COVID-19 waves and that many settled here in these hills along the border. We also know that refugees from Myanmar have been settling here for decades because of the tensions that have existed in the country since its independence. I get confused when I try to make sense of how the specter of colonization continues to affect so many issues we face in our parts of the world.

As we approach the border, the locals start to think that Mickey is one of them and frown confusedly when they hear that he's from India. There's a story that Mickey's ancestors on his mom's side escaped being forced to build the Great Wall of China and settled in the hills in Northeast India. It occurs to me that migrations and shifting borders have long been a way of life in these parts of the world. And as the global power centers shift, I find myself both uncertain and excited to reimagine the world.

I feel like I'm just starting to get to know my cousin brother. Mickey and I, we've been raised in very different parts of India and have seen one another irregularly over the years. I never knew that he was bullied in school because he looked different or that growing up, even we cousins couldn't say his name correctly—Melchizedek—which is why we have always called him Mickey. We only talked about this a few days ago when I heard him talking to the immigration officers. He speaks to me about the complexity of having an Old Testament name that is hard to pronounce and being the son of missionaries while living in an ancient Hindu city. He grew up reading The Bhagavad Gita and The Bible side-by-side. We've been talking about what it means to be Indian and Christian at the same time and to exist in these different worlds.

We've stopped in a shelter after getting caught in sudden heavy rains. A pickup truck has pulled over, and the few day laborers share our shelter. They cut a plastic bottle into makeshift cups and mix whiskey with water, and now they're passing it around. This is the kind of jugaad we see in India. They only share their potato chips with us; we share peanuts and sweets with them, especially with the little boy on his day off from school who is accompanying a parent. I'll keep writing more as we go along. I need to kick off my shoes; they are soaked, and Mickey is worried I'll get sick.

We're at the Thailand-Japan Friendship Memorial in Khun Yuam. The museum documents information about the Japanese army in this region during World War Two. These were staging grounds to fight the British. At that time, Myanmar was a part of India administered by the colonisers, and when there was the threat of Japanese invasion, Tamil migrant laborers employed to build the railways in Myanmar fled back to South India. Many didn't make it back as some of the ships carrying them were bombed out of the water by the Japanese Navy. Others were cheated or robbed of their possessions on their passage home. In the confusion, some ended up on other shores in the world. Those who made it brought back a unique culture that wasn't intrinsically South Indian, nor was it fully Burmese. And when I travel in Tamil Nadu, it's hard to miss the names of some of the restaurants: Burmese Kadai or Burma Hotel.

I read that many Japanese soldiers committed hara-kiri here in Khun Yuam when Japan declared an end to the war, while others stayed on and married local women. I'm thinking about your father, who was deployed by the British in Myanmar to fight the Japanese. I hadn't heard much of his story because he and I never spoke the same languages. I just know that he had been injured during the war, and when it was all finally over, the world in ruins, forever transformed— he sat by a river in Southeast Asia and used his service rifle to shoot at fish.

The places we're riding our motorcycle remind me of India, where there is a coexistence of the ancient and modern; we find old temples sharing walls with supermarkets advertising Coke in the local language. Like India, there is this romanticization of development and modernization. We ride past churches with large crosses, and it's stark in its difference to the temples, which have decorations, flowers, their pillars and ceilings full of carvings and local craftsmanship. At the shrines, people light incense and leave offerings of Nutella, assorted nuts, fruits, and various soft drinks, the bottles opened and complete with straws. The churches are concrete buildings; they seem closed, doors and gates are locked, the windows dark. In contrast, the temples are open, and the locals are always hanging around. Thailand was never colonized by Empire or Corporation; however, we wonder if, like India, Christianity here is also seen as a Western religion that destabilizes the local culture and ancestral religions. I remember you talking about how you became a Christian and after your baptism, you went to tell your father that your name was now John Samuel, and he was worried because the nearest mental hospital was three hundred kilometers away. I wonder what conversations you had in your life about being Indian and Christian at the same time. What was your thinking when you decided to change your name back to the name your family gave you: Krishnasamy Rajendran? I only know that the decision was made because of the important relationships: your cousins, brothers, sister, and with your father.

My sister has a memory where you sit by your father's coffin; he's covered with sweet-smelling garlands, and the women around you wail and sing folk songs of mourning. She watches as a single tear slides down your face. You have told me of a time when your father hadn't seen you for years and had traveled from your hometown to meet you briefly at Chennai Central. You barely got a glimpse of each other as your team of mission workers traveling across the country were late and trying to run and catch a connecting train. You would meet each other many times in later years, but you always painted this incident with pain and regret.

Mickey and I are riding slowly along windy roads; we've already crashed the bike once. We talk about the paradox of being Indian and Christian at the same time and the need to reimagine what this means for us, along with all the other layers to our identity. We've stopped at a monastery. I retreat to write in my notebooks. Mickey sits cross-legged to meditate but instead stares into space. We worry because a paradox is impossible to solve.

I've been remembering the time, a few years ago, when you started struggling with your speech. I later heard that, unable to speak, you were suddenly leaving conferences and speaking engagements without telling anyone. The doctors told us you had aphasia; I couldn't even pronounce it properly. As a young child, I have a memory of sitting cross-legged on the floor among the congregation, on mats woven from plaited river reeds. We were listening to you speak and were rapt with attention. I thought maybe your messages were so interesting because I liked you. As I grew older, I realized that you had a way in this world, and certain people recognized your vision, and they gathered around you like the leaves around a tree.

You needed speech therapy but were frustrated, sometimes getting up midway through consultations and leaving doctors' appointments. Soon, I was driving you on many hospital trips as other issues related to your health started to crop up, most of it during the thick of Covid. On one such trip, you were trying to communicate something to me; I was not understanding, and you started banging on the window of the car. I was tired too and started droning that I didn't believe that you had aphasia and you were just making it all up—just to get attention—and soon we were laughing our heads off from the strain and the absurdity of everything. There was one time you were not allowed much water, but you were being defiant and kept drinking large amounts. It had been long days in the hospital. I was tired, it was summer, you were probably just thirsty, and I was trying to remind you not to drink so much. But you weren't listening. I flung the bottle out of the window of the moving car, ignoring the honking behind us. The next moment, we were at a sweet shop trying to decide which sweets to eat and which ones to take home. I had decided that it was cheat day. You pointed out the sweets you wanted and wrote the amounts with your finger on my upper arm. We lay on the bed together that night. I asked you if you were scared; you replied in little whispers, with me straining to listen, "into the arms of Jesus." I asked who you wanted to see in heaven, and you said, "John Milton."

I knew a part of the story; I was told more of it later. John Milton and you were close friends as teenagers. He had become seriously ill, and at his bedside, you read him portions of his Bible. You were wailing when he died until an old woman got a hold of you and told you that if you wanted to see him again, you had to believe in Jesus. A few years later, when you were traveling the world as a missionary on a ship, I heard that you jumped into calm waters in the ocean, followed by other nutcase missionaries. And while you all were swimming, someone spotted a shark, and everyone scrambled onto the lifeboat nearby.

I prepared for weeks for tough conversations with Mom about your final wishes. The conversation, when it arrived, was full of love and trust.

I remember the sound of our footsteps as I marched through the darkened halls of the crematorium with your brothers; they refused to pay bribes to the officials. The walls were lined with paintings; one was of Shiva depicted as creator and destroyer at the same time, standing on top of a human pyre. My aunts stood in a circle, clutching at each other and wailing. Mickey walked around on his own and noticed that the coffin that we had brought you in, with its pure white polyester satin sheets that had been nailed to the frame and emblazoned with golden crosses, lay discarded in a corner. Workers placed you on a practical bamboo stretcher woven together with jute strings and slid you into an iron wrought structure. They worked a lever for a door to descend. I turned to leave, but they beckoned me back and lifted the door part way for me to see that you were alight and in flames. Our neighbor's daughter, who grew up around you and loved you, went into shock when she saw you on fire. While you were in a coma, she had been at your bedside reading aloud marked portions from your Bible. Those who had chosen to come to this end spoke to her in kind and comforting voices until she emerged. Mickey stayed on long after watching the thick smoke ascend from the chimney of the crematorium as you dispersed on the winds of Bangalore city. He said that you had become a part of a greater consciousness.

People from the Christian community ask me why, instead of a proper Christian burial, I chose to burn my father. I smile politely, but I just want to break stuff. I think about the people who rode in the ambulance with me, the final journey with you to the crematorium. They were all like you, Hindus who loved Jesus and were devoted to Him but had struggled with Christian culture. And then there was the unknown man who jumped into the ambulance and asked to see your face one last time.

I have a picture of you on my desk, and when I'm confused or just tired of this life, it looks like you are laughing at me. I complained about this to my friends. One of them is a poet, and he breaks into a folk song in your mother tongue about how you died before the banana trees he planted had bloomed. The other is a tree-hugger; she says the banana tree is actually a herb, and you are laughing with me.

As a child, I remember looking at you, deeply concerned when I heard a pastor say that we would have a different body in heaven, and I remember how you assured me, telling me that we would recognize one another. My sister tells me about a dream she has, and I see her in this place where the streams are like silver. There are no trees, and there is no sun. The skies are studded with stars that flicker in and out, luminous in the silence. There is a booming thunder when clouds like great armies crash through each other. Cold winds wet from the sea whistle up steep cliffs. Salty white waves burst elsewhere on beaches lit by starlight. She stands with you at the waterline and says she wants to see you. But you say that she can't because you are somewhere else, in a different place.

———

Pradeep Rajendran
Bramhall, United Kingdom; Lucknow
(Uttar Pradesh), Hyderabad (Andhra
Pradesh\Telangana), Bangalore
Bengaluru (Karnataka), Madras\Chennai
(Tamil Nadu), Basildon (Essex), Ooty
Udhagamandalam (The Nilgiris\Tamil
Nadu). The names of the Indian cities and
states changed during the writer's time
there, a shift that reflects the ongoing
effects of post-colonial localization.

Dear Mom,

As tears suddenly fill my eyes…I might finally know how you felt the first time our family moved abroad.

As we left our driveway in Kansas to go back to the airport in Colorado to move abroad, we had the tradition of slowly going out of the driveway and beeping the horn three times as you would stand there and wave until our car was well on its way. I did the same thing as my daughter and son-in-law drove away with their four-month-old, they beeped, and I cried while waving long after their car went out of view. They were leaving to move abroad.

Technology has changed a lot since my first move abroad in 1989. We added two kids, a cat and a dog while communicating with you but I never knew just how much you felt you were missing out on our lives. Once I opened a small gift from you at our new location in Australia and the card said, "Please send me lots of pictures as the kids grow up".

Today, my daughter went abroad for ONLY one month at this time, but I felt the huge hole of missing out on what she and her family were up to, and I knew it would only be for a very short time. I tried to put myself in your shoes knowing that this might be the first of many assignments not in our home country. I could not because I was just crying.

Thank you so much for allowing my family to thrive on our choices of working overseas and growing cultural smart grandkids for you. I hope I can be as strong of a mother as you were. I miss you every day.

Love,
Julia

———

Julia Simens
Kansas, Colorado, California, Texas,
Nevada, USA; American Samoa;
Singapore; Perth, Australia; Jakarta, Duri,
Balikpapan, Indonesia; Lagos, Nigeria;
Bangkok, Thailand

Dear Mom & Dad,

How you managed to bind together two of the planet's most different cultures, I'll never know!

Mom, I can't imagine moving from rural America to our small town in South India. You were so young. I don't know how you did it, but you embraced it so well. You learned Telugu and taught it to us. You never forced us to fit into a particular culture but put value in both.

Dad, you grew up in Andhra! Who knew you'd be living in Kansas City in your 50's in a house full of (mostly) daughters who barely know how to make pappu! I bet you never thought we'd be gathering around the kitchen island to eat chicken curry you made, or that you'd be peer pressured into having a mowed lawn. I'm proud of your adaptability, and the way you've kept your culture alive in us.

It feels like we've lived a million lives together, and I'm only 28! Culture is one of those butterfly-effect things where every action has impact, but unlike physics, it's never equal or opposite. Every cultural quirk has somehow affected us all uniquely. I'm writing this letter to share how those ripples have shaped me.

Childhood held so many wonders. Summers visiting Montana felt like a movie with the green grass, golden wheat fields, the sprinkler casting rainbows in the spray and a stomach full of string cheese, pickles and delicious local-grown beef. I remember selling lemonade and cookies to earn money for a clubhouse, and the independence of riding my bike to the pool, soaking in the water and sun until I was pruny and many shades darker. Our Indian side would be horrified if they had seen!

Then back to life at Nainamma and Thatha's house in Andhra with my baby water buffalo, Pinky. I'd drink her mother's rich milk with my Horlicks, collect broken glass bangles and bugs, gorge on juicy mangos and guavas and splash barefoot on the roof in the monsoon. At night, Shayna and Amira and I would snuggle into our shared bed with the fan and A/C blasting, watching shows or telling stories.

The hard thing about childhood, though, is that it ends, and society demands you pay the tax—conforming. Suddenly, I'm feeling awkward and excruciatingly aware that I'm different—wherever I am.

In India, I'm bigger than the other kids. They call my thick European thighs "tenkai" (green coconut). I speak Telugu, and I'm brown, just like them, but my hair is thin, my braids look like rat tails, and of course, I have a white mom. I'd been homeschooled until 4th grade, so the local school system doesn't make sense to me, and there aren't many outlets for creativity. Sometimes, the English teacher teaches us something incorrect—but I don't want to bring attention to myself, so I say nothing.

In Montana, I don't understand the cultural references—I don't know who Bob Dylan or John Denver or George Strait are. I've never done driver's ed, and I know nothing about branding or rodeos or combines. I don't know what team to support in the NFL, so I pick the Bengals because their mascot is an Indian tiger. Camping, hunting, and fishing are foreign—I've never even held a gun! My American accent means I can blend in, but I feel like I'm missing puzzle pieces. People here are kind, everyone in this small town knows us, but they're country and tough, and I feel like a silly city girl.

Boarding school was different, though. Almost everyone at Hebron had some unique background. Everyone was unusual, so no one was. I know it was a huge sacrifice for you to send me away, but it was undeniable that the learning system agreed with me, blending creativity and comprehension with the rigor of classical exams. I learned to play soccer (or is it football?)—and my favorite, basketball, a way to connect with my American cousins. I learned to sing, act, paint, I made friends, and I fell in love with my classmate, Josiah, also a TCK, with so many similarities! His mom was Telugu, and his dad was an American raised in India. Josiah just got me—I didn't have to explain myself or my family. In fact, you guys had already met his parents at the Cross-Cultural Christian Couples group. It was a natural fit, and our engagement and wedding was a whirlwind.

Adulthood in America has been an adventure together. He was there when I cried in Walmart because they had too many toilet paper options and I was overwhelmed. I was there when he worried his accent made him stand out. Sometimes pangs for "other home" catch us off guard and make us sick to our stomachs, but we're comfortable here.

The TCK still shows up, though, in different forms—one being code-switching. We speak two languages, but it's more like a spectrum of dialects—American English, Metropolitan-Indian English, Standard-Indian English, Biblical Telugu and Colloquial Telugu—each for different contexts. They aren't accents we "put on", they're all ours. Sometimes I use one in the wrong context and worry people don't understand me or think I'm being ingenuine.

Being a multi-cultural woman has challenges as well—the

expectations vary so much! Comments on role or appearance are unavoidable. Once, I was visiting India and an uncle commented, "Did you get fat here or in America?". It's common there but felt jarring after being in the States. Some Indian relatives put a lot of pressure on us to have children—almost making it a moral issue that we've taken our time. In America, it feels like many young people don't even want to have families! That's another thing—boundaries! In Asian families, they sometimes don't exist at all, while in America, people have cut off family members because of differing belief systems. People here find it hard to understand why we help with our younger siblings so much. It's challenging, but we've tried to exist somewhere in the middle, honoring our families while still trying to maintain our own family unit.

You know I've been exploring my cross-cultural identity and sense of belonging for a while. My bodies of artwork and undergrad thesis are about it—I've called this journey a "quest". When I catch a whiff of some cultural complexity, I feel like an archaeologist brushing away sand, trying to uncover the ancient bones of the matter. I dig into and talk about these complexities because I'm curious, but also because others might see themselves in my art or my writing and feel less alone. Sometimes I wonder if people think it's a waste of time or even vain to invest in it—but it's magnetic to me. One skeleton that I've been uncovering is an intense distaste for being defined.

People love to tell you who you are. Sometimes I hear, "You're very Western!" and sometimes I get, "That's so Indian of you!". Once, a close family member told me that he thinks I'm less Indian than him. It hurt to think I had "chameleoned" so well that even he couldn't see my Indian-ness. Being labeled is as magnetically repulsive to me as the exploration process is attractive. It makes me feel corralled and misunderstood. If I can't define myself with such specificity—how could anyone else?

Maybe we aren't fully knowable. Maybe that's part of being made in the image of God—The Knowable Yet Unsearchable One. He's One and He's Three, He's Justice and Love. The mystical nature of the search doesn't make it futile—searching the depths of God, being okay with knowing you can't fully know, asking for revelation though you'll never put Him in a definable box—this is the greatest quest. It might be presumptuous to compare these, exploring God and exploring ourselves—but all I mean is that I don't think it is a waste. The more complexities I find, the more awe I have for the Creator that made such complex beings. He wasn't satisfied with creating us as simple cells with a few actions, or creatures with concern only for basic functions. He made us infinite souls in intricate bodies, and I think he enjoys watching us be curious about Him, the world, and ourselves.

Recently I've been imagining my American-ness as a pane of red glass, and my Indian-ness as a pane of blue—but I don't see myself as pieces patched together like stained glass. Instead, I imagine the blue pane and the red pane layered on top of each other—a new color, but containing the fullness of red and the fullness of blue. I view myself as fully Indian and fully American, both my heritage, both at once. I am not "some" or "either". I will always be "and" and "also". I'm whole.

I want to thank you for the settling feeling of wholeness. Thank you for all the beauty, and the pain. Thank you for this rich heritage. Thank you for the siblings you've given me — my closest friends, who share a deep knowingness of being "and" and "also". Thank you for the assurance of an eternal place of belonging as a citizen of Heaven with Christ, who knows and understands me with clarity I will only have in eternity. I'll keep digging into the mysteries, but I'll be anchored.

I love you so much. Living together has been special, and we'll miss it. You're precious—like bangaram to me.

With gratefulness, mee kuthuru,
Simona

———

Simona Darshani Wiig
India; USA

Halo Pa,

As I tried to write this letter, I noticed that ternyata, kalo dipikir-pikir, meskipun kalo ngomong pake bahasa Indonesia, kalo nulis selalu pake bahasa Inggris.

Dad, you hate writing. I'm smiling just thinking about how stressed you get when you have to write. You mostly write to us on Christmas and birthday cards. Mom makes you write the main text and then she would just add a few words in Japanese. Whenever I read those cards, I am impressed and wonder, with a chuckle, how much time you had spent writing that one sentence or two.

You have really cool handwriting. I tried to imitate your handwriting. My first memory of your handwriting was when I was around nine years old. I woke up one Christmas morning (even though we weren't Christians back then) and was delighted to find that the milk and cookies I had left for Santa were gone and there was a letter for us kids—with a very complicated story about why Santa couldn't fulfill our Christmas wish list.

I had told Santa that I wanted a cabbage patch doll like the ones my American friends brought to school and kawaii pencils like the ones my Japanese friends had. But we lived in Indonesia. Still, I had faith that Santa could get anything since he knew how to get from the North Pole to tropical Indonesia. I did worry though that he would not be able to get inside our house because we didn't have a chimney like all those houses in all those books I read at school. But Mom had told me an elaborate story in the days leading up to Christmas: Santa can do anything; he doesn't need a chimney; he can turn into vapor and squeeze his big fat belly through the keyhole to enter the house. I believed her.

In the letter, Santa said that he had tried to come in through the roof instead, where the water tank (for the frequent blackouts that stopped the electrically-powered water pump) was installed but the cabbage patch doll slipped out of his bag and sank to the bottom of the tank and was ruined; the pencils also sank and he tripped and stepped onto them and broke them all. 'All of them?' I remember racking my brain trying to figure out how he did that. I remember being slightly disappointed that the doll was not what I had expected—it was a handmade, crocheted doll of Santa. I had never seen it in the Ratu Plaza department store (the only department store in the whole country back in the 1980s) though, so it was genuinely special in its own way. The pencils weren't Japanese but they were cute enough. I was happy that Santa had taken the time to write a long letter for us.

But that same letter made me wonder about Santa's handwriting. Eventually, I asked Mama why it looked so similar to yours and she decided that I was old enough to know. As her words landed on my ears, I wished it hadn't. Then she asked me not to tell my sister so that she would have a few more years with Santa. I nodded a slow, little nod as a tear rolled down my cheek.

I can't remember whether you wrote that letter in Indonesian or English.

Dad, you did your schooling in three different languages. You were born in Indonesia to Chinese Hakka parents. At the tender age of four or five years old you were sent away to study at a Chinese school in Jakarta, which was half a day's trip from your hometown back then. When you were around 11 years old, the school was forcibly closed down for political reasons. Your school bus was burnt in the chaos and the same campus was turned into an Indonesian school. Then at 15 years old, you were sent to Singapore to study in an English-medium school before going on to study engineering in Canada.

When you met mom, your rusty Mandarin came in handy. She had fallen in love with the Chinese calligraphy that had hung on the walls where she performed Japanese tea ceremonies and had come to Singapore to learn Chinese. You fell in love with her. You spoke Mandarin to each other when we were kids. You then learned Japanese when I was 11 years old and we spoke less and less Mandarin. Now I tell people that I speak 3.5 languages, with Mandarin making up the 0.5.

I once asked you which languages are easiest for you. You prefer reading technical and managerial business as well as faith-related books in English, and newspapers and other things in Indonesian. These days, you like to crack daddy jokes in Japanese (which make us cringe by the way) and know a lot more Japanese phrases and names of Japanese historical figures from the samurai era than mom does, thanks to all those 大河ドラマ you watch on NHK World.

Then, there was that one time when you met a Hakka-speaking couple. The husband didn't speak much but the wife poured out her heart. You would respond to her in Mandarin but you could understand their Hakka with some effort even though I had never heard you or anyone speak Hakka in my life. I guess your childhood language is still there somewhere in your memory.

Dad, you hate reading but I heard you finished reading my book about Third Culture Kids (TCKs). Mom tells me that you are proud of my work. But it's so strange that you've never once resonated with the TCK stuff that I've been droning on about for over a decade, even though you have 'TCK' painted over all your life story.

Pa, I love how we all speak the four languages that we do. I tell people, jarang ada lho yang bisa empat bahasa ini. It's a rare combination, and I like it.

Your daughter,
Danau

———

Danau Tanu
多伦多; Lampung, Tangerang, Jakarta;
東京; Singapura

Dear Daddy,

I miss you and Momma so much. Even after so many years, I miss you deeply. I think of you most days and often reflect on who I am because of you.

I am so grateful that you both were wanderers and explorers—grateful because it meant, as a family, we moved to unfamiliar places. Daddy, you left North Dakota to become a Naval Aviator during WWII. Then you flew in the Berlin Airlift. After retiring from the Navy, your career as a captain for Japan Air Lines took us to Yokohama, Japan, and later to Anchorage, Alaska. Momma left Iowa for a career as a medical technologist in Los Angeles. Somehow, you both found your way to Hawaii, where you met, married, and had me. We moved to Moffett Field in the San Francisco Bay Area, where my siblings were born.

Daddy, I don't remember the day you told us we were moving—or why. I was curious; I guess I got your explorer gene. One sibling was too little to remember moving, and the other felt anxious, since there was no explanation other than "we are moving to Japan."

I do remember the sad and confusing day we packed our things for storage. I stood in my bedroom, staring at my stuffed animals and dolls strewn across my bed, trying to decide what to take and what to leave behind. How did I know what to bring? I was only ten years old. We were supposed to stay in Japan for one year (which turned into six), so most things were stored, including our favorite giant stuffed animal friends—Lindy's black seal and my white-and-black ostrich with pink feet. Even my favorite dress-up doll that Santa brought (it was advertised on TV commercials for Christmas that year) was left behind.

We didn't see our beloved toys again for another five years, until our house in California was built. It was supposed to be home after leaving Japan, but it was never my home. By the time you, Momma, and Stevie moved there, I had grown up, so that house with glorious views of the Pacific Ocean became a place to visit. On my first visit after growing up, I walked into my bedroom to find the wallpaper I had so painstakingly chosen as a teenager—gone. No consultation with me, no warning. It was just gone. You all had moved on without me, which left me feeling empty, as if I'd missed something important yet unknowable.

I did miss out with my friends in the States, for instance. Luckily, they wrote newsy letters. Snail mail was truly slow back then. There were no long-distance phone calls (too expensive), and of course, no internet. So those long-awaited letters were exciting glimpses into life back in the States. Although I yearned for "home," Japan brought opportunities and new friends. I loved school and the chance to explore neighborhoods in a foreign country. I don't remember feeling terribly sad while living in Japan. Instead, I thrived on the discoveries each day brought.

Then one day you came home and told us we were leaving—this time, moving from Japan to Anchorage, Alaska. I did not want to go. Yes, it was back to the States, but not to where we'd come from, and not to the house built for our anticipated return to California. It was devastating and heartbreaking for me, as I had just become a cheerleader at my high school in Yokohama. Becoming a cheerleader was notable; to be chosen, you not only had to prove your cheering skills, but you also had to be a good student. It was my greatest achievement. Although I was painfully shy, I was finally included in activities and invited to parties. I was in the high school choir, on the gymnastics team, and about to become Honored Queen in our local chapter of Job's Daughters—but now we were leaving.

I cried buckets of tears. All I could envision was walking through blurry white snowstorms, pushing against frigid winds in an unknown, far-off, frozen place. We left at the end of my sophomore year of high school to start over in Alaska. After arriving in Anchorage and enrolling in high school, I learned that cheerleaders were chosen by a vote of the student body. Disappointingly, this meant it was a popularity contest—one I could never win, since no one knew me. I was lost in the crowd of a junior class as big as my entire school in Japan.

That first summer in Alaska was gray, cold, and drizzly. No swimsuits or sandals. Not my idea of summer. I loved warm weather and the beach. Our things didn't arrive from Japan for months. I remember sitting on the living room floor for what seemed like forever, playing cards with my sister. It was an empty room that reflected how I felt about the move to Alaska. We couldn't bring our piano, the company wouldn't ship it—but we could bring our cats. One cat seemed to thrive, while the other was distressed by the whole moving experience. Frisky got fat, and Marion lost weight. It seemed the cats reflected our conflicted spirits. Eventually, they settled in—just like we did.

Fast-forward four-plus decades: One day, while on a walk, I came across a man with a Shiba Inu (a breed of Japanese dog). To my happy surprise, he had gotten her in Kanazawa, Japan, where he and his Japanese wife had lived. It was enlivening to talk with him, since I had just returned from Japan. We shared favorite locations in Kanazawa—gardens and cafés—while I happily petted his dog, Sakura, which means cherry blossom in Japanese.

As I continued my walk, with a springier step, I smiled—exhilarated by my brief encounter with someone who could talk about places in Japan I knew and loved. Suddenly, it occurred to me: I feel Japan in my bones. It is a part of me—a place more like home than anywhere else I've lived. And yet, still not home, at least not as some people know it. I had that feeling of hiraeth, the Welsh word that's hard to translate into English, which implies a deep longing for something lost forever.

On my last visit to Japan, I noticed how "in-between" I am. I felt the interstitial cultural space that Third Culture Kids share. Although Japan is a part of me because I spent formative years there, the culture isn't in my physical DNA—after all, you and Momma were U.S. Americans. I'm not—and never will be—Japanese. Yet, somehow, it's in my psychological DNA, making me feel Japan in my bones. I pondered: How can I feel Japan in my bones, yet not be of it? My inquiry brought an odd sense of being part of somewhere, yet not really belonging, along with a feeling of loss.

Transitioning into adult life had its difficulties, especially because of the loss of adventure as trips became infrequent. That's what I miss—the anticipation of unfamiliar places and meeting new people. To me, it's like the hope of an opening rosebud. Going nowhere made life in the States feel humdrum. I eventually realized that what I missed most about our life of moving and traveling was the thrill of novel experiences. I wish I had understood this earlier. I might have made different choices; choices that allowed me to continue the life you gave me, a life I thrived on and loved.

Thankfully, a world of understanding and hope opened up when I discovered Cross Culture and Third Culture Kids. I began to connect with who I am—and why. You didn't know how your choices shaped me, but they did. Although our moving and your stoic, distant nature brought challenges, I am grateful. You gave me a gift most children never receive: the world. Now, I hope to help other TCKs honor their extraordinary childhoods by finding ways to incorporate that experience into their adult lives. Perhaps they won't feel as lost and bored as I did for so many years.

You also helped me learn to live with ambiguity, giving me skills I still draw on in a perplexing and unsettling world. As our heavenly Father teaches us to take life one day at a time, I realize that our life taught me that lesson, too.

Consequently, Daddy, you gave me world adventure. As Aunt Fern used to say upon our returns to the States, "The world travelers are back." Now, whenever I look up into the sky to follow a plane overhead, I think of you—and remember happiness with sadness, excitement with boredom, and knowing with the unknown. I cherish the memories—and I miss the life, too.

I love you, Daddy,
PattyAnn

———

Dr. Patricia Stokke
Yokohama, Japan; Hawaii, California,
Pennsylvania, Alaska, USA

Dear Mom and Dad,

Although you, Dad, were already physically gone from my life when I wrote *Letters Never Sent*, and you, Mom, have gone since then, I am glad for this opportunity to reflect and say "Thank you" again for the great parents you were to me.

Dad, as an ATCK yourself, you taught me so many things from that experience even though none of us knew there was a name for it then.

You taught me both by words and example:

To unpack my bags and plant my trees no matter where I moved. You reminded me others would one day eat from those trees even I had moved on by then.

To care for the poorest among us for they, too, have full human potential. I remember how each time before we went into town, you gave us money to give those begging outside the store with hands and toes eaten away by leprosy. When others tried to say, "They don't really have need as others give them lots of money." Your reply always came back, "Jesus said we are to care for the poor. If they are cheating me, they have to answer to Him. If they have need, I have to answer. So I'd rather they had to answer then, me."! How can I forget that?

To be a person of practical faith. How many times did I hear you begin your sermons with the question, "Moses, what is in your hand?" "A shepherd's rod, Lord." And you then listed so many commonplace things people had in their hands and how God could take the simplest, smallest things and turn them into something that could change a world. You were right.

To keep planting seeds. "Ruth, you never know which ones will grow. Some you think will, don't. Otherwise, you can't believe will, do. If you keep planting, when you look back you will see some giant trees that grew and, in the end, they can become a forest." Now as I write this when I am almost 80 years old, I look back and see the forest of Families in Global Transition (FIGT) that grew from four Indiana housewives sitting and wondering around kitchen table and wondering "What if…" and I believe you! Thanks.

Mom, you also taught me maybe more by example than the philosophical words of my father but teach me you did.

Through example…and some words, you taught me:

To not be afraid to go a bit against the stream, not in a rebellious way, but simply because it made sense. For example, no one else in our community home schooled their children. But after we, like them, went to boarding school for two years, you asked if we would like to stay home and you would teach us? Twenty-some years later an "auntie" from that boarding school met me and said, "Oh, you turned out after all. Everyone assumed when your mom home schooled you, you wouldn't be socialized."!! When I later asked you if you had gotten a lot of flack on that decision, you were a bit puzzled. "Well, I looked at the mission manual and it didn't say I couldn't. I guess I never asked. But why would it bother them?"

To be hospitable. Each week we had another family or the single people from the mission community in for supper, but not only them. Time and again you had local friends and families to come join us at our table for a meal or a meeting in the living room. All were welcome no matter their color, background or social status.

To be compassionate. Thank you for taking us to the Leprosarium nine miles away so we could meet the children's whose parents were being treated for the dread Hansen's disease. Seeing close up and first-hand how others lived made me wonder why "Not me?" It also helped to develop an awareness that with all I had been given came responsibility to care for others who had less. Even more to see and treat them as fellow human beings who had the same needs as I do and look for even small ways to help meet those needs.

To be efficient and pragmatic. Everyone marveled at how much you got done in your life. Teaching your classes at the school, teaching your children, working with the women's programs, helping dad with things like the financial reports for the school. Part of the capacity came from always thinking about how you could save extra steps by where you placed things in drawers or where waste baskets had their space to avoid extra steps. But it also came from not stressing about what, to you, were minor things. If you were painting a bookcase and the back was going to be against a wall, it was fine to not paint that part. "Who's going to see it anyway?" You majored on the majors and let the minors go. I appreciate that!

To you both, thanks for one big lesson you taught me together by word and example:

You explained the principles rather than just the rules. When I asked all the "But why?" questions that were second nature to me, when you set some limit I didn't like, you explained the principle behind your request. You never said, "Because we said so..." In the end, I remember often being inwardly convinced by what you said but not wanting to admit it! So, I often sulked but was glad when you didn't change just because of that. On the other hand, when the reason for the principle behind your edict changed, you didn't make up a new rule but lifted the earlier restriction as the reason for it no longer applied. I appreciate that example to this day. For me, it meant your reasons were honest, not simply legalism.

You received my journaling without defensiveness. Thank you for that when, despite my fears that I would hurt you, I showed you my journaling that ultimately became *Letters Never Sent*, you received it. You didn't get defensive or excuse yourself or go into deep blame. You simply said, "I read it and of course, I cried. If we had known then what you are writing now, we likely would have made some different decisions. But you wrote it well without blaming us and I just trust God will use it to bless others any way He can." If you had not blessed me or gotten upset, I would have never published it and my life would have taken a very different turn. Thank you for this gift. I trust your prayer for this to bless others has been answered.

I am sorry you have not lived to see the impact of your example continuing into your grandchildren and great grandchildren's generations. But again, thanks for living for eternal matters, including raising the children God gave you in caring, truthful ways—including me!

I love you,
Ruth Ellen
———

Ruth Ellen Frame Van Reken
Nigeria; Liberia; Kenya; Missouri,
Virginia, Illinois, USA

Dear Mom,

It's been eleven years since you've been gone. I am now older than you were when Dad retired from his career as a Korean diplomat. It took this long for me to step out of my habitual narratives of you as my mom, and revisit your life. I now see how your life was impacted by unexpected trauma and tragedy which in turn shaped my life.

You lost your dad abruptly at ten, the same year when Korea was liberated from Japan. Your twenty-two years older brother took you under his wing and doted on you. Nevertheless, you felt compelled to earn your keep by doing your share of cooking, cleaning, and ironing in the growing household. Come to think of it, where was your mother when your sister-in-law covered you with a thick blanket and paddled you? Was she, at fifty, too old and weak to protect you? I can't imagine what would have warranted such indelible abuse that left you with a perennial nervous twitch in your left eye. Four decades later, when this twitch stopped unexpectedly, you praised God. Only now I see how self-conscious you must have been every time we relocated, made new acquaintances with that uncontrollable symptom which worsened with tension. You used to wring a handkerchief damp with anxiety and migraines.

When you got married at twenty-one, you were assured you would be allowed to finish university. Instead, you bore three children and served four elderly in-laws; your mother-in-law, her mother, her sister, as well as her father-in-law. Family chores aside, your mother-in-law's vivid imagination fueled by the abrupt loss of her husband from an air-raid during the Korean War, led your brother to arrange counseling sessions with one of the first therapists in Korea. It took Dad to whisk you out of grandmother's clutches by becoming a career diplomat. Thus, you would come to spend the next thirty years living in eight countries, packing and unpacking through eleven moves, across five continents.

How was it for you to arrive in Washington DC, in the early 60s, speaking no English, with three toddlers? How did you adjust to the hierarchy and formalities of embassy life? Were you struck by the contrast between the US and Korea? I never got to ask you. I can only rely on the photo of you standing under a blooming cherry blossom, hair rolled up glamorously, dressed in a white polka dot dress, smiling meekly to the camera, hands gently on your belly. You are pregnant with me. Had it not been for your suffering, I would not have been a TCK!

Did it ever occur to you that your three-decade life overseas happened to match the period when the Republic of Korea went from being one of the poorest war-torn countries to a budding industrialized nation? The government's support for diplomatic families was at a bare minimum. Nevertheless, your overseas assignments were a source of envy for those back home whose travels were restricted until 1990, the year Dad retired.

I see you in Rome, on any ordinary day, lugging two bulky plastic bags filled with greens, meat, and dairy for this family of seven. It was a good fifteen-minute uphill walk, from the Supermercato. You were always either sewing, knitting, cooking or entertaining a diverse array of Korean guests that ranged from music students, Korean residents, Dad's visiting friends to Catholic priests including once a Cardinal. You wanted us to each look neat and tidy. You made sure we were dressed and fed appropriately, mindful that we each represented Korea.

No one had prepared you for the role. Neither your mother nor mother-in-law were equipped to guide you. At best, your few semesters in college, majoring in home economics, must have served you well as you ensured we each looked presentable, on Dad's limited salary. I still can't believe that when it was time for us to move to Brasilia, you bought this twelve-year-old a red raincoat. I only got to wear that thick, heavy garment once when we visited Iguaçu! Was that your way of compensating for our scrimping and saving through those years or was it simply your lack of information on the weather in Brazil?

You were all about fulfilling duties and obligations. During that brief year and a half back in Seoul, between one posting and the next, you managed to single-handedly sell the old hanok, get a loan, secure a new property and build a house. I heard you reminisce about this feat a few times, but it's only now that I am struck by the enormity of the task. Was this your way of reconciling the past and ensuring my grandmother's comfort in your absence? Did you know then that you would miss both your mother and mother-in-law's funerals?

Your duty station was always with Dad. So you probably didn't think you had a choice when you left two pre-teen daughters in Korea. You couldn't afford to send three children to an international school without a government subsidy. And it was another decade before you could afford to send me to an American school. Were you concerned when I began absorbing norms and values that contradicted Confucian virtues? Is that why you quipped I am not a blonde with blue eyes?

As kids grew and repatriated, did you think we'd someday reunite to live again under the same roof? I remember suddenly becoming the eldest, grown up enough to sit across from you at the kitchen table, listening to your woes and worries, wishing I could somehow make you feel better.

This is a letter that never ends. With my heart now open to all these questions and narratives, I will continue to engage with you and hopefully receive more from you.

I remember you.

I miss you.

I love you, Mom.

Isabelle

———

Isabelle Min
Washington DC; Seoul; Bangkok; Rome;
Brasilia; Tripoli; Milan

Dear Joan,

It has been quite some time since I have written to catch you up on the stories that you started. So here is the most recent update for the Planter family written across the continents, borders and generations.

The family constellation is shifting once more. Lucy has found her counterpart in Alan—a man whose gravitas would have earned your subtle nod of approval across a teacup's rim. Bailey has married and birthed new life to Evan, now living with his parents in Germany. And Carole's daughter Julia—oh, how social conventions evolve—has embraced motherhood without matrimony, cradling her child Wendy with a fierce independence that, perhaps surprisingly, echoes your own pioneering spirit. We are seeing photographs of adorable Planter babies cross our screens frequently since the family story seems to be currently written on WhatsApp, which is probably foreign to you.

Your influence persists. Eve is charting her course through Australian landscapes, and we frequently see pictures of her with her partner traveling the globe, running in races and being in constant motion. Lilly is interpreting South African horizons and seems to be building new campaigns for the Church there in between body surfing the waves of the Indian Ocean. This has become her most favorite pastime. We are all becoming cartographers of experience, mapping territories of the global heart across coordinates, just as you clearly modelled for us. Jack and I have transplanted ourselves to the Mexican highlands, to San Miguel de Allende, where the altitude thins the blood and sharpens the senses, we live about one thousand feet higher than Littleton. The colonial architecture stands sentinel over cobblestone streets that wind like tributaries through this mountain town.

You would appreciate how the bougainvillea here defies gravity, cascading down ochre walls in rebellious crimson fountains—not unlike how you defied the expectations of your generation. You would be thrilled to see the abundance of flowers and fauna around us, while we continue to weave lifestyles and patterns abroad. When we revisit the tapestry of stories you wove—of colonial Hong Kong with its harbor scented with salt and empire, to Malta's limestone fortresses standing defiant against Mediterranean tides, to Egyptian markets where spices piled in copper-hued pyramids—these stories have become our inherited memories.

You would be surprised to know that our memorabilia drawer

packs treasured memories of your daily journey to school, winding along the ancient banks of the River Nile where date palms cast dappled shadows on the path. You wrote to Lucy of your boarding school challenges at the height of her tweenage years and in preparation for her own journey. Born in Ireland under your father's service for the Crown, you crossed many cultures, adding a touch of alchemy along the way. You modeled how to transform foreign into familiar and familiar into foreign without diminishing either. Now, my husband travels under an Irish passport—a document that honors those first skies you saw and I bet you would be surprised that twelve of the family now carry that symbol of freedom—an Irish passport.

Your presence inhabits our lives when I find myself pausing over a delicate china teacup. The mini-Japanese metal bucket given to you by the American Officer's Wives Club at Miho Airbase sits on the shelf above my coffee maker. I assume it was a farewell gift upon your departure from the land where you navigated the delicate choreography of postwar diplomacy while gestating your sixth and seventh children beneath your heart. You embodied the structural integrity of your British upbringing, while allowing your heart's architecture to expand with each new cultural encounter.

Your counsel—pragmatic yet profound—continues to illuminate our decisions. "Dignity," you would pronounce with that inflection that transformed a word into a philosophy, "is portable". Indeed, you carried yours from continent to continent, from the twilight of empire to the dawn of new global orders, never devalued by circumstances nor geography.

It's been seasons upon seasons since we last conversed. Does eternity have seasons? Or have you transcended such earthly measurements of time? I wonder how you're acclimating to your new dominion, this final expatriation to realms unknown. On your own you created an embassy of memories where diplomatic relations between past and present were negotiated with grace.

Three years have dissolved since you departed this realm. Sometimes, in that liminal space between wakefulness and dreaming, I formulate questions for you before remembering the impossibility of your reply—at least through conventional channels. Yet you communicate still through the genetic and cultural inheritance you've bequeathed and through the stories we constantly tell.

When Jack speaks of distant places, I hear your cadence in his narratives, your gift for rendering the exotic to the extraordinary. I am resigned to imagining you now, perhaps sipping ethereal tea with your father the officer, while you recount the stories of your twelve children born across continents.

Until whatever shores next unite us, I shall continue to collect narratives worthy of your former audience. Your second son continues to embody the best distillation of your worldliness. Forty years together have etched countless lines around his eyes—your eyes—but haven't dimmed the curiosity that animates them.

I imagine when you first ventured beyond Ireland's emerald borders you discovered that home was not a place but a decision that delivers new perspectives to the corners of the globe that now harbor your essence. Heaven, I suspect, has acquired a formidable docent in you—one who can translate eternity through the lens of a remarkably earthly odyssey, because only after you live an odyssey can you describe it.

> With abiding fondness and perpetual
> wonder for the global journey,
> Doreen
>
> ———
>
> *Doreen Cumberford*
> *Scotland; Cameroon; Dubai; England;*
> *Japan; USA; Saudi Arabia; Mexico*

Dearest Dadito,

There isn't a single day that goes by when I don't think about you. I miss you more deeply than words can ever express. What I would give to turn back the clock—to have just one more moment with you. To hold your strong hand, to look into your kind, loving eyes, to see your beautiful smile, and to tell you—once more—how deeply and endlessly I love you.

I regret not flying to Ghana the moment I heard you were in hospital. I should have been there. You left us too soon.

I regret living so far away, even though you never once discouraged me from exploring the world. You always supported my curiosity and dreams. Your unwavering belief in me gave me the confidence to take risks, to go far, and to stand tall. That belief shaped the very core of who I am today.

I regret not sitting down to interview you and record your mesmerizing voice—your stories, your wisdom, and your extraordinary life. I wish I had captured your journey: the story of an 18-year-old Lebanese boy who left his homeland in the 1950s to provide for his parents and siblings. How it took you three long days on a propeller plane to reach Ghana. How, without formal training, you became a talented jeweller, a Judo black belt, a respected Rotarian, a leader, a radio amateur—and above all, a man known for his integrity, wisdom, and kindness. A man whose name meant honour, with a reputation beyond reproach.

I regret calling you a "small daddy" when, as a four-year-old, I overwhelmed you with endless "why" questions. After the tenth one, you finally answered, "I don't know." And in my little mind, I concluded that if you didn't know all the answers, you must still be a child yourself. I know this story always brought a smile to your face, and I wish you could repeat it to me just one more time.

I regret not organising a skydiving adventure for us after you expressed interest, inspired by hearing I had done it. You wondered if it would be possible, even as a double amputee. I wish we had flown to the UK and made it happen. You never let diabetes define you. Even when it took your legs, it never took your strength, your humour, or your spirit of adventure.

You have always been my hero—and you always will be.

Your strength and courage in every decision you made, and

in every challenge you faced, have been a guiding light for me. I strive every day to be even half the person you were—steadfast, compassionate, wise, and full of grace.

What I regret most of all is that my angel, your granddaughter, never had the chance to meet you in this lifetime. But you live on in me—in my values, my curiosity, my interests, and even my humour. So much of who I am is because of you.

I am deeply grateful for the memories we shared—from that first moment I smiled at you as a five-minute-old baby, to our very last phone call, when I told you one final time: I love you.

I'm proud to have been raised to see the world, to learn from other cultures, and to grow as a 'Cross-Cultural Kid.' That opportunity—one of the greatest gifts of my life—came from you.

I am proud of all that I have achieved so far, but most of all, I am proud that I am raising my child—your granddaughter—with the values you instilled in me, and that she knows all about her wonderful, brave, generous, and loving grandfather.

I am proud to be your daughter.

You will forever be in my heart.

"Who is Daddy's love?"
Koki.
"Who is Koki's love?"
Daddy.

———

Claudine Hakim
Ghana; Lebanon; England

Dear Dad,

I love you and I miss you way more than I can express in this letter; your death is a loss and a sorrow like a stone in the center of my body, smaller than it was, yet still present.

I never imagined that your visit to our new home in Tianjin, China, in January 2004 would be the last time I'd hold you in a hug, feel your strong arms, look into your warm eyes, or return that delighted, slightly mischievous smile of yours. The fact that you added a 'China leg' to your Asia and Europe tour that year, at the last minute, and ASKED me how I felt about it before you accepted the invitation was a double gift. You respected me for who I am as a person, an adult, a father, and as a new principal in a school for TCKs. You also gave us the gift of 'presence' after our first Christmas in China with your grandkids—the first time in their lives not celebrating the holiday with family.

Spending time together 6 months earlier at PFO (PreField Orientation) before leaving for China was also a gift. (Sure, it was complicated that we were 'just participants' and that you were a director and everyone wanted a piece of you.) But I was able to tell you again how proud I was of you as my dad, and how grateful I was for the life experiences, the exposures, the adventures and the downright FUN I had as your son. And you made the grandkids feel special, never 'in the way' of your work; they were always welcome to run to you and give you a hug. I miss that for them.

Do you remember that walk and talk in the woods before we left? You listened as I told you how sad and angry I was that you spent so much of my teen years with other people's kids, and then still didn't have the finances to take the family on a decent week-long vacation or to buy a reliable car. You seemed to grasp how painful it was for me to see Mom trying to hold it together while working and raising 4 unruly teens.

You listened carefully. And you had empathy for my expressed anger which included 'the Church'. I've forgiven, even after acknowledging that it was deeply unfair (and hypocritical) that so many people told you over and over how invaluable you were in their lives but didn't share back more of their 'valuables' that would have made your mobile life more palatable to our family and more sustainable. (And perhaps the relief of existential stress and the impact on your health could even have lengthened the time we had with you!)

Over the years, I've had countless conversations with other TCKs whose parents were in 'service' fields. I know I am not alone in this. And yet, like I told you at my wedding, after you officiated with that stubborn tear hanging from your eyelid; as glad as I am that you invested your life the way you did, my preference was to have YOU with us.

I don't mean to be sad and gloomy. There is so much that I want to tell you! Your grandkids: one just graduated with a Neuro-Science degree! One owns their own massage therapy business! One is an artist, poet, musician currently travelling and working amongst diverse farming communities and soaking up reams of knowledge. K. went on to get a paralegal certification to help marginalized people in the US legal system and worked for refugee organizations in Michigan and North Carolina, with the Red Cross during a hurricane induced disaster, and now a legal firm that provides services to marginalized and under-resourced clients in North Carolina. Yep, I'm super proud of all of them, too.

Who's your third grandchild? Oh good gracious, I'm getting misty again. She is our youngest, fostered in 2004 and adopted in 2005!! Oh my gosh, you would LOVE her, WILL love her when you meet, and wildly, she was born while you were still with us; we just had not met her yet. I see the tears in your eyes—and I'm crying, too. She should have had you as her Grampa, in person, not just seeing artifacts, pictures, and video and hearing stories. Yes, I too feel the timing was cruel. We met her upon our return to China following your memorial service in the States. Her story, woven with ours, is nothing short of miraculous. I'll have to write again and tell you all about it.

As for me—encouraged by you—I dreamed big dreams in China, and after five years as Elem. Principal, I created something new and called it 'Odyssey', in homage to the Great Journey of Life we used to talk about, to serve TCKs at all six of our schools across China. One aspect was leading trips across China to strengthen the benefits of the TCK life and to increase resilience for the hard aspects, while serving others.

Watching your wilderness slides—the hard-core canoeing, climbing, hiking slides plus all the hiking, canoeing and camping you did with us—paid off. I led one trip to Inner Mongolia; that was an amazing adventure. But I lost part of my heart out in the southwest, the province of Yunnan, where I brought groups six times into the majestic peaks and azalea covered highlands. Our hosts were Tibetan and Hui; pragmatic, hardy, rich cultured, fun loving, and warm once we had the introduction of a trusted friend. Good mountain folks. I know you are smiling, and have that joyful, 'I told you so' look (I don't mind—you were right). You told me that would happen while we were camping, looking out over the Green Mountains of Vermont and smoking pipes...

You said something like, "You can't invest your life in people and expect to hold on to your heart. Don't fight it. The hurt of losing is worth the gain. Paradoxically, letting go of parts of your heart expands your heart to a larger capacity." Good words, and true.

You taught me through example, Dad; that was powerful. Growing up with people always in and out of our home, even for extended stays, had me thinking that everyone must do that! Not true. I remember Ivy, with the crazy big hair and Italian vibes; Kevin the black track star who I later learned was gay; Giff, the troubled wealthy teenager that taught us to box; blind Timothy from Kenya who travelled far to meet you, and I remember many TCK students who didn't have a place to go for the holidays. I've tried to live out those values you taught me—to steward my possessions, my time, my gifts and home—rejecting the culture to be 'lord of the castle' with all the treasure I can hoard and the moat drawn up.

Dad, because I grew up the way I did with your example and encouragement to pursue meaningful work over money, I have worked with TCKs in their communities in some cool places—Like Taiwan, Korea, Germany, Ecuador, China, the Canadian wilderness, Baja Mexico, even Grand Rapids, Michigan, heh. And Papua New Guinea... remember how I once said I wouldn't like it there? Dead wrong. (Oh, haha, sorry Dad—yes, I hear you laughing—...ok stop laughing that was in bad taste, I know.) It was beautiful and reminded me very much of Kijabe.

Now I direct a non-profit called DARAJA—("bridge" in Swahili), to increase care and advocacy for Third Culture families and individuals. I wish I could say I'm as organized as you were, but you've set a high bar. The list of people and organizations with whom I've worked, trained, dreamed and collaborated with would take up reams! I am blessed, and deeply grateful. TCK care has flourished in recent years, and I know that would bring you great joy. You planted so many seeds. They've taken root and grown.

One last truth, Dad: I inherited your tendency to overwork. That has been a struggle for me. Like you, I've often placed others' needs ahead of my own limits. But I've learned, slowly, to set good boundaries (even when I crash through them). To say "no" when needed (most of the time). I even take real vacations, without friend-led interventions. (I'm poking you but it's true).

Dad, deep in my bones, in my soul, I know that I will see you again. Still, it aches to have lost so many shared years. You would be 87 this month! I think you would still be warm, wise, and funny. I miss your silly songs, puns, and hairy-dog stories. And what was it with squirting us with water pistols and beaning us with fruit that you made you laugh so hard? Good times.

I'm still learning to live in the 'both-and' of joy and gratitude and sorrow and pain. You lived that well. It's one more gift you left me.

So before I close, I'm sending you love, and a bear hug, and gratitude from my heart for the many precious and powerful gifts you have shared with me—I'm still opening and/or understanding some of them! And when the time comes, I'll be counting on you to be my transition coach to heaven, if you'll suffer me. (That was a joke Dad, put the clementine down, it's not funny, I mean it!)

Baraka, Amor, and Shalom.

Your son,
Michael
———
Michael Pollock
US; Kenya; China; England; South Africa

親愛的阿嬤(a-má)

It's me, 阿-Vi. I wish I could write this letter in your heart language. However, my Taiwanese 台語不輪轉 (liàn-tńg) and you could not read. In Taiwanese, liàn-tńg means flowing smoothly like a tire. I always wonder why the language I feel so connected in my ears could never flow out of my mouth without stumbling. Our communication is always full of barriers but somehow manages to push straight into our hearts. Like many CCK, I have two official names, but the one I love the most is the nickname you gave me, 阿-Vi. You said you did not know how to pronounce my proper English name Ivy and 台語發音 stuck. For me, it was never a mistake but your expression of love to your CCK 查某孫. I am blessed to have grown up near you. It is a privilege that many CCK do not have. However, the cultural barriers still stood between us.

Every birthday, you reminded me that you did not know my "real birthday" (lunar) because I was born in the US. You reminded me that our family friends and I are bí-kok-lâng. I guess it was natural for me to move overseas because I was never fully a 台灣人. However, I never meant to say that I do not want to live in Taiwan. I love this land as my home like many places I have called home. I wish I could

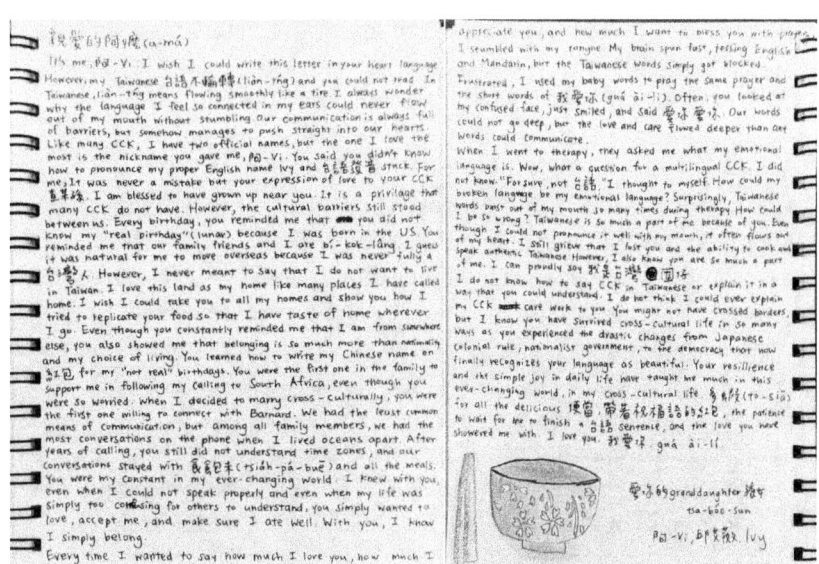

Ivy's handwritten letter to her Grandmother.

take you to all my homes and show you how I tried to replicate your food so that I have the taste of home wherever I go. Even though you constantly reminded me that I am from somewhere else, you also showed me that belonging is so much more than nationality and my choice of living. You learned how to write my Chinese name on 紅包 for my "not-real" birthdays.

You were the first one in the family to support me in following my calling to South Africa, even though you were so worried. When I decided to marry cross-culturally, you were the first one willing to connect with Barnard. We had the least common means of communication, but among all family members, we had the most conversations on the phone when I lived oceans apart. After years of calling, you still did not understand time zones, and our conversations stayed with食飽未 (tsiah-pá--buē) and all the meals.

You were my constant in my ever-changing world. I knew with you, even when I could not speak properly and even when my life was simply too confusing for others to understand, you simply wanted to love, accept me, and make sure I ate well. With you, I know I simply belong.

Every time I wanted to say how much I love you, how much I appreciate you, and how much I want to bless you with prayers, I stumbled with my tongue. My brain spun fast, tossing English and Mandarin, but the Taiwanese words simply got blocked. Frustrated, I used my baby words to pray the same prayer and the short words of 我愛你(guá ài--lí). Often, you looked at my confused face, just smiled, and said 愛你 愛你. Our words could not go deep, but the love and care flowed deeper than any words could communicate.

When I went to therapy, they asked me what my emotional language is. Wow, what a question for a multilingual CCK. I did not know. "For sure, not 台語," I thought to myself. How could my broken language be my emotional language? Surprisingly, Taiwanese words burst out of my mouth so many times during therapy. How could I be so wrong? Taiwanese is so much a part of me because of you. Even though I could not pronounce it well with my mouth, it often flows out of my heart. I still grieve that I lost you and the ability to cook and speak authentic Taiwanese. However, I also know you are so much a part of me. I can proudly say 我是台灣囡仔.

I do not even know how to say CCK in Taiwanese or explain it in a way that you could understand. I do not think I could ever explain my CCK care work to you. You might not have crossed borders, but I know you have survived cross-cultural life in so many ways as you experienced the drastic changes from Japanese colonial rule, nationalist government, to the democracy that now finally recognizes your language as beautiful. Your resilience and the simple joy in daily life have taught me much in this ever-changing world, in my cross-cultural life. 多蝦 (to-siā) for all the delicious 便當, 帶著祝福語的紅包, the patience to wait for me to finish a 台語 sentence, and the love you have showered me with. I love you. 我愛你. guá ài—lí.

愛你的granddaughter 孫女 tsa-bóo-sun
阿-Vi, 邱艾薇, Ivy
———

Ivy Chiu Modimakwane 邱艾薇
California, USA; Taiwan; Logos Hope;
Zambia; South Africa

April 27, 2025
Washington State, USA

Dear Grandma,

Yesterday, 2 years ago was when I saw you last. Your bony yet soft hand is still felt. It wasn't until a couple of weeks ago that mom reminded me you passed away 2 years ago, not a year ago. Time is a scary thing; when you're in the moment, it feels like it's so abundant, yet when life happens, it passes by so quickly.

It's been an insightful grieving journey since you passed. I'm fortunate and privileged that I was able to travel to Japan to go see you one last time and get my closure with you. When I heard you passed in your sleep seven or so months after, I hoped you were having a wonderful dream, and you still continue to live in it.

My grieving continues as I reflect back on your identity, not as my grandmother, but as an independent widow who lost her husband too soon, living alone and traveling the world, as you visited us in each relocation. You were the only one in the family who turned to religion, but through religion, you found community, belonging, and service to others.

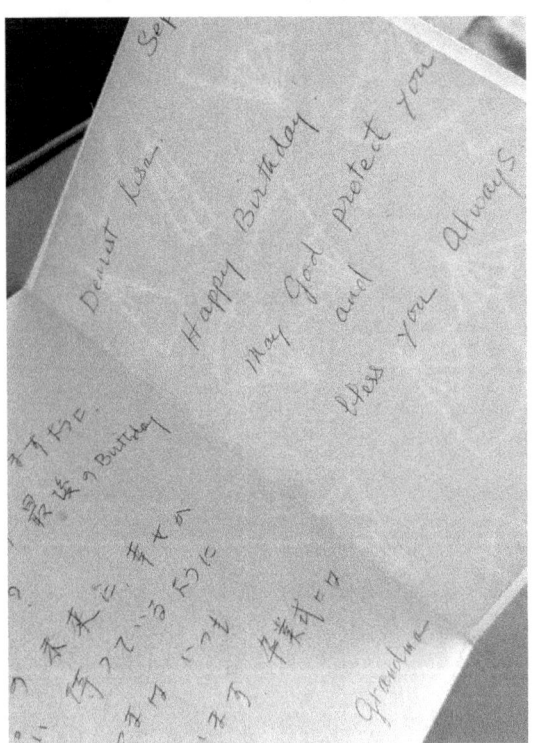

A card from Risa's Grandmother.

I need to process grieving the lost time I didn't get to ask you what the world looked like through your eyes. I'm currently in my early 40s and I look back to your life and wonder, what was it like for you? You too were independent, working your job in higher education, living with family, and maneuvering life as it came. Did dating ever cross

your mind? What were your goals? Did you accomplish them?
I share the same initials as you, and I take that to heart. I've gone through much of life switching it back and forth between R and L, and I've finally settled with RZ.

My grieving continues as I reflect on the time past and the time ahead. I want to do these initials proud, just like you set the example.

Thanks for holding space for me to write you letters, and later emails. You'll always be my favorite pen-pal. I'm sorry I never got a chance to teach you how to Zoom or FaceTime (that would've been handy, huh?) I'm glad I was able to teach you how to use a computer and email though. I have a few emails saved that you've sent, and they'll be kept til time immemorial.

Writing has always been a vehicle for communication between us. October of 2023, I wrote a long post on the online community Puttyverse, dedicated to you. A week ago, I was a guest on a podcast called "Show and Tales" and got to share the story of you and I and our love for Japanese stationery.

I truly believe the message behind the movie "Coco", and I promise to keep telling the stories that you took part in. I've yet to see you since your passing, but I'm hoping you see me and you're learning a thing or two about me; not as your granddaughter, but as an independent woman with communities to feel belonging in, service to others in higher education, and one processing grieving as she treks through life, one conversation at a time.

Miss you Grandma.

> Love,
> Risa
> ⎯⎯⎯
> *Risa Zenno*
> *Tokyo, Japan; Sao Paolo, Rio de Janeiro,*
> *Brazil; Mexico City, Mexico; Newcastle,*
> *Washington, Bronx, New York, Farmington,*
> *New Mexico, Oak Harbor, Washington, USA*

Dear Grandma Corinne,

I recently realized I am now the same age you were when you moved to Australia with Dad and uncle Jon as middle schoolers in 1952.

What was Australia like for you all? Did the boys settle in well? I know Dad learned to write in cursive while he was at school in Canberra—his handwriting is still very different from that of people who learned to write in the USA. It must have been tricky for them, arriving at a new school without much support, speaking "Yankee English", not knowing how the school system or even the sports worked.

I would have loved to hear from you how you helped them through this first move and the later ones to Turkey and Indonesia (I know from your diary that it wasn't all smooth sailing). But especially, how you all experienced the moves back to the USA each time. Was it difficult to re-integrate? Or did everyone just settle back in?

Do you remember the expression "that's a sunbeam" for clean cutlery that can be put away again since it wasn't used? I learned it from you and Dad and it is part of our family's lingo. I never realized until I heard an Australian friend use it during our time in Beijing that it was something you picked up there. And now it has been passed down through three generations. A little fragment of your life abroad. I love that.

I wonder what other traces of your life can be found in mine. Besides our experience of being accompanying spouses, raising Third Culture Kids and our shared name.

Our name. My name. Anna Corinne: Cori. How badly I wanted to keep hold of it, how much I feel this is my true name. But it was so difficult when I started school in Germany. At the time there were so few foreigners, so little acceptance of difference. It was hard enough as it was, so Mom suggested I just use Anna in school. It seemed the easiest thing to do and it was only for a little while.

But then we extended our stay and I had two names—one in English and one in German, one for home and the other for school. And then I moved on, studying, adulting, went to work, moved again. Since Anna comes first, people called me that. I did make attempts to switch back to Cori but it caused confusion and there were always people that were already using Anna. I eventually gave up. Today only my US-family uses Cori. It's one expression of the multiple variations of me. But it saddens me—the name that connects us has become a victim of the life I've led. I'm working on accepting that.

The good that came out of it? My experience influenced the names we chose for our children. We made sure they all have first names that are common and easy to spell. But don't think we stopped there—to express their birthplaces, family connections, and our dreams and hopes we gave each of them two more names. I regretted this a tiny bit every time I had to fill in forms to enter China or apply for documentation in South Africa. But boy-oh-boy do they own their names. They insist their full names are on school report cards every year and it makes me smile. Maybe acceptance isn't so far off.

I want to thank you for raising Dad to be excited and interested in the world and all its people and places despite the challenges and hardships along the way. He has passed his infectious curiosity on to his grandkids in a big way and I am curious where their lives will take them.

According to Dad every time you moved back to the USA you thought you were done adventuring—and then a few years later Grandpa would come along with another offer, another country and off you would go. We've settled into Germany now with no immediate plans to leave again but I wonder if my fate won't mirror yours in this aspect as well... Only time will tell.

Much love,
Cori

———

Anna Corinne Seidel
Oregon, USA; Germany; Switzerland;
South Africa; China

Dear great-grandmother,

In a few lines, I will attempt to navigate the labyrinth of my own existence, yet I find myself entangled in the branches of our family's history and anchored by the weight of your name—[Dama de Noche]. Born in 1923, they say you were so striking that your allure led my great-grandfather to chase you to that isolated haven painted in hues of sepia and nostalgia. There, in the heart of your secluded town, nestled amidst the tropical grasslands, fincas, and diverse wildlife of los llanos, you nurtured your children, including my grandfather and my father.

Though I was quite young when I last saw my grandfather, I still wonder what words he would share upon seeing me again, finding solace in the vivid memories we crafted together—long journeys to his modest home, the warmth of the plains, the echo of his bell calling us to meals, and the gentle swaying of hammocks where my brother and I sought refuge. Even in his absence, the essence of my grandfather's teachings steers me through the complexities of life, revealing that the heartache lies not in the absence of his physical form but in the enduring unconditional love that refuses to fade as I navigate the landscapes of loss. My grandfather lived and died as he wanted. Independent. Abuela, your son had his flaws, but on every visit, he welcomed us and showered us with love.

Abuela, you, the matriarch of our family story, you are my father's mother. He talks of you with so much love, as does my mother. After all, you raised my father. You sculpted his character with patience and love; you dedicated your life to his. You saw the child of a young uncertain mother and a frivolous father, and you raised him, transforming the chaos of his youth into a harmonious melody. There lies power in a name— yours, [Dama de Noche].

Abuela, what transpires after death remains a mystery. Yet I envision when we die, our consciousness remains intact without concern for the laws of space and time. We are and we are not. As I write these words to you, the veil between realms is thin. In the ethereal bloom of existence, you persist beyond its physical confines—not as a mere memory but as a presence. I wonder what your last thought was when Death dared to steal the final breath from you. Did you embrace its skeletal hand, surrendering to the cosmic dance of fate? You left behind stories, traditions, and pledged a ring for your first great-granddaughter. Little did you foresee it would be me, with a hunger for connection that transcends time. In my silent dialogue with Death, your spectral hand envelops mine, whispering,

"Not yet." Though I lack your promised ring, the weight of your guidance accompanies me. I know that when I learned to hold a pencil and I etched my first words onto paper, your hand gently passed through the pages in awe. Each stroke, an ethereal collaboration across the veils of existence. Abuela, my words are not from here or there. They are yours. They are the echoes of our generational storytelling.

Abuela, a veces siento que me oyes. En los silencios. En el aroma que deja la flor de Dama de Noche cuando no está. I imagine us talking—not a dream, more like remembering something that hasn't happened yet. I'd ask you things no one else can answer. Abuela, ¿cómo fue vivir cuando tus hijos crecieron y se fueron? ¿Cómo fue criar a mi papá, tan reservado? ¿Qué secretos me habrías contado mientras pelamos plátanos en la cocina? And I wonder what you'd say to me. You, who declared laziness a foreign concept in your daughters, what would you make of your great-granddaughter? Maybe you'd smile first, offer me un dulce de lechosa, and start answering slowly, letting your stories fill the air like steam from the pot. Maybe you'd tell me to stop trying to carry everything alone. Maybe you'd hold my face and say one of your refranes: "Ay, hija... el que remienda no estrena." Sometimes I wonder if you'd understand my restlessness. Or if you'd ask why I always carry my life in half-packed suitcases and unfinished poems. You were always moving, weren't you? They say you had a taste for the road, that you never hesitated when someone suggested a trip, a visit, a detour. You lived for reunions, and for new places. They say you made space at your table for anyone who needed a meal, or a story, or a place to breathe. That no one left your home with an empty stomach or a lonely heart. Entonces, ¿hubieras aprobado de mi?

I hold you in fragments. You live in the way I hold eye contact when someone is vulnerable. En mi manía de guardar las cartas y las fotos que apenas se ven. In recipes scribbled on worn paper. A veces siento que estoy continuando una conversación que tú empezaste. You, whose arms once held the whole family together like a carefully orchestrated dance. I carry you in every country I've landed in, in every border I've crossed. Y sí, maybe one day, when I get to the place beyond all this, we'll sit. I'll bring all my questions. You'll bring your stories. And we'll laugh about how time never mattered in the end.

We never met, but those fortunate enough to have met you say I bear your resemblance, a connection invisible to my own eyes. I was born in your country, in a city far from yours, where the araguaney cries gold, and the young generation mirrors its golden blossoms—for even in shedding, there is beauty and abundance. I left. I left. I left. Dominican Republic, Ireland, Jamaica, Mexico, United States, Venezuela... Unaware that windows would remind me of guacamayas soaring over the mountain ranges; that no sun compares to the Caribbean's, especially when compared to the arid embrace of the desert sun or the soft rain of the north; that an island is more than its coasts—it is its people, slang, food; that the anecdotes of all the roadtrips, ascending and descending hills, were destined to fade; and that we safeguard our sorrows within boxes.

Each relocation, each shift in pronunciation and culture, has taught me to embrace the chaos. Yet, I dream of returning to a land that no longer exists, Abuela, where childhood memories meld with the stories of our ancestors. It's a dream of returning to a memory impossible to replicate. And in this limbo, I dwell in a world where not many understand the nuances of my identity and the depth of my experiences. The only thing I can do is miss.

In the midst of these reflections, a question lingers: is maturity the awareness of one's own mortality? As I reflect on life and how home transcends all bounds, I find that, for me, maturity involves embracing the understanding that life is transient and that our time on this Earth is limited. We are moments. Like the chigüire gracefully navigating the river current, I find myself swept along by the current of time, where moments flow ceaselessly. This awareness shapes my aspirations and interactions, inspiring me to make thoughtful decisions, to nurture relationships that are profound, and to create a legacy that endures. In navigating this cosmic river, the stories of my family, especially yours, [Dama de Noche], emerge as guiding constellations that perpetually echo against its current. Our family's fragrance, rooted in resilience and love, mirrors the eternal flow of life and death. Thus, maturity is intertwined with acknowledging and embracing the finite nature of our lives, within time and borders.

In many ways, Abuela, I am the sum of these experiences—a testament that your devotion to life's beauty and the quiet wishes under the moonlight blossomed far beyond the garden where you once nurtured your children. Through joys and struggles, I promise to carry forward your legacy and the resilience that defines us.

With love,
Andrea

———

Anonymous
Venezuela; Dominican Republic; Mexico;
Jamaica; Ireland; Tennessee, Texas,
Florida, USA

Letters to Siblings

Dearest Marnie and Susan,

Our mother used to say you could tell how developed a country was by how long it took to cross the border. Do you remember that too? The more complex and time-consuming the process, she said, the less advanced the country.

Today I see a lot in there that needs to be unpacked—the colonial imposition of terms like "developed" and "advanced" for example. The time I most clearly remember her saying this was as we crossed by road the border between Kenya and Tanzania. There are innumerable past and current colonial impositions we could and should unpack there, and in fact across the continent and the whole of the Global South.

For the moment, however, I'd like to reflect on borders more personally. As a child we crossed a lot of them.

How have we crossed them, let me count the ways:

- National borders, by jeep, ship, plane, train. I don't remember: did we ever walk across a national border?
- Curricular borders in our many schools, from French to British to American-International to American and then again to International.
- Perceptual borders, Joan of Arc as savior versus rebel; the Algerian war as one of rebellion or independence. Do you share these too?
- Linguistic borders, from agua to l'eau with wasser in the background and ultimately water in the fore (tamasha and baraa kaam two of the few constants).

I could go on…

- Borders of cuisine, I think for all of us one of our favorites to cross.
- Borders of holidays, both spiritual and secular.
- Borders of friendships made and lost.
- Borders of landscapes known and loved and left.

One of the most notable border crossings for me was one I came to understand only after I discovered myself as a TCK, some 40 years ago when I was in my early 20s. It's the border I would name as my ethnic identity.

The way I remember it, we were raised to think of ourselves as American or, more to the point, as solely and fully American; our

Swiss nationality was always secondary in importance. Indeed, that's the thing about borders: society positions us towards them as if we have to choose. We're not supposed to exist on both sides at the same time.

It's American or Swiss, English-speaking or French, savior or rebel. Good or evil. You're either with us or against us. You're a part of or apart from.

But I like the in-between places, those liminal spaces that are more about holding the questions than on settling on a single answer.

In liminal space, I get to have two passports and I can choose which I use when. I've skipped past many a long line entering Europe and the U.S. respectively by choosing which passport to pull out.

In liminal space we get to identify as American AND Swiss. Even more to the point, we get to stand strong in our global nomad, TCK selves—formed by our mobile childhoods across countries, crossing borders.

In my more recent years, my border crossings have changed shape. I've crossed a developmental border from unconscious complicity in white supremacy and US/Western imperialism to a consciously anti-racist, anti-capitalist, abolitionist, and re-Indigenizing practice. (Yes, in my older years I've become what some might say is more radical; I would say more informed.)

I've also begun crossing a border in the way I conceptualize my sense of belonging. It used to be global. The disparate geographies of my childhood were threaded into a sense of belonging by the bodies of water in which I swam, and eventually by being able to name myself TCK and global nomad.

Now I am learning what it means (as Wendell Berry wrote) to make common cause with place. Belonging for me today includes belonging to the very particular singular geography where I now live, of water and land, birds and trees, people and commitments.

What I celebrate as I write is that this kind of border crossing, into making common cause with place, doesn't require us to choose between our global selves and our local. I can swim in the waters of a nearby lake and revel in memories of oceans and rivers and hotel swimming pools around the world. Beloved bodies of water span every form and every continent.

Of course, it's been much easier for the three of us to cross geographic borders than it has been—continues to be—for many others. We have passport privilege. The procedural complexities of that long-ago crossing from Kenya into Tanzania make me think of people now seeking asylum. I think of people seeking to cross borders not because they are tourists on vacation or expatriates sponsored to live globally, but because they are fleeing the consequences of the Global North extracting from the Global South. Recalling our mother's words about the more complex and time-consuming border crossings, adding in how dangerous and violent we make the experience, brings new meaning to the idea of which nations are in fact "developed" and in what ways. We have passport privilege, yes, and also passport responsibility.

And so I work for justice in my local community, and for the time when all people can cross borders of any and all kinds without being either forced into danger or being asked to choose. I return to liminal space, to that place of not-knowing and of possibility, and from there I can imagine that someday everyone will live as can the bird and the ant, crossing borders as our journeys take us, without being asked to show our papers.

Thank you for being my sisters on this journey,

Barbara

———

Barbara Schaetti
Oklahoma, Texas, Washington, USA;
Argentina; Algeria (first under French rule
and again after independence); France;
England (two separate times); Senegal;
Morocco; Malaysia; Singapore

Querida caropita,

Gracias por ser mi hermana. Empiezo esta carta en español porque en el último mes hablamos mucho español, mezclado con el castellano y portugués, pero ese tiempo fue una experiencia que comenzó a curar una herida abierta que no me había dado cuenta que existía—el español y responder la pregunta de dónde sois? La gente nos miraba raro porque la primera respuesta era siempre Brasil, pero nuestro español es uruguayo y nuestros documentos son de Portugal. Crecer entre culturas y lenguas trae desafíos que no se fueron, aunque ya estemos a once años en la misma ciudad y país (Brasil), creo que siempre tendré dificultad en todas las lenguas que hablo, mezclando la gramática y orden lógico de estructurar mis ideas, gracias por intentar ayudarme en ese lío de palabras y actuar de traductora cuando algo que digo no hace sentido. ¡Es una locura pensar que vas a hacer 22 el próximo mes!

Gracias por ser mi hermana, por aceptarme y amarme, por siempre ser honesta conmigo, de decirme cuando creías que estaba siendo muy impulsiva y ayudarme a pensar antes de seguir adelante, por ayudarme a procesar mi dolor y escucharme mientras procesaba hablando.

Thank you for giving me the strength to say no to life-draining groups and people and expectations. By seeing you taking your mental health seriously and setting boundaries, you have given me the example and the courage to do the same. You are my little sister, nunca me olvidaré de cómo eras chiquita, siempre fuiste más expresiva y vocal, creo que en parte también eres más curiosa, siempre haciendo preguntas e intentando entender las cosas. Tú me inspiraste a ser curiosa, a hacer preguntas, leer y continuar cuestionando, ya que me mostrabas que teníamos un espacio seguro para expresar nuestras dudas y miedos.

Gracias por tu coraje en hablar sobre tu salud mental y lucha con la depresión, as your older sister I wish I could have protected you from all kinds of harm, but it is not possible. I am so beyond grateful you had the strength and courage to ask for help before it was too late. I am sorry that during that time I was so lost in my own grief that I didn't realize earlier how badly things were and thank you for tackling head on our own family prejudices with medication and mental health.

Thank you for facing it and having pill-chan as your new best friend, and having the courage to talk openly about your experiences, bringing a lightness to such a heavy subject—especially when you can laugh after saying "I no longer want to kill myself", it is a heavy conversation starter but it is a good icebreaker that has had an impact in our family, maybe even more for those who are also treating their depression with meds and how we can talk openly about it. I am so happy to see how you are thriving and healthy, recognizing your limits and when you need more rest and being vocal about what you are feeling and how we can better support you through it.

It has been one week since you returned to Brazil, to our home in São Paulo, and I realized that home is where you all are, so I miss you a lot. Sorry that yesterday I was already sleeping and didn't hear your call, this week has been a rollercoaster of emotions and shit happening (mold in the car seats and a sick dog being some of them), remember you have a community and support system you can reach out to and ask for help when needed, we are a phone call away but sometimes timezones complicate things.

Talking about timezones, I remember how seven years ago was the first time we spent a prolonged period of time apart—four months— and I missed you so much. I feel that growing up in the same house we take for granted the fact that we will always be close to each other, cause your presence felt like a constant in a childhood full of changes and uncertainty. It is scary to think that we might soon be living in different houses (depending on where I get a job and how things go). If that happens let's have video calls to watch 'Avatar: The Last Airbender' together!

What the future holds is uncertain, and growing up as a TCK made me a bit afraid of making long-term plans, cause life can change suddenly and then we have to rethink everything, like the past six months of our life also showed—it turned out being way better than I could dream of but it was not easy to pivot our carefully made plans because of a visa being denied. We have different memories and experiences connected to being TCKs, because of our five-year age gap and memories of each place we lived. Now we are learning what it means to be an adult TCK, and it has brought forward many other challenges. The fact that we were so lucky to find a community that is full of CCKs certainly helps, and seeing you in a romantic relationship these past three years kinda gives me hope to embrace who I am and be more authentic in daily life and in my friendships, to stop trying to conform to the expectations of others and embrace figuring out who I am amidst the whole identity crisis of languages and passports and cultures I hold dear to my heart.

You are amazing, quero ser que nem você quando crescer (só muitas tattoos extras, hehe)

Beijos,
Juju

———

Ana Júlia Borges
Ribeirão Preto, Londrina, Paulinia, São Paulo, Brazil; Tokyo, Sapporo, Japan; Kyiv, Ukraine

Dear Joseph da,

Do you remember, in New Delhi, when we got into such a ferocious fight that we had to be physically pulled apart? I remember mustering all the strength from my five-year-old body into a bloodcurdling scream to tell you that you were the worst brother in the entire world and that I would never talk to you again.

Inevitably, less than a week later, I was back to chasing you around our apartment with adoring eyes. In every situation, at all times, you were always the cooler, shinier, older brother I longed to constantly be around.

Over the years, that adoration has grown, yet matured. I used to think that you were invincible, that nothing could ever shake you. That changed the other day.

I was talking with Mom, and she shared a recent conversation she had with you. Something I said off-handedly, years ago in high school, had cut you deeply. I was oblivious to it, but you've carried those words around ever since.

Guilt immediately flooded me, but more overpowering was the shock. The shock of hurting you so deeply. The shock of being capable of hurting you.

The worst part was that you never showed any signs of the hurt I caused. You continued to be my vigilant, caring, and protective older brother. Even now, when I'm out here working in LA and feeling homesick, you spend an exorbitant amount of money on flights and Ubers to help me surprise Mom and Dad for an unexpected weekend visit.

You were the same way in high school. I remember, one winter, my Chinese class had a gift exchange. We randomly pulled names out of a hat, not telling anyone whose name we pulled, with the intent of buying a thoughtful present for that person. A few days before the holiday break, we'd all exchange gifts.

When the gift exchange day rolled around, I was the only one who didn't receive a present. The person who pulled my name, a reclusive boy who always sat in the corner, had forgotten about the exchange. When we met at the end of the day to walk to your car, you kept asking why I was so quiet. Through tears, I finally told you what happened. You were silent, not saying anything.

A week later, I walked to my Chinese class and saw three,

huge, brightly wrapped presents lying on the front table. My teacher excitedly told us someone had dropped them off at her classroom that morning for me.

I remember tearing through the wrapping paper, finding the boxes filled with nail polish, lip gloss, a trendy cardigan, and a bomber jacket with my favorite band. After weeks of me pestering you, you finally admitted to being behind it.

You told me how you got a student in your orchestra class to deliver the presents (so my teacher wouldn't recognize you), how you convinced your friend to write the card (so I wouldn't recognize your handwriting), how you meticulously destroyed all your online and paper trails (so I wouldn't accidentally find out).

You even left a gift for that boy, an elaborate pocketknife, because you said that Christmas is a season for love and forgiveness. To this day, every time I think about what you did, I cry.

You've always brought me comfort. When we started at our new elementary school in Virginia, after spending the whole day feeling like a foreigner in my home country, I remember the relief wash over me as I climbed onto the school bus, grateful to spot your familiar face.

You looked out for me in middle school, too. By the time I reached sixth grade, we had been in Virginia for five years, the longest we'd ever been in one place. You were two years ahead of me, and during those two years, you paved me a crystalline path: talking me up to my biology teacher and assuring our orchestra conductor that I was a remarkable prodigy (to be honest, I spent more time giggling with my friends than playing the violin; apologies for mangling the reputation).

I remember walking into class on my first day, proudly telling my teacher I was "Joseph's little sister." I held onto that title with a tight fist, wearing it as a badge of honor.

Do you remember that fencing camp? It was the summer before eighth grade—you were going into tenth—and we had just moved to Indiana. No one at the camp believed we were siblings.

It makes sense: you have Mom's thick Indian hair and tanned complexion, whereas I have Dad's almond Chinese eyes and pale skin. It took us half an hour to convince everyone we were related, and even then, some refused to believe it. In retrospect, I'm surprised it took so long for people to realize. Usually, whenever we're in shared spaces, I never hesitate to single you out and claim you as my brother.

Aside from Mom and Dad, you've been the only constant in my life. Even if the houses changed, if the languages changed, if the weather changed, you were there. Because of you, I always had someone to sit with, someone to lean on.

Maybe you've gotten over the hurt I caused by those words. Maybe you haven't. Regardless, I'm sorry. I wish I could take them back, that I could wipe them from your memory.

There's a proverb that says, "A real friend sticks closer than a brother." For me, that person is the same: you. You will always be my best friend and my older brother, and I love you dearly for it.

Forever your affectionate sister,
Jasmine

———

Jasmine Hsu
Virginia, Indiana, Colorado, New York,
California, USA; Siliguri, New Delhi, India

Dear Goose,

I'm sitting here on the cold airport floor, missing you with everything inside of me. Each time a pair of sisters walks past—chatting, laughing, or even arguing as only sisters can—I miss you a little bit more. Every travel weary family that wanders past lugging suitcases, backpacks, and heavy hearts makes me grieve the chapter that is now coming to an end for me. Of course, I always imagined that this transition would be difficult on all of us, but I truly don't think I ever imagined the heartbreak I'd feel at having to grow up and move away from you.

My flight, the one that is taking me a thousand miles from home, will board in forty-five minutes. While I wait, I'm sitting here, cradling my way-too-expensive flat white, letting the comforting sounds of rumbling luggage wheels, boarding announcements and at least twelve different accents swirl around me as I write to you.

Do you remember that time we flew from America back home to East Africa with what felt like our entire lives packed into twenty-two bulging suitcases? We heaved each one onto the check-in scale, watching the airline attendant's face turn a shade paler with every thud. It took forever—standing there for what felt like an eternity while she tapped keys and printed tags. The whole time, we kept nervously refreshing our emails, silently praying that my COVID test would come back negative. When the result finally came through, I think we scared the nearby passengers with our celebration. And then, of course, came the epic journey through security—our crew with seven backpacks, seven carry-ons, and tearful goodbyes trailing in our wake.

My mind keeps wandering back to the first time we flew on a transatlantic flight without sitting next to Mum or Dad. Dad was somewhere behind us, and you quickly claimed the aisle seat, naturally leaving me to sit in the middle seat next to the stranger. Then, as if on cue, you fell asleep, sprawling on my shoulder and leaving me trapped. As much as I gave you a hard time about that seating arrangement, I'd give anything to be stuck in the middle seat again, if it meant you were flying with me, nudging my elbow off of the armrest or watching my film over my shoulder.

Do you remember that endless layover in the Middle East—the one where we just gave up and laid down in a ragged bunch? We slept for what felt like seven hours, and when we woke up, Dad arrived with a brown paper bag of chocolate croissants. We laughed—silly, sleepless, survival laughter—as we devoured the delicious pastries. That moment still feels so vivid, so warm. I wish that you were here right now, sitting next to me flicking flaky pastry pieces into my lap and making me smile.

I wonder if, when you close your eyes, you can still picture the winding dirt road from the airport up to Arua? I remember the truck bouncing over potholes, the sun brilliantly blinding the whole world in its dazzling light and the red dirt swirling in clouds around us. And of course we were all in the backseat, bouncing about and laughing uncontrollably for no reason we could name. Remember the juxtaposition of the Arua drive and the drive home to Bankfoot? Can you still picture the walls and sheep pastures? I wonder if that's what makes all of these memories so priceless—we weren't looking for crazy experiences, a certain number of homes or hilarious stories, we just lived the wild life that our family was called to and the experiences we've shared on this journey have been truly beautiful.

It's funny how the hard days have blurred—the bouts of malaria, all of the goodbyes, evacuating a war, being without a home—but so many of these golden moments—these flickers of beauty and life—they shine so brightly in our story. Not every day was easy, but looking back, it feels like we were part of something sacred. I think that's a gift and I'm eternally thankful that I share all of those experiences with you, Goose.

As we begin this strange new season of sistering across the sea, I'm holding onto these memories like never before. And I'm desperately counting down the days until I make this journey in the other direction to come back to you. I know distance will stretch and reshape us a bit, but let's hold onto the gift we've been given, the gift that is each other.

I'm not sure when I'll get to hand you this letter—pretty sure in-flight mail doesn't exist—but I'll tuck it into my bag and hold onto the hope that one day soon, you'll read it with a flat white of your own in hand.

Until then, know that I love you. I'm cheering for you and praying for you, despite this new distance.

Love always,
Elsie
——

Elsie Coppedge
Uganda; South Africa; Georgia, Kentucky,
USA; Israel; Scotland

Dear Mary,

This letter to you would have been written on blue air mail paper, if the British Royal Mail still sold them; but they don't. Remember the days I used to write to you on those fold-out thin blue sheets with the Queen's head on the top? I can't remember if I used those in Jamaica. I wish they were available again.

This letter would have also been written to you in my own hand, and now I'm using a laptop. Years ago, I would have emailed you, but I recall dad saying, "email isn't mail to me."

My friend Marlene recently looked out of her New York City apartment and saw a twenty-something young lady circling a Mailbox. Marlene left her building to go to work and as she did, she noticed the young lady still circling the Mailbox.

She crossed the street and asked, "May I help you?"

The young lady smiled and said, "I'm trying to send my mother a card for Mother's Day, but I've never mailed anything before.

Of course Marlene showed her how to open the Mailbox and drop in the envelope.

"Is that it? I don't need to do anything else?"

"That's it." Marlene smiled and added, "No passcode to remember, no buttons to push."

What I'm trying to say in this letter is that though technology enables us to send messages at the speed of satellite, sometimes it's still difficult for me to say what I want to say to you or even from the past wanted to say to you. It's always been difficult for me to communicate about my adventures from the days I first started living overseas, from the days of thin blue airmail paper and no passcodes needed. It's still hard to convey why I was someone who just "had to go. See the world," according to the words of a friend of mine in Families in Global Transition.

Ruth van Reken, the key founder of the Families in Global Transition organization, wrote a book on Third Culture Kids but today I'm thinking about another book she wrote, called *Letters Never Sent*. I believe there are so many letters I never sent to you. I never sent some letters because I didn't have the language, the words to use to explain myself to you. Writing from other worlds as I served in the Peace Corps was an experience so deep and I was so emersed in the here and now that it didn't even dawn on me that someone back home would want to know. I think I cut me off from you at that time. I told myself no one would ever understand except another Peace Corps Volunteer.

And yet, one of the commitments of the Peace Corps is to take back home what we learned. I saw other volunteers figure out how to do that, but I confess I never did. As you know, I've never really come back home. From Jamaica I went to Scotland, married to a former British Volunteer (VSO), then the north of England then the south of England, then London, then back out to the south of England via visiting mom and dad who lived in South Korea. I recall that when I took my husband and my kids to Taejon you said, "Doesn't anyone in this family want to live in America anymore?"

I didn't know how to write a letter explaining the incredible joy of celebrating my birthday in Seoul. With family. And at least a dozen unofficial aunties with whom I received so much love even if I hadn't learned their language. I still don't know how to write that letter.

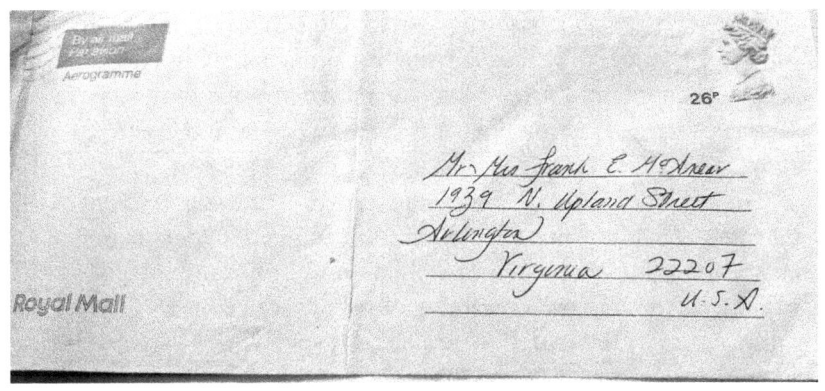

One of Kathleen's saved British Royal Mail letters.

So, I'll write this one. *Letters Now Sent* is a collection of letters written by people who have had third culture experiences. Inspired by Ruth Van Reken's book, *Letters Never Sent*, this book invited writers to choose who they wanted to write to. Some letters are ones we would like to have sent or want to send now and it's in honour of Ruth's big birthday and memoir *Letters Never Sent*.

I choose you. I want to write to you. I still don't know how to explain how I love living a global life, but I have learned in my years overseas to just try. I don't always have the words in Italian to speak to one of my grandsons, but I just try. I don't always understand when someone thinks that if I am "out of the country," I might not be interested in what's going on in their lives, but I'm trying. I don't always open my American accent mouth in meetings when politics seem crazy, but I've learned to try anyway.

So please accept this letter as an offering of wanting to reach out and say I am so sorry for missing so many events in your life. I am so sorry we couldn't live in the same town and meet for coffee on Saturday mornings the way our grandparents did with their friends. I missed most Thanksgivings. Most Christmases. Most birthdays.

Thank you for always keeping a guest room ready for me, when I did come back for a visit. Thank you for coming to England a time or two.

I remember the night I learned you were seriously ill and might only have days to live and so I just hopped on a plane to Atlanta and then had a car (Divine Chariots — isn't that a wonderful name for a car company?) drive me straight to you. Overnight in the hospital, sleeping on that bedside chair that I couldn't figure out how to set up; I plunged into a deep grief that I might lose you. Lose my sister, whom I rarely see these days. Then, something akin to faith rose up in me, and do you remember I leaned over the drips and monitors and whispered in your ear, "Listen here little sister, I know you love flowers; but you have never been to the Chelsea Flower Show — so you cannot die!" I know in my knower that I saw you give a little smile. I know it.

So, this letter will say this is your invitation for you to fly here (I'll come and get you, which should wreck the grocery budget but who cares?) and I'll take you to the Chelsea Flower Show. And we'll have morning coffee amongst something of my adopted country that you will love. Didn't there used to be an advert somewhere in the world that said, "say it with flowers?"

Saying I love you, with flowers, this side of the pond.

> Your big sis,
> Kath
> ———
>
> *Kathleen Smith*
> *USA; Jamaica; Scotland; England*

Letters to
More Family Members

Dear Savana,

I imagine you're thinking: "Why is my cousin writing to me all the way from Africa?" Well, I'm writing because I want to convince you that you should come and stay with us for six months! I know, it sounds crazy right now, but trust me, by the time you finish reading this, I think you'll be totally convinced to come!

Okay, here's why you should come:

1. You'll experience the great climate! Before it storms, the air is perfectly still. The intense humidity and heat seem to sit there, waiting. Then, a breeze stirs the silence. It stops…. then starts again with more force. In the distance you can see the clouds are dark and sometimes rain is already sweeping over the horizon. By now the wind is blowing every dead leaf off the trees which are swaying and bending from its force. Then comes the rain, at first big, fat droplets slowly tumble down, then, suddenly the whole sky opens at once and sheets of rain pummel the earth. Thunder cracks and lightning flashes. The water pounds on the tin roof. And then, as quickly as it had come, it goes, leaving vast puddles and a mist that covers the land. After a while, the sun comes out and the heat and the humidity return at full force. The leaves glisten, the birds chirp, the crickets sing their eternal song.

2. You'll learn a ton. You'll learn about different cultures and how to interact with them. And you'll go to school with us. Our main teacher organizes our lessons, and our parents come and teach some of them. There is kindergarten through 8th grade (11 students total) and everything's colorful and fun. I'm 13, the eldest. We have a classroom, older kids' room, library, and bathroom. They're the only air-conditioned rooms at the station (which is like a neighborhood where all the missionaries live).

3. You'll learn French. It would make whatever language you're learning in school so much easier, and you speaking French opens up a ton of job opportunities later on.

4. You can play soccer with us. People around here are obsessed with soccer. You could play every day with my missionary

friend and his Gabonese friends. But be careful, he's super athletic and sports-crazy, so he might totally beat you!

5. You'd go to church with me here and see how different it is to the church services in the US. In the US, the services are short, usually in air-conditioned churches, and the language spoken is English. Here, the services are long (4 hours), hot, and in French. Mommy teaches Sunday school, too.

6. You'll eat amazing food! We eat really well here and I can introduce you to some of my favorite foods. Gabonese food staples include chicken, fish, rice, and manioc. Manioc is a plant. Its leaves are ground into mush and cooked with oil, fish, onions, and some other things. Its roots are soaked, ground, boiled, and either frozen or eaten with the leaves. The leaves are the veggie sauce and the roots are the carbohydrate (like bitter potatoes). In English manioc is cassava (manioc is French). We don't eat the root and we put less oil, no fish, and add canned chicken and canned beans to our manioc. The names of the other dishes are all French versions of what they are in English. We grow our own manioc in our garden.

7. You'll see the coolest animals. There are so many animals here! My favorite are the orange and black lizards that do push-ups! Clouds of bats fly over our house each night. There are Christmas birds who migrate here during December and follow our lawn mower guys looking for bugs to devour. There are millions of bugs, like army ants that march in a straight line for miles. There are monkeys, snakes, and panthers, but the Gabonese eat them, so they stay away. Want to join our hippo/snake-infested-river-tubing?! Sounds like fun, right?!

Lastly, I have a few travel tips for you before you come. Before going through security at the airport, make sure you dump out your water bottle. You can refill it after security. The flight is about 17 hours, so settle in to your "home" on this plane! I recommend you try to sleep, eat all the food they serve, read books you've packed in your carry on, and watch movies on the personalized screen in front of you. It's not a direct flight to our capital city, so you have to take another plane after that 17 hour one! And then you need to drive 8 hours to our house! It's a long trip, but it'll be worth it.

I really hope you'll come visit, and I can't wait to see you! Love you lots!

> Love,
> Esther—your TCK Cousin (TCK stands for Third Culture Kid, not Treacherously Cat-like Know-it-alls or Totally Confused Kit-Kats!)

P.S. Being a TCK is great! It gives you compassion, flexibility, international experience, open-mindedness, understanding of others' cultures, thinking outside the box, and willingness to do wacko things. P.P.S. Oh, and I'm sending you some French phrases to learn before you get here. You're gonna need them for the plane ride and the market! Bonjour (bone-joor) means hello. Merci (m-air-see) means thank you and S'il-te-plait (seal t play) means please. Oui (we) and no mean yes and no, and "Where is the bathroom?" is ou sont les toilette? (oo sone lay t-wa-let).

———

> *Esther Hofman*
> *Oklahoma, Nebraska, New Hampshire,*
> *USA; Gabon, France*

01 August 2021

Dear (Great) Aunt Margery,

I did not get to say goodbye to you, and now you are gone. I did not even make it to your funeral, which is what happens sometimes when you live on the other side of the world. I guess you knew that better than anyone, though. You lived longer and traveled farther than most, teaching in northern India before coming here to where I now live in Taiwan. You were an American farm girl far away from home, and your adventures influenced my life more than many realize.

"Can you guess what this word is?" you asked me when I was young, writing a Chinese character that looked like an E that slipped on its back. "It's the word for mountain. See?"

Three strokes rose up from a horizontal line on the paper, the middle one taller than the others. The pictograph did, indeed, look like a mountain. As a Midwestern preschooler, all I knew of mountains was the 70s panoramic wallpaper on the walls of my room.

"Mountain," handwritten by Jenessa.

I had a flashback to this memory, of the first Mandarin characters I learned, when I accepted my first teaching position in China. I was visiting you at your retirement community in Iowa. You sat me down at your dining room table and—a teacher through and through—you asked me, "Can you guess what this word is?"

I was twenty-two, still a child. I did not know that in my career I would teach in northeastern China, at a Chinese immersion school in Minneapolis, and eventually, in Taiwan. These days I travel some of the same roads you did, although you would not recognize most of them now. Taipei, like me, has grown up.

When I was young, you gave me a Taiwanese flag that I hung on the bookshelf in my room. Its large, white sun nearly glowed in the dark as I slept under the flag each night. Who knew I would someday teach under one in my classroom?

Looking back, I can see how out-of-place a Taiwanese flag was hanging in a suburban American girl's bedroom. And how unusual it is to have learned to write the character for mountain before having learned to spell the English word. But part of me does not think it is strange at all. Perhaps even then my path was winding towards Taiwan.

I have lived here a long time now. For my sons, this is the only home they have ever really known. My little family knows now what you knew all along: Taiwan is a very special place. What a privilege to know so well this place you called home for so long.

Some people are hard to say goodbye to simply because I owe them so much. To me, you were so much more than Grandma's big sister—and you gave me so much more than my first language lessons and a flag. Thank you for everything, Aunt Margery.

> Love always,
> Your great-niece, Jenessa
>
> ———
>
> *Jenessa Van Schooneveld*
> *Minnesota, USA; China; Taiwan*

Dear military husband,

We joke that God has used our marriage to teach me American geography, as the military bumps us from one side of the US to the other (and back again). But in truth, there's a lot that we've had to learn for the sake of our marriage and each other.

We started out in two very different places as two very different people. Who would've thought that the girl raised on the overcrowded island nation of Java, with its volcanoes and rice paddies and mosques, could find enough common ground to stay married to the southern boy raised in Mississippi farmland and Tennessee suburbs, with water moccasins and rodeos and accents you could scoop with a spoon?

I had an unfair advantage. I got to know your family years before we even started dating while my family was still a twelve-hour plane ride away. I got to sit on the porch swing that hung from your back porch. I got to hold your baby sister and rock in your mother's rocking chair.

Marian's handwritten letter to her husband.

You met my dad two days before our wedding. You have never gotten to visit the land that shaped my growing up years, to hear the cacophony of street vendors, to eat roasted corn on the side of a mountain, to watch the mist drift over the green of the tea plantations. My parents have moved, so even if we bought exorbitantly expensive plane tickets to fly halfway across the world (with or without our herd of kids), I will never really get to take you home.

But you...I have seen you try so hard to connect with the

Indonesian half of your tall, blonde wife. Everywhere we move, you look for Indonesian restaurants. You order Indomie and sambal and kecap manis on Amazon to make sure I have my comfort foods. You celebrate when I cook rendang and gado-gado. You encourage me to teach our children to speak Indonesian. You love that I hang maps and angklungs on the walls of our home. And when a hurricane destroyed our home, taking with it the wooden chest I had brought back to the States with me upon graduating high school, you held me as I wept and did not once tell me that it was just a thing, knowing that it was, in truth, a tangible memory and one of the few ways I could share with our children where I'd come from, who I'd once been.

Our marriage hasn't yet been celebrated by matching stamps on our passports. I did all the traveling before we said our vows, and you've done all of it since. One day I hope we can do it together. But until then, thank you, you wonderful man, for all the ways you help me bring my home with us, for all the ways you encourage me to share it, for all the times you've resisted the urge to make fun of me for using the excuse of "I didn't grow up here!" even though I've now lived in the US longer than I lived in Indonesia.

I didn't realize when we got married how much being a cross-cultural kid would prepare me for life in the military (which is its own weird culture, to be sure), nor did I realize how life as a pastor's kid turned military man would prepare you for marriage to a third culture kid. I didn't realize how much resilience and flexibility my life overseas had given me, how much perspective it enabled me to have, or how often I would need the reminder that home is where you make it. I didn't realize how much your upbringing had prepared you to love adventure and exploration, how much it had trained you in the desire to listen well to other's stories, how much it had taught you to love the stranger, the minority, the one who had no home. Our differences have ended up giving us more strength than we sometimes credit. And our differences have deeply enriched our marriage.

It hasn't always been easy, but, with seventeen years' worth of hindsight, I do believe it has always been good.

Dengan semua cintaku,
Your cross-cultural kid wife

———

Marian Frizzell
Indonesia; United Kingdom; USA

26 March 2025
Gabon

Dear future lover,

I haven't met you yet. Someone is mowing their lawn somewhere around my house, and the noise is infernal, but my inner calm prevails. It's actually a serene day here in Libreville; the loud neighbours are away, and I'm just writing this letter.

I wonder what you're up to—where you are, how you're feeling. Of course, the image in my head is blurry beyond meaning. I don't know your face, or the container of your life.

But still, I wonder about you. I wonder about us.

For so long I have pictured you with hair as dark as mine, skin the same shade of pale honey. My parents spoke to you in their mother tongue—simple, melodic Malagasy—and they loved you because they could. They loved that you were one of 'us'.

But then we moved to a place where my black mane wasn't the norm. Gabonese women were curvy and gorgeous; their long braids adorned with gold and silver; their dancing laced with confidence my male friends called 'womanly'. Suddenly, I wasn't your ordinary teenage girl—I was too shy, too Asian, with hair too thick and a frame too small. I can still feel the lingering spite of watching my brother be called 'Chinese' on the bus, blamed—absurdly—for youth unemployment in the country.

Somewhere in the chaos of surviving this new home, learning that accents were cool and so was breaking the rules, your features lost their clarity, and I, the certainty of who I was. Was I Malagasy, and did you need to be? Would we doom ourselves to cultural mismatch, like my father warns we would, if you weren't?

Thinking about you became a refuge. A place where I could be my wholehearted self, and be not only accepted, but understood and echoed with. When I transferred to an international school, I dreamed you spoke both French and English, and we could connect in all the languages I exist in. I began to think of you in terms of hobbies! One day you loved music, the next, you played football. There's even a corner of my mind dedicated to the Disney song you'll sing the night you propose.

My friends used to find all these filters odd. My mother definitely thinks I'm being too picky. She says to content myself with who's already there. The young and tall, the handsome ones. She openly wishes for 'Chinese' grandkids and might not know what to do if I fell for a Black man.

How do you feel about her criteria? It's hard not to care, but I try anyway, because I know why and where my touchstones fit. Because I know I'll want to argue in English, then tell you how much you mean to me in French. Because the deepest, truest definitions of who I am are rooted in the way Pixar movies make me cry. In dancing around my room when the world feels too heavy and speaking to trees as fellow Earth dwellers.

I hope you share the values I have nurtured over the years. Acceptance. Connection. An unrepentant drive to delight in living. I've had a large and unstable palette to draw values from, but I think I've done a good job. I'm kind, you know? And thoughtful. I weave homes around laughter born from tearful intimacies. I see the best in people and strive to bring it out of them.

I hope that where you are on your side of the world, you're also carefully crafting a self that you love. I hope that in the midst of our mortal aliveness, we will find one another and be each other's safe landing. Where the full scope of who we are, no fear or performance, has space to exist, to be craved, saved a seat for. A place to be and to belong.

And yes, I wonder if you smiled reading that last sentence — because maybe, like me, you hate it when the experts are right about things like 'belonging'.

Mostly, I just hope I make sense to you. That my hasty disclosures don't scare you away, and my meta-discussions leave you charmed. I hope you see the light I create in a room and appreciate the way I listen with my heart.

I hope you love me for all I've become — eclectic, profound, endearingly unorthodox — and that you never tire of becoming with me. You'll likely find me quaint, perhaps 'fascinating'. And I'll admit to dreaming you're overwhelmed that I exist. But I hope, in time, you'll grow to see beyond that awe and meet me exactly where I am instead.

I'm so excited to meet you.

Love,
Kate
———

Kate Rambolamanana
Antananarivo, Madagascar; South Africa;
Gabon; Mauritius

Letters to
Friends, Mentors, and
Mentees

Dear Chris P.,

In elementary school, you threw a ball at me. I mean, right at me, on purpose... and it was likely the kindest thing anyone had done for me as a new student in that school.

Just in case you don't recall, I was the new kid in second grade at a large public elementary school in Las Vegas, Nevada. It was the late 1980s, and neon colors had only just been discovered. Everybody dressed like they had been attacked by a giant set of highlighter pens. I came to the school from a very small village in the UK. The late 80s didn't come to the UK until 2003, so I still dressed as if it were the 1970s... I looked different. I was the only student in a very large radius with an English accent (which can have some charm and allure later in life, but nothing that makes you stand out is really helpful in elementary school).

It didn't take long for many students' preferred recess activity to become shoving me (the funny-looking, funny-talking, British kid) up against a wall and then cajoling me into saying words that everyone thought sounded funny in my English accent. It was a bizarre form of bullying, and I didn't enjoy it. I just wanted to belong... and every day I felt like I was being pushed further and further away from the shores of acceptance by the relentless waves of kids' laughter and unflattering interest in all that made me stand out.

Then you came along. You were in my class, so I'd seen you around. You had yet to join the "Shove the British kid against the wall and extract unique phonetic expressions for amusement and ridicule" club (that's not what they called it, obviously... "STBKATWAEUPEFAAR" is far too difficult to pronounce as an acronym). But then one day you made up for lost time and disagreeableness by throwing a ball at me. You skipped right past intimidation and opted for projectile violence.

Except that you threw the ball with such a high arc from where you were standing (quite a way behind the circle of kids verbally poking at me), that I had plenty of time to see it coming... in fact, I caught it without having to move anything but my arms. From the vantage point of the encircling children, a ball had practically materialized in my embrace without warning. Amidst their shock (and still quite a way removed from all of us), you yelled at me, "Hey! That's my ball. Bring it back."

Without saying a word, and with no protest from the still shocked group of kids around me, I walked right through and brought you the ball back. You said you were heading off to play kickball and that I should come too because I didn't look like I was enjoying myself with the other kids.

That day marked the first of countless days of kickball, and of our friendship. I was a cross-cultural kid, and you were not. You made fun of how I spoke from time to time (you'd earned it), but you also helped me perfect my American accent. It took me a while to adjust—it was my first cross-cultural experience (who knew the seemingly simple UK to US transition could be such an ordeal?)—but it was made so much easier because of you and your willingness to take me on as a friend, provide some safe space, and take an interest in what was behind my accent (which you thought only really existed on TV shows), or my clothing (which you said you'd seen in your mom's old collection of catalogues).

Your empathy was subtle but powerful. You didn't dramatically threaten to fight a crowd of kids who weren't really intentionally mean as much as they were ignorant to the feelings of others. But you did creatively help me escape and offered me companionship... we never talked about it directly. But seeing you waiting for me as I got off the school bus dramatically changed how I felt about getting out of bed each day.

I'm sad that we lost touch when I moved away just a few years later. We were young, social media hadn't been invented yet, and honestly neither of us knew how to say goodbye well. I missed you more than I let on. I was heading into the unknown again. Switching countries, being the new kid again, I hoped and prayed a kind soul would throw a ball at me at whatever school I landed at next.

I'd built some resilience, honed some adaptability, and knew a little more of what I was getting into in that next move—and I kept building on those skills in subsequent moves. I think I soon realized I didn't have to wait for someone to throw a ball at me: plenty of people around me were in need of someone to bring them into a kickball game... or a friendship, or sometimes even just a conversation.

Chris P., your demonstration of empathy (even though we didn't have the words for it back then) was foundational in shaping how I saw other people. Unknowingly, you inspired me to be moved by others in different cultures spanning the globe. Honestly, that skillset has been an ingredient in so many of my endeavors. As a CCK armed with a lot more language and framework now—I can confidently say that you contributed in setting the course for where I am now. Thanks for throwing a ball at me, I'm still reverberating from it... in a good way.

Gratefully,
Chris O

———

Christopher O'Shaughnessy
United Kingdom; United States; Belgium;
Turkey; United Arab Emirates

March 28, 2025
Indonesia

Dear Isabella,

I wanted to share with you what it's like to be me, since we haven't really talked much about my life outside of the States. So, as you know, I moved to Southeast Asia six years ago when I was seven (almost eight). Which is a pretty hard time to move; you're old enough to have made a lot of friends (including you), have a rhythm (a.k.a. have a pattern of what you do every week), and be close to your family. But you're also young enough to not entirely understand what's happening.

I remember being excited about making new friends, trying new foods, and learning a new language. However, it doesn't make it any easier when you see your favorite toys sold off without your consent or full acknowledgement of what you just agreed to. But a good thing is you do have friends you can come back to, but they change overtime, which can be tough. Still, with you, I feel like things won't change that much.

Anyways, once in Indonesia, we landed in a heavy downpour of rain. Now, I'd heard about monsoons, but no one told me there were monsoons in June (which was when we landed). It was also very hot and humid, especially when compared to Washington state, which is where I'm from. My first birthday there was over a month after we arrived and only my family was at my party. After a little while, we met some other English-speaking foreigners. There were four girls who were all one year older than me (for some reason that makes a difference, so I never became as close to them as they were to each other). When Covid came, they all moved somewhere else (although Covid may not have been the only factor), and soon I was the only girl in all of the city over the age of ten that was a foreigner. I became really lonely and on top of that I had really bad stomach problems. We went to multiple doctors and none of them could figure out what was wrong.

But one day God answered one of my prayers. I joined a traditional dance class at one of the language schools where I lived and during that class I met an amazing girl. She's one year younger than me and soon became my very best friend. We're still friends to this day. Also, after a while God healed me (while my family was praying for me) and I've never had that pain again.

When we went back to the States for a couple of months when I was eleven, one of my best friends shared that when I left, she cried every night for months. I didn't find out about that until four years later. I was so sorry to hear this.

Back in Indonesia, some other kids moved to the city where I lived, but some also moved away. Although I'm used to it now, it's still really hard to say good-bye.

At the moment, I'm the oldest girl in the city, which is the complete opposite of when I first arrived. Two years ago, I moved six hours north of the city. The road isn't great, but at least there aren't too many sharp turns. I also have the cutest cat in the world, Rayo, which means "thunderbolt" in Spanish. It's in Spanish, not Indonesian, because, as you know, my dad is from Mexico.

I feel like God is calling me to create a TCK camp somewhere outside the U.S. when I'm older. I've already made a lot of plans for one somewhere in Asia. I also want to get a degree in counseling to help other TCKs, because it can be really hard, and I don't want anyone to feel too lonely. Personally, I've said so many goodbyes, but I've also said plenty of hellos. As a TCK here I've not always fit in because I look different, my first language is different, and I just act differently.

My life isn't horrible, but it isn't all sunshine and rainbows. But then again, no one's life is. So, in that way, I'm at least "normal." I've heard that people in the States often say that being "normal" is a bad thing, but I actually wish I were "normal" sometimes. You might think that's strange—and honestly, sometimes I do too—but I wouldn't trade my life for anyone else's.

I've traveled to so many places, tried so many types of food, learned new languages, and made at least a hundred friends (and that's not an exaggeration). I love my life, and I hope you'll see the good in your own life too, even when you face challenges. If you focus only on the bad, you'll miss how blessed your story is and how God has guided both of us along the way.

Love you, Isabella!

> Your Bestie,
> Eva (Zelly)
> ———
>
> *Eva Hernandez*
> *Washington, USA; Indonesia*

Dear 李阿姨 ,

I think about the Panda Express orange chicken and chao mian that we have here in Southern California, and I know that nothing compares to your cooking that you did for our family all those years in China. When my friends ask me about where my passion for baking cakes, and cooking dishes like tikka masala or curry came from, I always tell them about the impact you made on my childhood. Cooking alongside you after coming home from school propelled my love for food.

I remember coming home from 书香园 elementary school and bolting to the kitchen to see what you were cooking for dinner, bombarding you with questions of how I could help. Soon, I became your sous chef! The first thing you taught me to make was 饼, a Chinese flatbread that you let me form into different animal designs like a bear face or dog. Then, we would put it on the stove, and you would flip it for me so that I could see all the nice golden patches on the underside. Whether you were making Chinese pickled radish buns called 芽菜包子 for our family, or 猪肉白菜水饺, delicious cabbage and pork dumplings, you gave me a deeper appreciate and pride for my culture's food.

Some days, I would find you making 拉面, Chinese hand-pulled noodles in our kitchen. You always set some dough aside for me to play with and roll into different shapes, as I watched you roll, pull, and twist homemade noodles with your hands. Watching this art and gift you had for food set my heart on fire for cooking. Whatever you did, I had a curious desire to learn how to do the same! Whenever I was still in Kindergarten, I decided to make my family an apple cobbler for the first time, and you helped me as I struggled to follow the recipe instructions. When I came home from school and wanted to make my family a snack, you helped me cut an apple, but after a while taught me how to do it myself!

When I think about why so many of my American friends in the U.S don't like vegetables, it's because they grew up eating it the wrong way. My love for potatoes came from your 土豆丝, a hot and sour Chinese stir-fried shredded potatoes dish that you always added the perfect amount of chili peppers so that my sister and I could enjoy it. My love for cucumber came from your cucumber and peanuts dish, 黄

瓜花生米. As a kid, my eyes would stare in fascination as I watched you use your big knife to peel the garlic, crush the peanuts, and smash the cucumbers with authority!

The most humbling thing of it all was witnessing your love for food become your ministry. When we had the college students over at our apartment for Saturday night Bible studies, you would make a big batch of 白菜粉丝. As you prepared these dishes, you would invite students into our kitchen to have conversations with them and teach them how to cook these foods. You revealed to me the gift of fellowship that came with food; a pattern I discovered as I started going through the Gospels and read about Jesus's heart for fellowship over meals with His disciples.

Food connects us. It's a universal language that everyone in the world can find both comfort and pride in. "Thank you" is not sufficient enough to express my gratitude to you for sharing with me this gift of cooking and love for food.

God places people in our childhood for a purpose. I can only hope that I would have the same impact on someone like you did for me.

Love,
晓惠
———

Haley Hsu
Dalian, China; California, USA

Dear Irina,

How are you, Irina? It's me—Sophishka. I often find myself thinking about you and the time we shared. It was such a brief chapter in my life, yet you've stayed with me, woven into the person I've become. Over the years, I've written so many letters to you, but I've never truly thanked you for what you did for me. Maybe neither of us fully understood what I was going through back then, but your kindness and presence gave me the strength I needed at exactly the right time.

I remember the day we first met. We went out to the Kazakh countryside for a welcome picnic with all the international teachers and their families. I can still picture the dried fish laid out on a picnic blanket, the crusty bread, my parents raising vodka toasts under the open sky, but most of all, I remember being in complete awe of you. You were so powerful, so beautiful, so magnetic. That day, I went home and wrote you the first of many letters. I painstakingly wrote every word in a different color. When you told me, 'I've had lots of letters from my students, but nobody has ever written to me in different colors,' I felt an overwhelming sense of pride.

At the time, you may not have realized it, but as a family, we were starting our third new school in three years. I was fourteen, caught in that awkward stage of adolescence when you're supposed to be discovering yourself, but I was simply trying to keep up with the constant changes.

Astana was a world apart from what I'd known. I went from the warmth of tropical Malaysia, where life was badminton games, big stage productions, and pool parties, to a stark, frozen landscape where I was the only foreign student in my year group. On the first day of school, when everyone introduced themselves in Russian, I was blindsided. I hadn't expected to be the only one who didn't speak the language. Most of my lessons were solitary, PE felt like a military drill, and the weather was unimaginably cold. The culture shock was overwhelming. I was only there for a year, and honestly, I'm not sure I ever fully acclimatized.

Our relationship wasn't exactly conventional, but I don't think I gave you much choice. I wanted to be by your side, and I made sure to find a way to be near you. I idolized you, and I can imagine that, as a headmistress, that must have been a little tricky to navigate. I convinced you to give me Russian lessons, did my homework in your office, and even had your boyfriend teaching me guitar. You took me to your dacha in the mountains of Almaty, and you even let me stay with you when my parents were away. You gave me so much of your time, and I'll always be deeply grateful for that.

It's taken me years to understand why I needed you so much. Looking back, I realize just how lost I felt, desperately searching for a sense of connection. I didn't have the time to fit in or adapt to yet another new world, but you saw me. You didn't ask me to change, to blend in, or to be anyone else. You liked me exactly as I was, and that meant everything. That connection was my lifeline. It got me through.

After I left Kazakhstan, life became a whirlwind of moves: Russia, London, Cardiff, Bath, Bristol, and finally the Philippines. With each place, I found pieces of myself, and somewhere along the way, I discovered my true calling. I became a teacher in international schools, working with children just like me, kids who navigate the ever-changing, often chaotic world of being "from everywhere and nowhere." Every day, I try to be their anchor, their connection, their safe place. Because I know how much it matters to have someone who sees you when you're struggling to find your footing.

So, thank you, Irina. Thank you for holding my hand when I needed it the most. Thank you for seeing me, for accepting me, and for showing me that being myself was enough.

And one day, I dream of standing in your dacha with my own children by my side, introducing them to the extraordinary woman who shaped my life in ways I couldn't fully understand back then. I want to look you in the eyes and tell you, face-to-face, just how much you meant to me.

All my love,
Sophie
_____

Sophie Wycherley
Wolverhampton, London, Bath, Bristol,
England; Wrexham, Wales; Yokohama,
Japan; KL, Malaysia; Astana, Almaty,
Kazakhstan; Moscow, Russia; Manila,
Philippines

Dear Alex*,

Come in, have a seat.

Yeah, you kind of sink into my sofa, right... it's so comfy sometimes I don't want to get up either. The smell in here? Oh, that's vanilla, yeah it does smell a bit like cupcakes.

Hey, hey, it's okay. If you're going to cry anywhere in this school, it's the counselling office, right? It's okay, cry as much as you need to—I have some tissues, let me grab them for you.

I can see you're searching for the words to express how much you miss your home(s). You're missing the way the air smells and how the food tastes half the world away. The sense of knowing what you are doing, where you stand—heck, even how you stand. To queue or not to queue, that is the question! Well, probably not the question, but a question nonetheless.

It might not be one home in particular you miss, but the sense of belonging you get with the people who know you. You can't articulate it yet but I sense you are also missing who you used to be, in that place, at that time. One day who you were when you were there, will be a story in the tapestry of your life, but right now, your past and your sense of self seems ripped from you and lies scattered all over the floor.

And you sit here, with me, crying big silent tears. Unable to find the words to describe this encompassing loss you mutter: I miss home.

You want to be back there, but you can't, you're here in my office, sitting on a strange sofa in a strange room, in a strange city, in a strange country, talking to a stranger about home.

My heart aches for you.

Who are you in this new place when no-one knows your story? Can you still be a 'really good student' if you are struggling to navigate what is expected of you in this school? Are you still an 'athlete' if you can't make the team? Are you still the 'popular kid' if you are so sad you can't pluck up the courage to talk to anyone? Are you the same person? How will you piece together the remnants of your identity? Who will you become here? Every move comes with the option of reinvention, but with reinvention comes loss.

Later from now, I will ask where is home? Everywhere you've

lived and nowhere, you'll reply. Not here, not yet.

You'll sigh as you wonder out loud if it's worth the bother of even trying to make friends here because it hurts so much when they, or you, leave again. But you will, you will try again because you always do. We all need people.

Over time you'll tell me all the things you loved about your last country—your friends, the things you used to do, the pillow you had on your bed... I'll gently laugh and tell you I know that feeling—I still miss my mattress I left behind last time. It's the small things we miss, the things that aren't always obvious, the hidden losses. The quirks of living in places so tiny everyone knows everyone, or cities so gigantic we can get lost for days. We grieve everyone we have loved, and every place we have ever called home. I'll tell you these live within us in the way we eat noodles and what we do with our shoes, through to our slightly strange accents that no one can seem to place. You'll ask if I'm Irish and look at me slightly quizzically when I say I am not.

You will smile as you tell me about your family back in your passport country but say you don't go back as often as you like. If I ask your nationality you define yourself by your passport but note that you feel different to that, not quite that nationality, but something else. You sound different, you do things differently, you don't quite fit in your passport country. Like traditional food when the chef has added a ton of extra ingredients. A dash of this, a dash of that—like chucking chilli in a cottage pie to make it more delicious.

I will explain, when you're ready, that these pieces of us, our culture and customs from our passport country are all jumbled up with the culture and customs of every place and every person we've called home. You'll say that makes sense and give me a ton of examples in your life. Your eyes will widen when you find the term 'Third Culture Kid' encapsulates all of this. Finally, you have a word for this feeling; this difference, yet affinity to others like you. Belonging with people not places.

You will settle here. You will thrive in a way which may be similar or completely different to your last school. You will figure out what is the same in this new place and adapt to what is different. We will smile at each other as we pass in the corridors, and I will see you laughing and having fun again. You will no longer need me.

You will find your people. With your people you will find home.

Years from now, I will occasionally think of you and hope you are happy. For now, though, here, in the room with the cupcake smell, you are safe with me.

Ms. Aylssa,
Your School Counsellor

———

Aylssa Temple
Gateshead, Newcastle upon Tyne, United
Kingdom; Majuro, Republic of the
Marshall Islands; Bandar Seri Begawan,
Brunei; Phuket, Thailand

*Please note the name has been anonymised to protect confidentiality. And in my heart I am addressing every past and future TCK student I have and will support in transition.

Lieve Anja,

You were definitely my favorite primary school teacher, and I cannot remember a single thing you taught me. I will always remember the way you made me feel: heard, seen, and safe.

I will never forget the moment I walked into that school building in Gouda. I was nine years old and we had recently moved back to the Netherlands (to the little Dutch town where I had spent the first five years of my life) from Switzerland, where I had attended an international school since kindergarten. I was nervous, scared and excited all at the same time.

Early that morning, my mom and I walked into the school building and the hallways were still quiet. All the other kids were playing outside in the courtyard. You walked down the stairs and greeted me with a warm smile.

"Hi there, can I help you? Are you new here?" you asked.

"Yes, I am."

"Which class will you be going to?"

"Third grade," I replied.

"Oh, what a shame—I teach fifth grade! I wish you'd be joining my class."

We stood there for a few minutes as you asked me questions about where I had lived and how I felt about being back in the Netherlands. All I could think was, I can't wait to go to fifth grade. And even now, forty years later, third and fourth grade are a blur. Fifth grade was probably my happiest year at school ever.

And as the years passed, you weren't just my teacher anymore— you became like a second mother to me and a dear family friend. You welcomed me into your life, into your family, and we created so many memories in different places, from Gouda to Switzerland to Ghana.

You stayed in touch while I moved, again, and again, and again. You encouraged me to always follow my heart. You taught me that life was not always going to be easy and gave me the confidence to manage the tough times. When things got difficult, you always encouraged me to "chase the bears away" whenever I'd find them on my path. For our wedding gift you gave us Going on a Bear Hunt, a story that has been read with so much love, so many times, to Josephine and Madeleine. And whenever I came to you in tears, I always left our conversation with a smile on my face and usually a good belly laugh.

Almost two and half years ago you called me on my birthday—to wish me a happy birthday and also because you finally had found the courage to tell me that you were suffering from Alzheimers.

The road was quick from there and unfortunately it all happened while my father was also very sick. I was not with you in those last years as much as I wish I could have been. Meanwhile, my dad also struggled with his memory as mostly dark clouds settled over his mind in his final years.

You, however, always found ways to highlight the bright side, at least to me. You always reminded me to find the light and to treasure those we love. "Life is nothing without friendship" you once wrote to me and then years later you sent me the song "You can't make old friends."

People often ask me if you actually gave me a version of a *My Moving Booklet* when I moved, as you were featured as 'Juf Anja' in my book *B at Home: Emma Moves Again*. You never did.

You did model to me what it looks like when a teacher cares. You did model what it looks like to approach difficult conversations around identity and belonging when we're only 10 or 11 years old. You did model that even in your fifties there's no reason not to jump off the mountain with a parachute. You did model that value and purpose cannot be measured by your bank account and that sharing the little we have can be even more rewarding. You did model that we can make small changes that have big impacts. You did model that transitions happen through all walks of life to people everywhere, and how to support them. And you did model that you can dream big no matter what.

The last time I saw you, just a month before you passed away in November 2024, there was nothing left of the larger-than-life woman I was so proud to call my favorite teacher and my friend. However, you—your soul, your being, your presence—left such an incredible mark on all of us who were lucky enough to have known you.

You always encouraged me to write. As a teenager I was mortified that someone would find my writing so I would put it in sealed envelopes and send them in packages to you instead. You kept them safe for me for years. Unfortunately, they became my letters that never arrived—when I was finally ready to read them, you sent them back to me and somehow, they must have gotten lost in the mail. Perhaps they were never meant to be read and only meant to be written. It only seems fitting that my letter here is written to you. I trust it will reach you somehow.

I treasure all the memories that we built together. Yet, it is that welcoming smile and those words of kindness on my first day of school that stand out to me the most. And as I became a teacher and passionate about the transitions-care work I do, I often reflect on the power of a simple act of kindness, especially in the moments when we feel in between worlds and unsure of where we belong. I am so grateful that at an early age you taught me that a strong sense of belonging can be planted in a very small gesture of kindness.

Dankjewel lieve An—ik hou van jou.

Kus,
Valérie

———

Valérie Besanceney
The Netherlands; Luxembourg; United
States; France; Germany; Ghana; Egypt;
Myanmar; Bolivia; Aruba; Switzerland

来自： 被收养的哥哥
收件人：我的弟弟妹妹

你好，亲爱的弟弟妹妹，

我有好消息带给你！

请允许我称呼你为我的弟弟妹妹。我是一位十几年前被收养到美国的孩子，今年二十七岁。 我曾经也是一名孤儿，和你一样在福利院生活。 我是2002年进的儿童福利院， 在院里生活了八年。 你的经历我都知道，我可以感同身受。

我知道你挨过饿，为了好吃的饭菜或者零食你会去讨好叔叔阿姨，或者去抢去偷去骗。这些事情我也做过。

我知道你受过冻，手脚都有过冻疮，鞋子里进过水，能换洗的袜子和衣服就那几套，衣服几乎都是捡别人穿过的，二手的。 这些事我都经历过。

我知道你住的地方不理想，没有自己的空间，冬天挤空调房，夏天挤空调房。也许你的环境改善了，但是你应该和我一样想象着哪天有自己的房间，自己布置安排。

我知道你身体上有缺陷，心里有自卑，深处也有质问"为什么我和别人不一样呢？为什么被抛弃的是我？" 我和你一样，身体也有缺陷，心里有过自卑，也质问过。我有白化病，头发和其它的毛发都是白色的，视力很差很怕强光。我身体不对称，有大小手和大小胸。 你身心的挣扎我能理解。

我知道你是免费的劳动力，你被别人要求洗衣服，刷鞋子，打扫屋子，给别人跑腿，给别人按摩，给别人洗脚。 有的时候你也会要求比你弱小的人听你的话，去为你洗衣，刷鞋，跑腿，按摩，洗脚。 这些事情我也做过。

我知道你的惶恐和惧怕。比你强壮，比你大的人打你，骂你，他们用言语威胁你， 恐吓你，甚至要你罚站，罚跪。不过有的时候你也会打骂，恐吓，体罚比你弱小的人。 这些事情我也做过。

我知道有的时候 你胆子还很大，为了好吃和好玩，你偷过别人的吃的，玩的，喝的，还偷过别人的钱，别人的自行车。你没有觉得偷东西不对，如果被抓了还要辱骂抓你的人， 这些我都经历过我都知道。

我知道你脏话和谎言不离口，骂人和撒谎对你来说都是家常便饭，因为你不骂人别人就会骂你，你不撒谎就不能遮盖你和他人做的事，有时候你不撒谎还会得罪人，所以撒谎已经成为了你的本能。 我不是要来指责你，我说的也是我的经历，我的心路历程。

我知道你心底的渴望，也知道你做过的白日梦，"为什么被收养的不是我呢？我要是被收养了该多好，如果有一天我有钱了要怎样，怎样…我要是有爸爸妈妈该多好!我也想有个家!"我和你一样有过这样的想法，做过这样那样的白日梦。甚至有的时候你还想过更深刻的人生问题，比如"我活着有什么意义呢？人到底从哪儿来的？人死了又会到哪儿去呢？"这些本不是你这个年龄该思考的问题，但是这些都是你内心最深的想法，最深的渴望。这些我都想过，我都知道。

作为哥哥，我非常理解你的处境，我经历过你经历过的事。我想与你分享一个极好的消息。这个消息改变了我的人生，给了我希望和对未来的憧憬。我亲身体验过的，经历过的，我才来与你分享。我希望你能把这个好消息记在心里，常常去思考，常常去依靠。

我带给你的好消息是这样的"耶稣爱你！耶稣爱你！耶稣爱你！耶稣认识你，祂比任何人都了解你，祂知道你一切的经历。祂要带你认识你的创造者，就是你天上的父。祂为了救你脱离罪恶附上了生命的代价。祂看你为宝贵，祂要来接纳你，要来爱你。"

耶稣是创造宇宙万物永生神的的独生子，祂两千年前来到这个世上为了让人能够重新回到神的面前，祂劝人认罪悔改，教导人认识他们在天上的父。为了让人与神和好，祂被钉死在十字架上替我们而死，在第三天祂从死里复活，战胜了死亡，为的是给我希望，叫我们悔改，重新认识我们在天上的父我们的神，让我们得着真正的生命，这生命是从耶稣那里流淌出的永生。，如圣经上所说"神爱世人，甚至将他的独生子赐给他们，叫一切信他的，不至灭亡，反得永生。"这是人类历史上最好的消息！

感谢神让我在被收养后的第一年就听到如此好的消息，让我认识到我需要被拯救，因为我深陷罪恶和黑暗的泥潭，我自己救不了自己，就连收养我的美国家庭也救不了我，因为这个家庭也破碎了，父母离婚了。我的生命没有希望。我急切的需要耶稣的拯救。我承认自己是个罪人，常常做恶事，心里装满了诡计，淫邪，恶毒，和嫉妒。我的罪让我与神隔绝，让我无法看见神，认识神。

耶稣听到了我发自心里的呼求，他医治了我心底的伤，祂给我永生的盼望，祂收养我进入祂的家，祂的国。祂带我认识我在天上的父，让我成为神的儿女。祂给我新的生命，新的身份，和新的盼望。祂永远不会抛弃我，祂的爱永不改变，因为耶稣昨日，今日，一直到永远，是一样的。耶稣是我的救主，祂带我出黑暗入光明，

我相信耶稣替我而死，成了我的替罪羊，我相信耶稣第三天从死里复活。我相信耶稣是永生神的儿子，我接受耶稣成为我生

命的救主，我愿意通过耶稣被永生的神收养，成为神的儿女，与我天上的父和好。我接受永生神的圣灵进入我心里，常常提醒我悔改，信靠，顺服耶稣。我愿意打开自己的心门让耶稣进来与我同住。我愿意把生命的主权交托给耶稣求他带领我过地上的生活。我相信在耶稣里有永生，因祂胜过了死亡，并掌管着所有的一切，因为神已将天上地下所有的权柄赐给了主耶稣。耶稣是万王之王，万主之主，祂配得一切的颂赞，荣耀，尊贵，能力，权柄，直到永永远远。

耶稣爱你，你愿意接受他的爱吗？你愿意通过耶稣认识你的创造者你的天父吗？

你愿意通过耶稣被永生的神收养，成为神的儿女吗？如果你愿意就在心里祷告接纳耶稣，开口回应他的爱，说"主耶稣，我愿意悔改，我接受你成为我生命的救主，我相信你为了我的罪被钉死在十字架上，第三天从死里复活，我接受你的爱，我邀请你的圣灵进入我心里，求你带领我走人生的路，带我认识你，认识我在天上的父.

我要为你祷告，求神带给你一本圣经或者有声圣经这样你可以更深的去认识神和了解主耶稣对你的爱。

要记住我给你带来的好消息"耶稣爱你！耶稣爱你！耶稣爱你！"

被收养的哥哥

English Translation from Titus:

From: Your Adopted Older Brother
To: My Younger Brothers and Sisters

Hello, my dear brothers and sisters,

I have good news to share with you! Please allow me to call you my younger brothers and sisters. I am someone who was adopted into the United States more than ten years ago. I'm now 27 years old. I was once an orphan like you, living in an orphanage. I entered the orphanage in 2002 and lived there for eight years. I understand your experiences—I truly empathize.

I know you've gone hungry. To get better food or snacks, you've tried to please the staff, or maybe you've stolen, fought, or lied to get what you wanted. I've done all of that too. I know you've suffered from the cold. You've had frostbite on your hands and feet, your shoes got soaked, and you only had a few sets of clothes to change into. Most of the clothes you wore were second-hand. I've been through all of that.

I know your living conditions weren't ideal. You didn't have your own space. You crowd into air-conditioned rooms in the summer and winter. Maybe your environment has improved, but you've probably dreamed like I did—of one day having your own room, decorating it yourself.

I know you have physical disabilities, you feel inferior, and deep down you've asked, "Why am I different from others? Why was I the one abandoned?" I've asked those questions too. I have albinism—my hair and body hair are white, my eyesight is poor, and I'm sensitive to light. My body is asymmetrical—I have mismatched hands and chest. I understand the struggles of your body and mind.

I know you're used as free labor. People make you do laundry, wash shoes, clean rooms, run errands, give massages, even wash others' feet. And sometimes, you've turned around and made those weaker than you do the same for you. I've done that too.

I know your fear and anxiety. People stronger and older than you have hit you, scolded you, threatened you with words, and punished you by making you stand or kneel. And at times, you've done the same to those weaker than you. I've done that too.

I know sometimes you've been bold—for the sake of food or fun, you've stolen things from others: snacks, toys, drinks, money, even bicycles. You didn't feel stealing was wrong, and if you got caught, you'd curse at the person who caught you. I've been there too. I know cursing and lying are part of your everyday life. You curse because if you don't, others will curse you. You lie because it hides what you and others did—sometimes lying is the only way to avoid offending someone. Lying has become instinct. I'm not here to judge you—I've been through it all too.

I know the longing deep inside your heart. I know the daydreams you've had: "Why wasn't I the one adopted?" "How great would it be if I were adopted?" "If I had money one day, I'd do this and that…", "How amazing it would be if I had a mom and dad! I want a family too!" I've had all those thoughts. I've dreamed those dreams. Sometimes you've even pondered deeper questions like, "What's the purpose of my life? Where do people come from? Where do we go after death?" These aren't questions kids your age should have to think about, but they are your most sincere, heartfelt questions and longings. I've thought about them too, I understand.

As your older brother, I truly understand what you're going through because I've been there. I want to share with you the best news I've ever received. It changed my life. It gave me hope and a vision for the future. I'm only sharing it with you because I've personally experienced it. I hope you'll remember this good news, reflect on it often, and lean on it in your life.

Here is the good news I bring to you: Jesus loves you! Jesus loves you! Jesus loves you! Jesus knows you—better than anyone. He knows everything you've been through. He wants to introduce you to your Creator—your Heavenly Father. He gave His life to save you from sin. He sees you as precious. He wants to accept you and love you. Jesus is the only Son of the eternal God who created the universe. Two thousand years ago, He came to earth to bring people back to God. He called people to repent of their sins and taught them to know their Heavenly Father. To reconcile humanity with God, He was nailed to a cross and died in our place. On the third day, He rose from the dead, conquering sin and death to give us hope, calling us to repent and return to our Heavenly Father, to receive true life—a life that flows from Jesus and leads to eternity. As the Bible says: "For God so loved the world that He gave His one and only Son, that whoever believes in Him shall not perish but have eternal life." This is the greatest news in human history! Thank God that in my first year of being adopted, I heard this incredible message. I realized I needed to be saved, because I was deep in the mud of sin and darkness. I couldn't save myself—not even my adoptive American family could save me, because that family also broke apart—my adoptive parents divorced. My life had no hope. I desperately needed the salvation of Jesus.

I admitted I was a sinner. I constantly did evil, my heart was filled with deceit, lust, malice, and jealousy. My sins separated me from God and blinded me from seeing and knowing Him. Jesus heard the cry of my heart. He healed my wounds. He gave me hope of eternal life. He adopted me into His family—into His Kingdom. He introduced me to my Heavenly Father. He made me a child of God. He gave me new life, a new identity, and a new hope. He will never abandon me. His love never changes. Because Jesus is the same yesterday, today, and forever. Jesus is my Savior. He brought me out of darkness into the light. I believe Jesus died for me, taking my place as the sacrificial lamb. I believe He rose from the dead on the third day. I believe Jesus is the Son of the living God. I accept Jesus as my Lord and Savior. I want to be adopted by the eternal God through Jesus—to become a child of God and be reconciled with my Heavenly Father. I invite the Holy Spirit of the living God into my heart, to constantly remind me to repent, trust, and obey Jesus. I open my heart to let Jesus live in me. I surrender the control of my life to Him and ask Him to guide me through this life.

I believe in eternal life in Jesus because He has overcome death and holds authority over all things. God has given Him all authority in heaven and on earth. Jesus is the King of kings, the Lord of lords. He deserves all praise, glory, honor, power, and authority forever and ever. Jesus loves you. Are you willing to accept His love? Are you willing to know your Creator—your Heavenly Father—through Jesus? Are you willing to be adopted by the eternal God and become His child? If you are willing, pray in your heart to receive Jesus. Respond to His love by saying: "Lord Jesus, I am willing to repent. I accept You as the Savior of my life. I believe You were crucified for my sins and rose again on the third day. I accept Your love. I invite Your Holy Spirit into my heart. Please guide me on the path of life. Help me know You and my Heavenly Father."

I will pray for you. I'll ask God to bring you a Bible or an audio Bible so you can grow in understanding and come to know the love that Jesus has for you. Never forget the good news I bring you: Jesus loves you! Jesus loves you! Jesus loves you!

Your adopted older brother,
Titus

———

Titus Theis
China; Thailand; United States

May 30, 2025
Alaska, USA

Dear Best Friend Back Home,

I miss you! And you'll scarcely believe what life is like here. Everyone drives everywhere, it's hard to walk places and often unsafe to go walking! The food is mostly fake; rarely do people eat real food. Everything runs at such a fast pace, it is hard to find peace here. I haven't heard my Mundart* heart language in months; my own voice inside my mind is becoming quieter each day that I go without speaking our language. I feel like I am losing my voice, like I am going silent. People live life so far apart; no one greets me with kisses on the cheek and embracing arms anymore; my body is in shock about the separation, the static charges from all the plastic clothes, and about the loneliness. And yet, everyone is telling me to focus on the good about this transition, to see the nice things here. It is hard for those who care for me to sit with uncomfortable emotions, and so they tell me I am wrong for feeling my big hard feelings. I am trying to shift my attitude, even amidst the grief feeling so overwhelming and heavy, but I also feel like in order to survive I have to be invisible, and that feels like I am dying inside.

...I am missing you less, but I still miss you dearly! I have moved several times since writing to you last; sometimes multiple times per year. I appreciate how I can always address my letters to you to the same address that you had when we were little. The consistency of your location gives me stability and helps me to feel less afraid here. One time I had moved so recently that the wee music box you sent me was the only time I heard "Happy Birthday" played to me that year. I wish that we could speak our Mundart language together. Even though it wasn't fully the language of our parents, when I got to speak our mix of languages together, it felt like home. I felt like my authentic self. Now, I feel like I am losing myself. It's really hard to be an immigrant, in order to survive here I have to adapt and let parts of myself go that otherwise I would rather hold onto if I could.

...I have been meeting people who study languages, and they taught me that our Mundart/Swiss German language doesn't actually have grammar. I don't know entirely what that means yet, but somehow maybe that's why studying German grammar was so challenging for me. It's hard to have to write to you in the languages of our conquerors because our Mundart is not a written language.

I spend so much more of my time looking at papers and computer screens now, than I do looking into others' eyes as we speak together. I worry that the loneliness that I feel also many around me feel it too. I am concerned that the advice here to get a pet when you feel lonely is actually not helpful, because then you spend more of your time caring for the pet than you do looking into each other's eyes and speaking together. I miss your eyes, and our cherished times together.

…It has been a whirlwind getting to know my now-husband and his family; we organized several wedding receptions in the countries that we have called home. I am sad that you could not be at my wedding, because you have been like a sister to me and your parents like my parents. I am so thankful to have met someone who shares my beliefs, values, lifestyle, and goals. Such an amazing blessing to get to walk together with my beloved husband. He is an artist, and his art is so amazing; he paints portals of love for those who are hurting! He is a musician, and his music is so beautiful, the music from my dreams! Even though he only speaks a few words of our language, his music reaches that same part of my heart. He is a teacher, so good with children, he wants to be a parent with me! I am so thankful that God brought us together in Iowa. I hope someday we can take our children on hikes together to roast Bratwurst over the fire and sing songs into the natural amphitheaters of the Alps together again.

The challenges that we have been navigating since getting married have been extreme, and we are weary. We long for the stability, walkability, balance, peace, and beauty of that place I once called home. Each time we start again to make our home here, we learn from the prior attempts—so it is not lost effort—and each time God places generous people into our lives who come alongside us and help us with the painful grief and the losses and the rebuilding. The healing process will take us some time yet. We need prayers for the indoor air quality here, it is overall quite bad, and the harmful air can be damaging to my voice. It hurts to be silenced by the air; I want to sing freely.

Thankfully the outdoor air is pristine here in Alaska. We are so thankful that God brought us here, to wide open spaces! As we were making the drive across North America last fall, we were struck by how similar the landscape here is to the forests that Jacob grew up with in Slovakia and to the mountains that I grew up with in Switzerland. We could see ourselves making a life for our family here, especially since making good friends who share our values and are walking journeys that allow them to understand and relate to us in loving ways.

My heart still wants to translate, record, and release the songs that soothed my soul and led me to a peace that surpasses understanding even amidst abysmal circumstances. I hope to connect with people who can teach me music production and who can help me with making sure the songs are translated into Mundart/Swiss German appropriately. Do you know of anyone who might be interested in working on a project like this with me?

Cherished friend, I am so thankful for our childhood that we got to share together in Switzerland. I am hoping for a future filled with peace and love and joy.

Sincerely,
Rebecca
———

Rebecca Lesan
Switzerland; Canada; Connecticut,
Massachusetts, New Hampshire, New
Jersey, South Dakota, Iowa, Idaho,
Alaska, USA

*Note: 'Swiss German' is an English misnomer for the 'Mundart' languages of the people groups in Switzerland. Mundart is the heart language of the people, the language of family and friends, and it is not a written language. It is a poetic verbal art form that can't adequately be captured by the written word. Thus, developing a method to translate English worship songs into Mundart would allow for us to connect better at a heart level.

May 29, 2025
Melbourne, Australia

Dear Ruth,

I have just re-read your *Letters Never Sent* (1988) cover to cover. I confess that although I knew about your ground-breaking book in 1988—it caused a sensation in western missions and MK communities, I avoided reading it for several years because it was rumoured to be attacking MK boarding schools. 1988 was also a big year for our family as Janine and I arrived in Nepal, with our two older children aged six and four, to serve with the United Mission to Nepal 'for three years'. This stretched to eight, after which we moved to India for another 20 years! When I did read *Letters Never Sent*, I discovered it was not specifically 'anti-boarding schools' at all, for that was only a small part of your much fuller and broader cross-cultural life.

David Pollock described *Letters Never Sent* as your "autobiography by epistle". Reading it again, I was struck by the raw honesty and vulnerability with which you wrote, reflecting on your deepest thoughts and feelings as you wrestled with issues of family dynamics, spirituality, loss, love, anger, grief, joys and sorrows. From the childhood experiences of Ruth Ellen Frame to the newly wed bride of Doctor David Van Reken and the trials and lessons of becoming a missionary family, you share your emotional and spiritual struggles in themes of obedience, sacrifice and perseverance (themes that are uncomfortably unpopular today) juxtaposed with the realities of God's clear direction, guidance and blessing in your life.

I found myself resonating deeply with your letters—smiling, chuckling and crying as I joined your emotional roller-coaster ('Who said it was a sin to cry anyway?' *Letters Never Sent*, p.72. 'Tears are good!' has become one of my personal mantras). Although we grew up as MKs in different continents and you are my senior by less than a decade, we have much in common. The details of our growing up cross-culturally differ, but many of the experiences, issues and emotions are remarkably similar.

Yes, there were hard times—mine came not when I started as a boarder at Hebron School in south India (3000kms from my parents in Nepal) at the age of six, but when I transitioned from boarding school where I belonged and felt comfortably at home, to Melbourne for my last two years of high school. The 'hidden immigrant' experience as a teenager was excruciating at times—but I survived, even as my parents and three younger sisters returned to Asia. Looking back, it took me nearly 18 years to overcome the nagging, incessant desire to escape back to my Asian roots and to accept that I was now an Aussie. During those years I was not dysfunctional, but I needed to reconcile my multi-cultural childhood experiences and integrate these into a healthy, wholesome identity. You describe that so well: 'I think I have finally come to terms with who I am as a missionary, a missionary kid and, most importantly, as a person uniquely made by God. I like being me.' (p. 157)

You and I grew up knowing we were MKs, but the term TCK was still decades from becoming commonly used (nor fully understood) in mission circles. After the International Conference on MKs (ICMK) in Manila, 1983, you and Dave Pollock began introducing the TCK concept and despite initial resistance the term TCK gradually replaced MK because it was more than a descriptor, it encompassed and shed light on the experience of living cross-culturally, of 'growing up among worlds'.

The three ICMKs (Manila 1983, Quito 1987 and Nairobi 1989) together with *Letters Never Sent* (1988), were the catalysts needed to open the pandora's box of MK/TCK emotions that had been overlooked and all too often repressed. Now that box was open it could not be ignored. The MK/TCK experience needed to be listened to, researched, written about, understood and acted on. I was unable to attend any of the three ICMKs because I was busy as a pastor of a small country church and then moving with my family to Nepal. I first heard Dave Pollock unpack the TCK concept at a conference for school boarding staff in 1996 at Faith Academy in Manila. That was my 'Aha' moment of discovering my TCK identity. In 1999 you and Dave published the first edition of *The Third Culture Kid Experience— Growing Up among Worlds* (it has become the TCK 'bible') and the floodgates opened. The TCK concept gained traction, then acceptance, and the term spread widely—at least in global north missions and the non-mission expatriate sectors. It is gradually becoming recognised and appropriated in the global south—something that I have been striving towards for two decades.

Whilst we have much in common in terms of our MK heritage and experiences, our work has been on different trajectories. You have had a truly global impact through your research, writing and speaking (in collaboration with David until his death in 2004), and as founder of Families in Global Transition (FIGT) that has had an exponential influence on families living cross-culturally. For the past 20 years you have broadened the scope of TCK to Cross Culture Kids (CCKs) to address the growing complexities of cross-cultural experiences in the 21st century. Most of my life has been immersed in the lives of MKs/ TCKs in boarding schools—first in Nepal and then in south India, and for the past 15 years more broadly in missions throughout Asia.

Boarding school communities provide opportunities for deep, rich and lasting relationships with staff and students as we live cheek by jowl in close proximity over years. Janine and I were privileged to share life with hundreds of young TCKs watching their lives mature and blossom in a melting pot of dozens of cultures. We saw the TCK phenomenon described so clearly in *Growing up Among Worlds*, taking shape before our eyes—it was a rich and remarkable privilege!

I return to *Letters Never Sent*. Your penultimate letter (July 1984) concludes with: 'God gave me a whole new vision of how much he really cares for His children and how He expects us to care for one another.' You have been true to that vision. Before you moved to Liberia your dad, Charles Frame, shared with prophetic wisdom: "Ruth, you'll do a whole lot of seed planting. Sometimes it may look as though none of the seeds are growing but keep planting. When you look back, you'll see some trees. You just never know while you're planting which seeds God has chosen to grow into trees." He also advised you to 'never be afraid to plant fruit trees that you might not be around to eat from. Someone else will receive them as a gift from the Lord'. I don't think he could have imagined how those seeds would grow into trees and become vast forests and how true his words and advice have been. Thank you!

Yours in the cause of TCK care,
John
———

John Barclay
Nepal; India; Australia

27 January 2025
Hamburg, Germany

Dear Ruth,

As you hide in the dark, crouched between the bed and the big standing lamp, quilted blanket drawn over your head, listening to the pounding in your ears and the void in your teenage heart, remember that I am, though on another continent, still right in the room next door.

Everyone has a place in their remembrance where they had hidden, where they had felt most without a home, without attachment, without guidance. Those of us who have moved about the globe especially so.

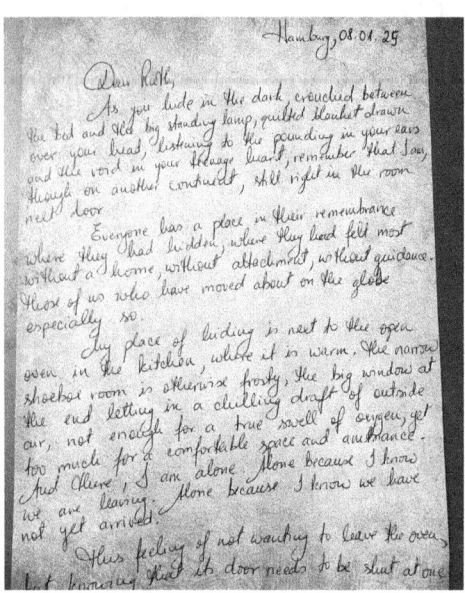

My place of hiding is next to the open oven in the kitchen, where it is warm. The narrow shoebox room is otherwise frosty, the big window at the end letting in a chilling draft of outside air, not enough for a true swell of oxygen, yet too much for a comfortable space and ambiance. And there, I am alone. Alone because I know we are leaving. Alone because I know we have not yet arrived.

Handwritten letter from Henriette to Ruth.

This feeling of not wanting to leave the oven but knowing that its door needs to be shut would haunt me, and the cold would follow me onto beaches and places where everyone else was rather at ease and well. When we are forced to leave the womb too soon, to leave our place of refuge for the world, the shock stays with us for life. Ruth, I know your ghosts resurface when others are relaxed and feel together. Ruth, I know you understand.

You had to leave your trees and smells and faces. You had to leave your little girl behind. I climbed the trees and hung on their branches, yet in the end, I too had to replant. I ate and breathed and tasted, and tried to write every recipe down, but in the end, it did not matter, the ingredients didn't stay the same. And the faces turned to masks, theirs and mine, and ours. Masks of fitting in and forgetting. Masks to help leave my little girl behind.

But oh, what a gift we carry within us. We can translate the absurd. We can untangle the lines. We see the shadow and the light and live in nuance. We have been on both sides of the door.

We can look at the other and see their own pain. We can look at the box and not only see what is within. We can see the dots and connect them, across the table, with our family and friends, through countries and nations and valleys and deserts and waters and lands. We find solutions that matter, because we care and because we comprehend, because we have left behind and have been forced to find again.

There are many like us Ruth, many little girls who had been left behind, but found again, rediscovered, loved again, and taught to feel sheltered. Many of us who have learned to lay brick on brick, solidify one relationship after the other, connect in disconnect and live on in a better world.

My house is now cozy, insulated, and safe. In some ways, it blocks out the outside, and I am in absolute control of what I let in. On the other hand, it is a home full of breezes and the perfumes of near and far. The oven is closed. I do not need it for heating or to hide behind. I can now use it as it was intended. And the darkness has been replaced by lights, and the memories and yearnings by children of my own, a boy and two girls who I hope will never need to hide.

So, Ruth, let us remember our little girls who hid and wrote letters and cried. Let us embrace them and keep comforting them forever, because they made us who we are now.

> Love,
> Henriette Javorek—aka Dr. J (-:
>
> ———
>
> *Dr. Henriette J. Runte*
> *Kolozsvár/Cluj-Napoca/Klausenburg in*
> *the Carpathian Basin; Romania; Hungary;*
> *Texas, Kansas, USA; Paris, Besançon,*
> *Avignon, France; Guadalajara, Mexico;*
> *Caracas, Venezuela; Cyprus; Argentina;*
> *Hamburg, Germany*

Dear Ruth,

Your letters have been sent... and received by countless people all around the globe. Your work has profoundly touched the lives of expatriates and third culture kids (TCKs), offering them understanding, validation and a sense of belonging. Through your lectures and, above all, your ground-breaking book with David Pollock, you paved the way for a global movement of support and recognition for TCKs. I don't think I can ever fully express my gratitude for the impact you have had—not just on the international community, but on my own life as well.

I was 24 when I first met you. I had just moved to the Netherlands and thought of myself simply as Greek with Assyrian origins. That was the extent of my identity, or so I believed. Then came that unforgettable day at Robbie Zein's place. As you shared TCK stories, something stirred deep within me. I found myself in tears, overwhelmed by a flood of memories: most vividly, the image of my grandmother speaking Assyrian when I came home.

You noticed, sought me out from a crowd of nearly 200 people, and gently asked, "Why?" I told you what had moved me, and then you asked about my aspirations. I explained that I was studying psychology and planned to return to Greece to pursue work as a clinician. I still remember your response: "Think about it. You have something in your heart... you need to help more in the international community."

Those words stayed with me. I read your book, and it was a revelation. It helped me connect with my Greek-Assyrian roots, embrace my international identity and, ultimately, find a sense of wholeness. That realization changed the course of my life and career.

Years later, as I continued working in the international community in the Netherlands, I started to see, more and more, the unique challenges faced by expatriates. This inspired me to create Expat Nest, combining my love for psychology with my passion for serving those navigating life across cultures. At the time, providing online psychological support for expats was almost unheard of. When I shared the idea with you, you were both honest and encouraging: "Hmm, it sounds like a good idea. I haven't heard of this before but go for it."

Starting something new is never easy, but your words gave me the confidence to persist. Looking back, I realize that this was also a deeply personal journey of rediscovering my identity. In many ways, Expat Nest mirrors the experience of the Assyrian people: a nation without a country, scattered across the world, yet still close and connected. This is how I created Expat Nest, with nests across the globe in different languages but all connected under one global home. Without embracing my own heritage and integrating my own experiences as a TCK, I couldn't have built this space of belonging for others.

And I owe this to you.

Your wisdom, your faith in me, and your profound understanding of identity have left an imprint that will last beyond this lifetime. I promise to carry your legacy forward; to continue serving, guiding and supporting the international community, just as you have done.

You have been my mentor, my friend, my source of strength. You have prayed with me, cried with me and celebrated with me. From the depths of my heart, thank you for what you have done for me and for the many lives you have touched.

I have so much love and respect for you!

> With endless gratitude,
> Vivian
> ─────
>
> *Vivian Chiona*
> *Greece; The Netherlands*

Letters to Younger Self

February 25, 2025
Kingston, Ontario, Canada

Dear 14-year-old Mathieu from 1994,

Here I am in 2025. Man! Time flies! I'm sorry it took me 31 years to write this letter.

I'm writing it because if I remember correctly, you just came back to Canada after years of growing up in Côte d'Ivoire, Haiti, Switzerland (etc.) and I wanted to check on you. Recently, I was remembering that you are having a hard time, that you are crying yourself to sleep every night. I know you wait for nighttime, so no one hears you. I know you think you are the only one hurting. I wish I could be there to comfort you. But I don't exist yet in your timeline.

Still, if I could reach you, I would tell you that these painful feelings—the confusion, the loneliness, the emptiness, the groundlessness, the sense of artificiality and powerlessness—will one day evolve into sources of great meaning, connection, and belonging. It's going to take some time of course: you will run away from these emotions over and over again, constantly attempt to numb them out, and definitely get lost along the way.

Bit by bit, your sense of identity will become disconnected and disjointed, and it will feel like you are somehow broken. You aren't. Or maybe you will be for part of your journey. But not for all of it. One day, you will piece it all back together, even adding new parts accumulated along the way. I know because I've been through it all. I've seen it all unfold. From your current perspective, none of this could be predicted or even understood. But from mine, all of it is obvious.

By the way, I'm not writing this because I want you to stop crying or feeling sad, lonely and confused. This is not a "cheer-up" kind of letter. From where you stand, now is the time to experience loss, sadness, loneliness, confusion, and disconnection. Yeah, yeah, easy for me to say, I know. But it needs to be so. Please trust me. You see, your life so far—and please remember, you're only 14, there's so much more to come—has been a rich, unique and complex journey that will take time for you to unpack and appreciate. Because it is all you've ever known, you can't yet grasp how meaningful it is. That will take time. All you understand right now is the pain of separation and loneliness. That's ok. From where I stand, however, that pain is like a compass needle pointing towards future meaning. No one grieves things, places, people, and cultures that meant nothing to them. So, for now, cry, as many tears as you want. Also, don't get me wrong, none of these feelings will fade away or disappear completely. Rather, they will evolve into sources of love, depth, attachment and connection. One day, they will help you be of service to a community that you love and with which you feel profound kinship. Your people. Your tribe. And you will meet incredible people along the way: Ruth, Megan, Andrea, Cynthia and countless others. None of these names mean anything to you, of course. But they will.

I also know you are having a hard time adapting to your new school. I know the stress and worry you carry deep in your belly every day. How alien it all feels. I know everyone seems to be part of a group except you; how you somehow feel outside of it all, like a detached invisible observer. I remember you sitting alone in the staircase to eat lunch instead of going to the cafeteria, waves of fellow students passing by around you as though you were a rock in a stream. As though you did not exist. I remember you hiding in the library to escape and find relief in fantasizing and daydreaming. I even know that you created an imaginary friend to help you get through the day. You speak to him in your mind, don't you? And he helps you to go on, doesn't he? That's ok. All of it is ok. You won't always need him. You will eventually make new friends at school. Real ones. Not many... 2 or 3... but good ones. I can't promise you these will be lifelong close friends. People grow apart. People move away. You'll move away a few times too. That's just the way life is. But just know, there will always be friends wherever you are.

Anyway, I can't reveal every little detail to you. That would be too much. But I just wanted to let you know that I care.

With love and tenderness,
48-year-old Mathieu from 2025
———

Mathieu Gagnon
France; Morocco; Côte d'Ivoire; Haiti;
Switzerland; Québec, New Brunswick,
Ontario, Canada

Dear younger Calvin,

You are writing this letter after returning to Indonesia from Singapore after being interviewed by the Singapore National Museum for their upcoming exhibition titled, "Once Upon a Tide: Singapore's Journey from Settlement to Global City". Pretty cool right? As a kid, whenever you visit a museum, you often wonder how these great men and women shaped history, and now you can even make a claim "Hey I'm a part of a museum exhibit!"

Of course, if I only shared the beautiful parts of this journey I'd be betraying the mindset you established during your quarter-life crisis: "Do what you need to do, not what you like to do, to get what you want!" At the same time, I know you are just an 11-year-old boy living apart from his parents without fully understanding its impact. So, for now, I'll share a few pieces of your life.

You used to hate Soekarno-Hatta Airport because it always felt like the monster that took Dad away. Believe it or not, Dad developed a love-hate relationship with that place too. I never knew how he felt until a few years back when I picked up Uncle Jamal there—who, by the way, is now a police chief. Dad was always reluctant to let you go and study abroad, but he didn't want you to grow up spoiled.

It's funny how a place can hold so many contradictions—back then, Soekarno-Hatta felt like a black hole, always pulling Dad or me away from each other. But as I grew older, I started to see it differently. Airports became a symbol of possibility—a gateway to new adventures and a reminder that leaving isn't always about loss.

I know you hated practising Mandarin at Grandaunt's place... sadly I am still having difficulty with the language, though at least it gets somewhat better at times, and why did I bring this up? Because our time abroad actually gave us a certain appreciation that learning another language exposes a new dimension of ourselves; this is known as code switching. Each time we practise a new custom we learn something new about ourselves, I think this phrase encapsulates the experience "每一次离别，都是成长的机会"。It means every farewell is a chance to grow.

Even though the airport breaks you apart, it pieces you back together with new perspectives, which makes you stronger for each return. Which makes me wonder, each time I step through an airport gate, who am I becoming this time?

Life in Singapore felt ideal at first, but like learning to ride a bike, the training wheels had to come off. You fell—figuratively and literally—many times. You faced judgment from society and your environment. Not everyone likes you, sometimes for no reason at all. I wish I could have helped you tone down your tough-guy act or that heavy accent you picked up from imitating Schwarzenegger and Stallone (who, ironically, had his own speech issues). Maybe it would have made adjusting easier.

Growing up, our ideal image in everything is what Mum and Dad do and who they are—and I am proud to tell you that they are still your everything. Being called a "mama's boy" is a badge of honor for me, unlike those stereotypical media messages that grown men at home are undeveloped manchildren who 'fail to launch'. You did live on your own for a good number of years in Singapore and then you returned back to Jakarta. However, when dad passed in 2022 you decided to remain in our family home.

I really want to tell you everything is alright, but it really is not. I miss him every day and I still question and wonder if I will ever be enough to fill his shoes. I am not him nor will I ever be him. At times I realise that I don't have the same work ethic or values that allowed him to survive here; and there are times I worry if I can ensure there is money at home; it is my responsibility as an adult now and as the man of the house. But my constant desire is to always be abroad and I feel guilty that I have never held a strong attachment to settle down in Indonesia.

I need to have a hard conversation with you about this as you base everything on the exemplary behavior of our parents and sisters. I'm so sorry that we actually never see their imperfection, as this results in us still continuously searching for parts of ourselves. We always believe everything about them is how it is supposed to be. However, you have the right to forge your own path, and some of their beliefs might fit you but some don't and there is no shame in that, notably because what I mentioned on how travel and our time abroad reveals a new dimension of ourselves.

For years and even till now I still struggle in fitting in both of our homes. Many moments made me feel like I didn't belong, even in my 'home' country or even our second home. However, connecting with the TCK community and finding a creative outlet became my saving grace. I don't have all the answers but for anyone who is struggling with cultural reintegration, my advice is this: Don't erase parts of yourself to fit in. Instead, seek to understand why customs exist and find a way to integrate them without losing your identity.

In the opening I mentioned you were being interviewed by the museum of Singapore. As a creative outlet, I created a podcast called Global CKtizens. It's a livestream show featuring guests from diverse cultural backgrounds. Can you believe it? You—who once needed your form teacher to get classmates' phone numbers—have now interviewed over 100 guests and earned public recognition for it.

If I could speak to you in person, I'd tell you this is one part of our life I would never change. It's a major milestone. Though, if I'm to be honest, it didn't start for the happiest reasons. One reason was the constant cultural and generational clashes with Dad. Another? Getting your heart broken by a girl who believed dating a Caucasian man was her ticket to a luxurious life. Don't take it too personally though, you realized that this international life you live moulds you in a certain way that others who are not so fortunate enough to have experienced it since young, didn't.

These truths may feel heavy and unpleasant, but you'll learn over time that running away from a problem doesn't solve anything. You'll realize that life has a unique flow; sometimes you have to rotate with the motion or sometimes press on straight forward.

Flexibility is a lifelong journey—I'm still learning it myself, and I am glad I get to share it with you in this letter. On this piece of paper we communicate our peace.

Warm Regards,
Your Future Self

———

Calvin Karuniawan Widjaja
Indonesia; Singapore

Dear Helen (aka Eleni, Elen, Helena, Hélène)

I'm reading your diary entry from October 3rd 2001. You were a 10th grade student at the Anglo-American School of Moscow. Somewhere in the middle of this diary entry, you go:

"I want to do something about all the evil and the unhappiness in the world. Don't know how, don't really care right now. I just know I'm going to do something in that direction in my life."

This is a letter to you from your future Adult Self. I can see how deeply you care about wanting to help people when you grow up. You're not fussed about the how. Your primary motive isn't to chase some fancy job title, social status, or financial gain purely for self-serving reasons. You genuinely care about helping to make the world a better place. I love that about you.

It's now April 1st 2025. I'm writing to you from our beloved homeland, Greece. I want you to know that I'm proud of you for staying true to your intention via the choices you went on to make in your professional and personal life.

On that day, as you often did, you had turned to your diary for comfort. Your basketball coach had just announced who had made it onto the Girls' Basketball Team to represent the school at the upcoming tournament in Istanbul. You made it. You were on the list. But as you said in your diary, you felt "confused". Because even though you absolutely loved playing basketball, so you really wanted to go, you were terrified of boarding the plane to get there.

Even just thinking about getting on that plane filled you with terror. "Basically, I'll be frank", you confessed to your diary:

"I'm terrified of being hijacked. There you go. Now I know why terrorists are called that. But it's terrible. I want to do something about all the evil and unhappiness going on in the world. Don't know how, don't really care right now either. I just know I'm going to do something in that direction in my life. That means I need to work on writing well, history, problem solving, talking, convincing people."

You watched as innocent human beings trapped in two planes that were hijacked by terrorists, die a cruel death as they crashed into the Twin Towers. 9/11 didn't just impact America. It impacted you, too, as you watched what happened replayed again and again on the news.

272

And I get why. Because you knew what it was like to feel terror from emotional contagion while being trapped in a plane. It's understandable that watching the footage of that horrific moment for those people, replayed again and again on TV, left a mark on you. It makes sense that just the thought of having to get on a plane again brings up big emotions after what you saw and what you have experienced.

I get that you're angry with your mum for taking you to "that weird 'psychologist'" who had no clue how to help you. All that psychologist had done was make you feel worse. Forgive your mum. She was just trying to help. She didn't know.

Cover of Eleni's diary from 2001.

I get that you're frustrated; seeing a psychologist felt like a complete waste of time. She wanted to help. She just didn't know how. Most psychologists in 2001 didn't know how to help teenagers overcome a phobia or process unresolved trauma. What you needed was someone who could help you neutralize the triggering thoughts and distressing images replaying in your mind of planes crashing into buildings that were adding fuel to the fire of your pre-existing huge fear of flying. She didn't know how to do that. Forgive her.

I'm glad that at least you could fall back on the mindfulness, breathwork, and journaling practices that the School Counsellor at the International School of Islamabad had taught you a few years back when you went to her for help after experiencing that massive panic attack in a plane. You managed your anxiety with your existing self-regulation tools and skills. You didn't let it stop you from going to the tournament. I'm proud of you.

I'm sorry that you had to go through about 10 years of painful exposure therapy as the child of a diplomat to overcome your fear of flying. You had no choice but to keep boarding planes, again and again, because of your family's expat lifestyle.

Know that your commitment to working on your speaking skills to help make the world a better place will pay off. In 2023, you will go on be interviewed by solution-oriented people, like Rhoda Bangerter, who has a podcast called Holding the Fort Abroad. You will talk about how tapping can be applied to calm intense emotions for expats and expat kids. Expat mums no longer need to despair when talk therapy doesn't work to help their child overcome their fear of flying, like your mum did. EFT helps.

Thanks to your problem-solving approach to EFT therapy and coaching, when you grow up, you will help many kids and adults tap into happiness as they overcome their fears and phobias in a matter of weeks or months. Not years, like what you had to go through.

You will not only help others access their inner happiness—it will also make you happy.

And your happiness matters, too, my dear.

With love,
Your Adult Self, Eleni

———

Eleni Vardaki
Harare, Zimbabwe; Sudan; Belgium;
Pakistan; Russia; England; Greece

Dear little Jo,

"Where are you from?"

This question will haunt you. Voices will overlap, and eyes will glow bright and curious. But as you open your mouth to answer, anxiety and grief will twist together in your lungs, leaving you to mumble, "It's a long story." Because the truth is, you will call too many places home to only give one answer; an avalanche of feelings and pictures will flood your mind as you ransack your memories for the right words to say...

Red dirt rises in clouds, bare feet slap on tile floors. Children's voices rise and fall in the thick, heavy air as heat shimmers above dirt roads. Cars jolt over potholes and little eyes stare out the window for hours at a sea of green punctuated by small huts peopled with bright, patterned cloth and headwraps crowned with wobbling jars. On market day, flashes of red, green, blue, mud-stained cloth, bananas spilling over teetering baskets, cheap jewelry glittering under the tents. Sweat trickles, and little hands stroke the soft fur of a new kitten and jerk away when they play too rough, nursing scratched fingers.

This is Lola, West Africa.

This is home.

Dusty pages, yellowed and ripped, infused with the musty scent of years of waiting on a cool, dark shelf. Wisdom whispers: the characters of classics speak in stilted language, strange yet magnificent. Old formalities, traditions, and expressions, thrown out as outdated and stuffy. And yet there is an elegance that the delicate, browning pages can't wait to communicate. The characters breathe in those pages— laughing, crying, living in a way that young books wonder at. With graceful poise they dance through their story, their distinguished clothes lending them at once an antiquated yet cultivated appearance.

This is Austen, Montgomery, Alcott, Tolkien.

This is home.

Dusky green vineyards, a gray sky stretched out like a blank canvas above them. Chattering voices, staring eyes, anticipation mingled with fear. Desks lined up in neat rows, an unfamiliar language looping and mocking until it's finally untangled. Outcast, until accepted. Walking for hours, gazing in awe up at towering spires that articulate their nobility through the whispers echoing in their ancient halls. Breathtaking, immaculate gardens depicting the refined royal blood that curbed their imperfections. Mist falls in a hazy blur, hills making soft slopes against the clouds as boots skip through the mud to be with the horses.

This is Luynes, France.

This is home.

Hope budding, only to be blighted by the sudden frost of reality. Heart strings attached to another place, another house, another school, another future. And then... new shoes, shy eyes, bright hallways, voices in a familiar language bringing comfort to the chaos. Schoolwork, friends, and laughter suddenly made it easy again. Lacing up running shoes, feet pounding on the pavement, lungs gasping for air, sun shining down bright, wisps of hair tugged loose. Sweat trickles again, except the red dirt is nowhere to be seen. Classes weigh heavy, deadlines loom on the horizon, but suddenly friends laugh and joy glows bright. Sorting candy, building balloon towers, painting huge paper banners, gathering at early hours to plan, plan, plan. Finally, the labor in the shadows is displayed in full glory, exhilaration exploding as the hallways sparkle and pulse with energy.

This is Dallas, Texas.

This is home.

Clothes and treasures and suitcases stacked up high. Packing up a life... again. But away from family? Anticipation and anxiety twisting, stealing appetite, stealing sleep. Driving, driving, driving— new faces, new names, new surroundings, new traditions. Sitting up late, talking and laughing, hoping for the future. Pulling words from the air, whispering ideas, click-clacking steadily. Cold bites, snow stings, but sunshine gently warms, spring breathing her perfume. Eyes skip over pages of dark print, eagerly drinking knowledge. Bright lamps illuminate sleepy faces as they struggle to find the right words to draw from dusty tomes. Unexpected adventures dart through a busy schedule, each moment an opportunity to explore new freedom. Friends put their arms around each other and share their deepest fears and desires.

This is Columbia, Missouri.

This is home.

"So, where's your hometown?"

Don't let this question haunt you, dear one. It's ok that you don't have a boxed-in-perfect-normal answer. I know there will be days when you wish you were "normal"—a normal kid, a normal student, a normal TCK. I know there will be days when you wish you had never left, when you wish you could leave, when you wish you didn't live every day afraid of leaving or being left.

Your story is beautiful because Jesus wrote it. He is the stability you crave. So, take a deep breath... and let your answer be complicated.

Love,
College Jo

———

Jo Sellers
Columbia, St. Louis, Missouri, Dallas,
Texas, Fresno, California, USA; Chambéry,
Luynes, France; Lola, West Africa

March 5, 2025
Philippines

Dear little Marie,

I hope this letter finds you well. I know moving back to your passport country in the Philippines doesn't feel all that great right now. I know you miss South Korea, your home, the place you felt the safest and felt the most understood by the people around you. You know your neighborhood, the streets you need to walk through to get to your favorite 붕어빵 (red bean paste cake) stall right next to the Baskin Robbins you and your family go out to after dinner. You know the old lady and her husband that mans the closest stationary store close to your house where you bought your very first paper dolls. An obsession you had growing up anticipating new releases of your favorite characters and if they had a new edition of paper clothes. You can walk to your favorite VHS store with your eyes closed, reminding yourself of the weekends your family will rent out movies for the week. You love music class because you learn new instruments and can audition for school musicals. And I know you'll miss soccer club and AWANA because you enjoy playing soccer and memorizing Bible verses that will be converted into points at the end of the year so you can buy all the fun things from America that were brought in. We can't forget about your love for slap on bracelets and glitter pens. And the friendships you made all throughout your childhood. This was all you have ever known, then for all of that to be taken from you all in a single plane ride, is just awful. I would know we do that a handful more times as we grow up.

I write this to you to let you know I get it, I see you, I know how sad you are leaving it all behind. Despite what your parents say to look forward to the new friends you will make and to stop crying, I'm here to tell you that it's okay to let it all out. Cry if you need to, do nothing if you must. This is a normal part of transition, to miss the things that were so close to your heart. Any move will affect anyone, you may not see it, but it's hitting your parents too, they just like to keep things from you so you don't worry about it. Everyone is adjusting to a new life, and even though your parents grew up in the Philippines they have also changed a lot from the 7 years they have been away. They have become completely different people too, so they are also learning to navigate the changes that took place in their own country while they were away. To a degree they also have adjusted to becoming more Korean, just like you, but in your case that's all you have ever known.

You don't have the same relationship to the Philippines as they

278

do, so you don't have to feel guilty not knowing things. I know the language sounds strange, and some of your relatives don't get it. You can be sad about it, they are being rude by calling you names telling you that you have to go back to Korea because you don't belong. That would make anyone mad or sad, or both. You are allowed to feel those things. You are allowed to feel misunderstood; you are allowed to feel a plethora (that means a lot, a word you will learn from your favorite teacher in Egypt, yes Egypt where we will be moving to next) of emotions. I know you weren't brought up learning about your emotions, but they are there, and they are a part of you. Don't be ashamed when they come up, it's a natural part of your beautiful sensitive soul that is worth celebrating. You my dear, are worth celebrating. You are smart, kind, empathetic towards others, and never pass up an opportunity to sing your heart out. You are uniquely you. I felt like you needed to hear that because we are a words of affirmation kind of girl.

I know at this point you are crying your eyes out wishing you were back in Korea, wishing you could just go back. I know, and that's okay to miss it, despite people around you telling you to try and "be strong". People in that time period didn't understand themselves and their needs well enough so they try to get people to act according to what society expects them to. So you don't have to worry that in a few years that will change. Just continue to be you. Emotions are a funny thing, they want to be seen and acknowledged, the more you push them down the more they will cause chaos in your life. So write out how you feel, process what you are going through, it's okay, you are safe.

As you learn how to process your emotions you will inspire others to do the same, we are going to be doing some incredible things later on in life, things will work out, God will take care of you in every season of your life. It may not look like it, but He is leading us exactly where we need to be. It's going to be fun, challenging, but definitely an adventure. Take it a day at a time, enjoy the present because you can't get that moment back, breathe in the memories you are making, especially in college because that's the time you will long for the most, and rest your future in God's hands.

> With all my love,
> Marie
> ———
> *Marie Suazo*
> *South Korea; Philippines; Egypt; Oman;*
> *Canada*

Dear Younger Me,

You always felt like you could never fit in from the beginning. You moved, and then—just as you adjusted—you moved again. By the time you were eleven years old, you remember selling all of your toys at a garage sale. Your American Girl doll, the one that was a gift and your favorite, was gone. All the things that symbolized your childhood had been sold, and you felt like you had to grow up. You packed up your things and said goodbye to your friends because you thought you'd never come back. But you did—about three months later—and then moved in with your Bapa (Grandpa) to help him during his cancer treatment. It wasn't easy but you knew every day was a blessing since he ended up living five weeks longer than he was supposed to.

During that time, he was able to start a blanket for your little brother who was on the way, and you were able to talk and laugh with him a few last times. Two weeks before he passed away you held a birthday for him, and this was the last time you saw him not in complete pain. You welcomed your youngest brother shortly after Bapa passed away. Then you came back—and somehow, you were okay.

You kept going back for the summers every year until you graduated high school, but it wasn't that simple. You would be gone, and it would feel like no one could ever understand you. You became very good at hiding how you felt by becoming very bubbly. One time while at a youth retreat for a group overseas you found a guy who was very nice and also from a different country but you later found out that many of the girls liked him and so that day by trying to make a friend you lost 5 potential friends and that wasn't the only time something like that happened.

Little did you know you weren't alone. While you were in it, you didn't realize there were others like you. You'd arrive in the country you were stationed in for a short time and try to make friends—but everyone already had theirs. You'd return home, go to school, and find that everyone had their groups there too. There were a few consistent ones, a few who stuck around and didn't leave. Many did leave—not because of you. I know you wanted to take it personally (and sometimes you did), but it wasn't you. That's just how life happens—there are things outside of your control.

Your experiences didn't match those of your peers from back home. When you returned and entered middle school, the kids thought you were strange. They didn't understand everything you had seen—or why you didn't care what you wore. While they were thinking about going to the mall or keeping up with the latest trends, your thoughts were different. You had seen people who had almost nothing—some without shoes. You focused on other things, and that made you feel out of place.

One time we were playing cards in Ecuador and a lady walked up to your youngest brother and started petting his head because such blond hair was so foreign to them. My siblings laughed and then she walked away, and my brother moved to the other side.

When you moved to a new country and the culture didn't make sense—because of language barriers, unfamiliar traditions, or even needing to pay to use the bathroom—you tried so hard to fit in as if you already understood. Not understanding wasn't your fault. You just needed time to learn how to navigate the blocks of a new place. You were set on a course to live a different kind of life, one of wonder and discovery—not one that everyone was meant to understand.

Even though you felt alone, you would slowly realize that you weren't. It didn't happen overnight. You took a risk and told someone about your experiences—and they turned out to be a TCK too. It wasn't the first time you had met one, but she was from the same kind of culture and you were able to talk about how you never felt like you had lived anywhere long enough to be a "True TCK" even though you were. How it was weird coming back and seeing how the US was unaware of many things going on but also way more ahead than other countries. You were able to compare how many places you had lived and what you thought would be a 30 minute to one hour conversation turned into a three-hour conversation. And she wasn't the only person that happened with. You bonded many more times and realized that you weren't an island, but a person—someone who needed to take a chance and reach out. There are many people like you who also struggle to fit in, who are searching for belonging. Soon, you realized there was joy in that. You could be a light to others who also felt like they didn't belong.

You went to college and moved again—but this time, it was on your terms. You were able to go through the change with lots of others who were trying to figure it out. On the nights where it was hard for some girls you were able to be the strong one who guided them and was able to bring a few laughs in the midst of stress. The first semester of college a girl you knew had a panic attack and you helped and you later found out she thought you were an angel, but you didn't do it for the recognition. You did it because that was how you embraced the change and that is part of who you became.

Life is full of change, and that's okay. It's how you embrace the change that matters. You learned to surround yourself with people who love you and push you toward what's best, even when it's hard. You learned to slow down, rest, and work through the tough emotions that come with moving. Most importantly, you learned that our God is a God of deep love. He wants to hold your hand during both the painful moments and the joyful ones. He doesn't expect perfection.

When you make a move, it won't always be easy—but try to find a little joy in everyday life, and don't give up.

People are like mosaics—pieces of everyone they've encountered. But we also leave pieces of ourselves with others. We're not the only ones affected. You've impacted many people. You brought joy to the hopeless, love to the lonely, and reminded people that they matter. What felt small to you might have been huge to someone else. We don't always get to hear those stories, but when we do, let them fuel you to keep going. Someone smiled one more time because of you.

You often felt like you had to hold it all together—that you had to be strong and have all the answers. But you didn't—and that's okay. Once you accepted that, you began to embrace the community of others who also didn't know where to call home. One time while staying at a place for missionaries there were some kids and they asked, "Where are you from?" And I looked at them and then laughed a little as we realized what I was going to say. "The world" or "Everywhere." Those were my normal responses since I never knew if they meant where I had lived the longest, was born, or where I felt the most at home because most of the time they weren't the same answer.

Life isn't simple. It's not a step-by-step plan. It's an adventure—and change is part of it. So, forgive yourself. Give yourself grace. You are brilliant and strong. Just because there's no clear path doesn't mean the journey stops. Embrace your gifts. Don't be hard on yourself when things aren't perfect—nothing ever is. Don't be afraid to speak up. When you do, you'll discover that many people feel like their voices are being muffled, and they just need someone to speak first.

So don't hide. Be a light in other people's lives—they'll pass it on. Just because you may not find one place to call home doesn't mean you haven't found home in a thousand different places. You learned young that home is where the people are—not the buildings. That's a lesson many take a lifetime to learn.

You are strong. Keep going. Be bold. Be funny. Make someone

smile—because you can be the impact someone else needs. You can be the voice that helps someone become the change. Our voices matter. And so do theirs. You are not alone.

There are so many people who feel just like us—hidden, unsure. But when you reach out, when you feel like you're falling—someone will catch you.

You are seen. You are loved. You matter. Keep shining,

Maleena (Your Future Self)

———

Anonymous
Oregon, Texas, Florida, Oklahoma, USA;
The Middle East; Germany; Ecuador, and
other short-term places in Europe and the
United States

Dear younger me,

I haven't talked to you in a while—come to think of it, I can't remember the last time we encountered each other. I was showing my friends at college pictures of you and telling them about the life you lived. I noticed all the pictures were of your smiling, holding hands with friends, letting your curiosity run wild. Not one of them captured the days you were sick or bored or sad. My life got busy; people expected things from me, and I guess we lost touch. I never meant to forget you or move on without you. In fact, you show up in my life every day, even without me noticing. We haven't talked much lately, but I think about you often as I tell and retell stories of when we were together—what seems to be so long ago, so far away, so out of reach.

I wanted to say I'm sorry. I'm sorry for all the tears you cried in your bed, burying your face in your pillow, unable to breathe. Like the one Christmas you hid in your bed because you were scared of the storm outside. Or in high school, when you locked yourself in your room and cried when you were told you were leaving yet again. I'm sorry you lived life afraid of being alone and of uncertainty—our lifestyle definitely didn't help with that. I'm sorry for the moments you needed something—even if you didn't know what that something was—but weren't given it.

I'm sorry that you had to say so many goodbyes. I'm sorry for the season of life that was filled with feelings of unsettledness even though you lived in one place. I remember the day you found out you were leaving again; I remember the anger, confusion, and brokenness you felt towards your parents and your God. It seemed like you were always leaving, or, when you finally had the chance to stay, someone else left. I'm sorry you had to watch your friends leave.

I'm sorry you felt left behind. There is no other way to put it—you felt constantly left behind and replaced. That is why my greatest fear now is being replaced and forgotten.

I'm sorry you felt so different when you came back "home"—or rather to your parents' home. A place that felt like anything but home; a place so foreign an unfamiliar. I'm sorry that you felt left out and much too different to make friends. I'm sorry for the way you felt so lost and out of place at school when the other kids talked about things you had never heard of. I remember the time you were introduced to secular music. You felt so foreign not knowing any of the words and so ashamed for listening to it in the first place. I didn't know I could feel so much like an alien in a place that was supposed to be "home". It was as if they were speaking another language. Who knew two worlds could be so opposite. I'm sorry for how confused you were when you tried to listen and understand and how dumb you felt when they looked at you, waiting for you to say something back. You got good at making things up and sounding like you knew what you were talking about—a skill you never should've had to develop.

I'm sorry that you felt lonely growing up, wanting friends but not knowing how to make them last. I'm sorry that every friend you had said they would keep in touch when you left yet again. I'm sorry for how disappointed and insignificant you felt when they forgot to call or were too busy to write. I'm sorry you had to start over every time you returned to America because your friendships weren't the same as when you left. I'm sorry making connections with people was so hard, all you could see was how different you were when you looked in the mirror. When, in reality, there were so many similarities—they were just hidden under layers of differences.

I'm sorry that your innocence was taken from you at such a young age. I remember the first time a man asked to marry you—a man you thought was a friend. You were only eleven. I'm sorry for the moment you realized men not only assaulted you through words when his hands grazed what was not his to touch. I'm sorry for all the moments that made you want to hide, curled in a ball, and scream "Just leave me alone!". I'm sorry that because of the actions of others, you had to walk around with your guard up because you felt unsafe. You didn't deserve to feel the eyes of lustful men when you walked down the street or have to scan your surroundings when you stood still. I'm sorry for the times when you felt cornered because of people's questions. I'm sorry for the way they treated you, like you were something exotic, placed on a pedestal to be admired. "The Little African Missionary Kid" was stamped on your forehead—or so you thought—begging people to stare, point, interrogate.

Dear younger me, most of all, I'm sorry you were not given the freedom to simply be a kid. You understood safety as within a set of walls, and that was only safe as long as the outside world stayed outside. You didn't have the opportunities to do activities like sports or dance—luxuries you only experienced through movies. You were forced to grow up before it was time. You witnessed and lived through things and hold onto memories of things a child shouldn't have to remember. Memories replay in your mind so vividly of moments when you were sad, disappointed, scared, lonely, misunderstood. "Normal" was not a concept you were familiar with; it wasn't even a word in your vocabulary. But then again, is anything normal?

Here we go again—back to the inconsistencies.

Dear younger me, I'm sorry I couldn't be there for you when you needed someone—someone to notice that everything was in fact not ok, that you were struggling, you were lonely, you were uncomfortable, and all you wanted to do was run because that seemed easier than living in the discomfort. I'm sorry I wasn't there when you simply needed a hug, when you needed someone to hold you. I'm sorry I wasn't there to make you smile and remind you of how amazing and special you are.

I'm at college now, trying to navigate life in America. Learning what it means to live in one place. Life hasn't been easy in this transition; it's an uncomfortable blend of wanting to live with a "this is permanent" mindset when I'm stuck in an "everything is temporary" mindset. You visit me a lot—most of the time I don't recognize you. But you're there. You're there when I cry in bed at night, into the arms of a loving friend who listens patiently as I try to articulate the desire to be somewhere not knowing where that is because I'm restless everywhere I go. You're there when I look through pictures and relive memories and tell stories about you and your world. You're there when big emotions overtake me as I realize things from my past affect me now. You're there when I get excited, remembering I'm living my college dream. You're there when I get anxious knowing that someday I will have to take the next step, saying more goodbyes and walking into another change, another unknown.

My aunt told me that the only consistent thing in our lives is change. Excuse me? No thank you! After a life of change after change after change after change after change, I would like some consistency. Let's be honest, you deserved some consistency—something, just one thing that stayed the same.

I hope you realize that during every step, in every season, you had a friend that never left your side. He held you as you got on that plane when you were one. He guided your feet as you toddled barefoot through the sand. He held your hand when you were scared at night or when you stepped on the school bus in America. He held you as you cried. He embraced you when you questioned your life and doubted yourself. He protected you when you felt vulnerable and unprotected. He renewed your life when you thought you couldn't keep going. Through all the valleys you endured, Jesus was your faithful, consistent friend. And he hasn't left me, just as he never left you—not even for a single millisecond.

I love you, little one. And I'm proud of you!

All my love,
Grace

———

Grace Shaarda
USA; Uganda

Dear Hannah,

Right now, you're on the top bunk that 엄마 set up just a few hours ago, running your hand on the new bed sheets that feel stiff and crinkly, like tissue paper. You've just spent an hour in the dark, excitedly talking to Jane about tomorrow and your first day at Taejon Christian International School. You're proud that you coolly said bye to 엄마 and 아빠 and don't feel homesick for your room back in Yanji with the dusty pink curtains and direct view of the sandpit where all the Peace Town kids hangout during the long summer evenings.

But tonight, in your dreams, you'll walk past the sandpit, climb up five flights of unpolished, concrete stairs, unlock the green metal door on the left, and walk into an apartment bathed in sunlight. And you'll repeatedly have this dream because this was home. Sadly, you won't realize this until you revisit Yanji 6 years later and the dreams stop.

You'll realize this home no longer exists in a physical and metaphorical sense; it's been swept away by new tenants, urbanization, and growing up too fast. We still mourn this loss, even as I'm writing this letter to you 18 years later. But don't worry. You'll glimpse home again, sometimes in conversations with adult TCKs from countries you've never heard of, sometimes when you host dinners and insurmountable differences melt away because you're just people enjoying good food.

You'll also learn this the hard way, but Christians and adults are imperfect and broken people. Sometimes, the most twisted and unsafe spaces are religiously affiliated. At first, you'll think it means you can't count on anyone, then you'll realize you can't even count on yourself because you too are imperfect and broken. Then after years of peeling off all the layers of hurt and pride, you'll finally understand grace. You'll see that God redeems people and situations that seem too far gone.

Right now, I know you feel overwhelmed because you're navigating three different cultures and languages while developing your own identity. To be honest, code switching never ends, but I can promise that you'll develop some roots that don't tear off each time you replant. Also, detaching from your feelings to stop hurting only brings temporary relief. To feel is to be alive and to not feel is to choose a slow and lonely death. So, keep feeling, keep observing, keep questioning, because you grow up to become an adult who is brave enough to choose adventure over safety, new friendships over never-ending goodbyes, and gratitude over regret.

You got this. 화이팅! Add oil,
Hannah

———

Hannah Jang
South Korea; USA; China; India

Dear young Yvonne,

Be warned, your first trip to Walmart upon returning to the United States in 1994-1995 will be a complete shock to your system. As a six-year-old, you become completely overwhelmed by the choices. It was all so bright and loud. Looking up at the shelves, your mouth will hang open in shock. The shelf, an intimidating giant, will make you dizzy looking all the way up to the top. Then you look to the left and right and you will be inundated with colors, words, shapes and numbers. Imagine sitting on a carousel horse, the background going bleary as you spin faster and faster. I still feel that way sometimes when I walk into some grocery stores.

Before returning to the US, you will have spent two years in Zimbabwe, the country will have been in a drought for much of that time. The shelves at the grocery store will often be bare or sparsely stocked. Your parents are going to be heavily involved in various food relief programs in addition to teaching at the local high school and doing student ministries while you are in Zimbabwe. I don't ever remember going hungry. You will be blessed. Although, I do remember your sister sneaking Kapenta (dried minnows) from one of the food relief bags. You are old enough to know better. Don't try them!

You and your family will have the ability to acquire food. It just means that sometimes you will have to drive three hours away to get your groceries, instead of one hour. People will consider you rich, you will have a car, a house, electricity, and semi-regular running water. In the little town of Sanyati, Zimbabwe, you will see several houses typically consisting of villages with dirt floor huts with no running water or electricity.

Unfortunately, things will happen, and you will not be able to stay in Zimbabwe. This is typical for missionaries with conflicting governments. They sometimes have to leave. You will return to Oklahoma and Arkansas between overseas assignments. Many of your relatives live there or in close proximity, so this will become your "home base." Oh, and try not to be mortified when you hear the elderly lady at the church say, "I remember you. I changed your diapers in the church nursery. We are so glad to have you home!" People will use that statement a lot: "Welcome Home". It is awkward that they assume your home is where you stay in between assignments and not the last location that you spend years of your life before being forcefully removed. The best word I have for it... weird. Sometimes, you will lie, replying, "Thanks, I am glad to be back." Sometimes you will say it and might even believe it a little. There will be times that you will be glad to be "home" to see family and a very few close friends. Enjoy the American food, candy, and sweets. Oh, and the air conditioning and heat! Realistically, you will spend a lot of time away from "home" as a child. Your life away from the US will dominate your memories. You will look like an American, mostly speak like an American, but something in the back of your mind will always make you feel like a foreigner. Oh well, off to the next assignment (or two).

You will return to Zimbabwe at the age of eleven, but first you take a detour to Central and South America for a few years. Enjoy those times. You will have great memories of those countries, and your future family wants to know about it. However, when the opportunity to go back becomes a reality, your family will jump on it. Now, at this point, you will have spent more time overseas than in the US. You will have to go without American candy and junk food for a while. You won't realize it, but you will miss Welch's grape jelly. In fact, it will have been so long since seeing grape jelly, you probably wouldn't have even remembered it and continued to live contentedly without it. But then it happens...

One day around twelve-years-old, you go to visit the little apartment where some new short-term volunteers were staying. You will open the door to their refrigerator and the first thing you see? Welch's grape jelly. To the utter shock and maybe even horror of the volunteers, you will start exclaiming loudly, "Welch's grape jelly! Welch's grape jelly!" As the excitement waned and the looks of surprise from the volunteers bring you back to reality, don't worry too much. Just apologize for your explosive reaction and explain that you haven't seen or had Welch's grape jelly in a very long time. If you do so with the right expression and maybe even a little emphasis in your voice, they will promptly make you a PB&J sandwich. Then when they leave the country, you get to finish the jar.

There is some expectation that this kind of thing may happen when you leave your country of origin, moving to a new place. However, this grape jelly paradox may happen just as often when you are back in your country of origin and are no longer able to return to the country that was part of your life for so long. In fact, it may become even more of an intense emotional response when reminded of or seeing something from the country that also became your home. The reality is that as a missionary kid, you almost always return to your country of origin, but that homebase was never really your home. It was a place to visit and rest. Your home will change here and there. Sometimes you will go to another country for extended periods of time, waiting for your chance to go back home. There will be times when you can't go back. When that happens, there will be those back at your home base that won't understand. Don't hold that against them.

So, young Yvonne. In these moments of a "Grape Jelly Paradox", remember that it is okay to suddenly have an emotional outburst of excitement, a moment of sadness, or even anger at what once was part of the life that shapes you into who God is molding you into. Your life will be a large intertwined web of many realities. You will adapt to many things, you will have lost so much but gained significantly more. You become the person you need to be to survive the situations, the trials, and the tribulations.

Here are some quick life tips I want to give you. Keep your hair in a braid or ponytail so that the little Zimbabwean kids can't constantly touch it. You will have to pretend to understand the numerous colloquialisms that come from entertainment that the average 1990's and 2000's kid enjoyed. You are going to miss out on a lot of them. Learn how to use them even though you have no clue where they come from; it helps in the long run. Sometimes, you may even be "in style" without realizing it. Learn how to make your own jellies, they will comfort you during hard times and make great gifts to friends. Figure out how to make traditional Zimbabwean dishes such as Sadza and Oxtail soup. You will be so excited about it. Cherish those ice-cold, glass bottle Coca-Colas in Zimbabwe, you won't realize how much you will miss them when you get "home". Climb the mango trees, you will love the experience and the snack, once you master it. Most importantly, cherish the memories. Share them with those you love and take time to grieve as needed when you desperately miss things unique to your many home countries.

God is always with you. It doesn't matter what country, village, state, or house you are in. He won't leave you.

Sincerely,
Older Yvonne

———

Yvonne Keller
Arkansas, Oklahoma, Louisiana, USA;
Zimbabwe; Costa Rica; Venezuela; Kenya;
South Africa; Ecuador; South Korea

1996

Dear 5-year-old Courtenay,

You are so angry to be in China, so far away from your familiar home, your grandparents, your friends. You feel pent-up and are searching for a release, for regulation. You suggest drawing out how you feel on the wall in your bedroom, convincing your brother Hanno to help you. Big, angry X's line the walls, each stroke releasing some of that charge in your little body. Baba is very upset about this at first, but he doesn't stay angry. The angriest you will ever see your dad is when the men at the market target and assault you. You're riding on the back of Mama's bike and feel eyes burrowing into your back as laughter erupts behind you. Turning around, you notice two men pointing directly at you and laughing. Confused, you turn back around to face Mama's back, and that is when you feel the blinding pain of the bb entering your back side. You scream out as Baba jumps into action, taking off after the two men who shot you. This will become one of the first long-term memories of your life; but life is not as scary as this one incident.

1997

Dear 6-year-old Courtenay,

While in China, you learned "not to be the nail that sticks out of the board, or you will be hammered down". When you return to the Friends school in Pennsylvania one year later, you learn that in the American context, Black kids like your friend B. cannot afford to be the "nail that sticks out". Your white friends get away with seemingly everything, but not B. One day, you feel scared and helpless as your teacher loses her temper with B., grabbing him by his shirt collar and lifting him clear off the floor. You freeze in fear and surprise as you watch your teacher scream at him for using an expletive in self-defense, after another classmate had called him a N-----. This memory will stick with you for the rest of your life; and you will always wonder what happened to B. and his family. You never see him again after kindergarten. When you eventually become a teenager, you don't freeze when you witness bigotry and racism, but you do when it comes time to speak in class. You learn that it is safe to speak up for others, but speaking up for yourself is terrifying. One day, this won't always feel so scary; you will have experiences that support and encourage you to share yourself. Courtenay, your voice has always mattered to me; and one day, you will learn that your voice matters to others as well.

2000
Dear 9-year-old Courtenay,

You are about to leave everything and everyone you consider "home". Again. This move feels different; you were not expecting this one. You were not expecting to leave again. This news devastates you; I remember how viscerally you feel this loss in your heart, diaphragm, and stomach. It crushes you; it feels like someone close to you has died, and in a way, that is true. When you leave with Mom, Dad, and Hanno, the part of you that anticipated growing up here with your Friends School peers, is the part of you that dies. You try your best to understand why this is happening again; on some level, you already do. But it is important to me that you know this: It is not your job to protect your mom. You were never meant to be her "little hero". It is her job to protect and parent you, not the other way around. It is also not your job to protect or take care of your brother, who is only a year younger than you are. You are still a child, and you are about to need both of your parents more than ever.

2003
Dear 12-year-old Courtenay,

When you find out you are moving off the Rez, you are so excited. After 3 years living over 2,000 miles away from Pennsylvania, you will finally be back on the East Coast; this has felt like an eternity to you. You don't realize until after you leave, just how connected you are to this place, including the people. Shortly after you move, you receive the devastating news that your friend J. was killed by a drunk driver. She had been riding in the bed of her family's pickup truck, like a lot of Navajo kids do, when the glonnie hit her family's truck, sending her flying out; she did not survive. When you find out, you lose yourself in waves of tears, unable to pry yourself from the soft carpet of your grandmother's living room. J. was one of the few Navajo kids who went out of their way to be kind to you and befriend you; an outsider, a Bilagáana. She affectionately called you "Corndog". You won't find out until you are in your 30's that it was her father who designed the Navajo Nation flag. When your family arrives in Vermont, you think there has been a mistake; this is not close at all to Pennsylvania. The school mascot is a racist stereotype of a disembodied Plains Indian head, and your white peers (and their parents) are wearing headdresses, "war paint", and making the "Indian war whoop" sound at sports games. When your dad raises the issue with the local admin, our family becomes known as people who create unnecessary problems, and we are criticized for questioning the local "tradition". You learn to stand up for your values, to assert yourself against injustice, and you also struggle to feel connected and a sense of belonging with your peers. Do not forget to keep seeing your peers as people too; they want to connect with you, even if you don't recognize it at first. It is a great skill that you learn to reject and push others away, especially in the face of injustice, but don't let this isolate you; you need community and connection too, especially with peers your own age.

2009

Dear 18-year-old Courtenay,

It's okay that you don't know what you want to major in; it's okay to not have all the answers. It's okay to be interested in many subjects; how could you not be? For the first time in your life, you have the time and space to explore what you want, what you are interested in, and what brings you joy. You are going to meet friends and partners who will shape you in ways that you are not always comfortable with, and you'll eventually recognize how important and necessary these experiences are for your growth. One day, you will move to the San Francisco Bay Area for one reason, only to establish roots for another. All the people, places, and things that make up your past will play a role in the future you form for yourself. Every experience you have ever had, has had a purpose and has helped to shape the adult that you are becoming. Most importantly, you will learn to love yourself; you will learn that putting yourself first and forming boundaries is anything other than selfish, and that "good girl" conditioning has kept you quiet and small. You are going to feel so proud of yourself when you grow up; you will achieve things that you have been dreaming about, for your entire life.

———

Courtenay Houk
Pennsylvania, Navajo Nation (New
Mexico), Vermont, USA; China

9 May 2025
Turtle Island (USA)

Ay-ayaten nga Sheila,

Daytoy ni Myra. Isabali dan to ti nagan mo no dumakkel ka. Ti kinaadu ti iskwelaan nga inattendarak, saba-sabali nga nagan ti inkabil da ti pappapelis tayo. Isunga imbis nga Sheila iti tawag ti tattao kenka, nagbalin nga Myra, ta daydiay kano ti "first name" mo. Urayno ta balay ken ta gagayemmo ket Sheila latta ti tawag da kenka.

Ragsakkem am-amin nga gagayemmo ita ISKL. ISKL iti agbalin nga paboritum nga iskwelaan. Umalis ka manen, ngem nagadun to iti agbalin nga "bes fren" mo. Ammok nga nagsakit iti umalis manen, ngem umadu-nga-umadu laeng ti naragsak nga panawen. Umadu-nga-umadu laeng ti gagayemmo. Ken umadu-nga-umadu laeng ti katawa ti biyag mo.

An-anusam laeng ni Mama ken ni Papa. Umadun to iti panawen nga mailiw ka kanyada, kasla idi ub-ubing ka idiay States idi addada idiay KL. Isuda laeng ti makalagip iti am-amin nga gagayemmon to. Ken pati isuda, nagadun to met ti kailiwen da nga gayem da, ken agba-bawi dan to nga nagsina kayo no dubduma idi obeng ka pay. Pakawanem isuda ta saan da ammo nga ti kinaadu nga alis mo, natipon dagidiay sakit ken ladingit mo nga saan mo maritna angana dumakkel ka. Urayno ammom nga umalis ka, nasakit latta ta kailiwem amin nga gagayemmo ken nanim-adu kan nga nabiglaan.

Ngem, uray no kasatno, saan ka latta nga ag-sardeng nga ag-katawa. Uray no kasatno, saan ka nga ag-sardeng nga maki-gayem. Saan ka met nga ag-sardeng nga ag-sangit, ta dagita luam ket katawa nga nakadulin idta pusom.

Addan to ti anak mo nga saan na kayat ti alis-nga-alis iti lugar. Tatta, ipagarup mo ket saan mo kayat nga umalis no dumakkel ka. Ngem addan to ti panawen nga kayat mon to ti alis-nga-alis. Lagipem laeng idi obeng ka tapno maramanan met ti anak mo iti ag-gyan iti maysa nga lugar nga nabayag. Tapno mas ad-adu met iti katawa na ngem pagsangit na. Ken addan to met iti gagayem ken inayayat mo nga saan mo kayat nga panawan wenno makisina. Lagipem met idi obeng ka, paspas ka nga dimakkel. Paspas met nga dumakkel iti anak mo, ken paspas met nga bumaket ken lumakay ni Mama ken ni Papa. Lagipem nga awan iti maysa nga aldaw nga ma-ulit. Ti pamilyam laeng iti mabalin nga haan kayo nga agsina, no mabalin.

Addan to met iti gayem mo nga mas-agkataros kayo nga dua ta alis-met-nga-alis isu. Maragsakan ka no adda iti gayem mo nga ammona met ti alis-nga-alis. Naynaymon to nga malagip isuda ta man-mano iti kasdiay nga gayem. Mas-nauneg iti pag-gayem yo ta ag-tinnarus kayo nga dua ken saan nyo kailangan nga ipalawag am-amin nga bagay.

No adda iti ay-ayatem nga maisina, lagipem laengen nga am-amin nga lua ket katawa nga nakadulin idta pusom. Ti kinaadu nga katawa, adun to met ti lua, ngem regalo latta ti lua, ta naggapu ti nagadu nga katawa . Naynay mo lagipem nga ag-katawa ka latta angana mabalin, ta awan iti maidulin mo nga katawa no adaywam iti naragsak nga panawen.

Daytoy Agay-ayat,
Myra

English Translation from Myra:

Dear Sheila,

This is Myra. They will change your name when you grow up. Because of all the schools I attended, they put different names on our paperwork. That's why instead of Sheila, people will be calling you Myra, because that was what they considered to be your first name. Although, at home and with your friends, they still call you Sheila.

Enjoy all your friends at ISKL. ISKL will become your favorite school. You will move again, but you will meet many who will become your best friends. I know it hurts to move again, but you will keep having more happy times. You will have exponentially more friends. And you will only have more and more laughter in your life.

Have patience with Mama and Papa. There will be more times in the future when you will miss them, just like when you were in the States when you were younger and they were there in KL. They are the only ones who will remember all your friends. And they too will have many friends whom they will miss dearly and they will regret that you are sometimes apart while you're still young. Forgive them, because they do not know that due to all your relocations, you will accumulate hurt and grief, some of which you won't feel until you're older. Even though you know you will move, it still hurts because you miss all your friends and each of your many moves has felt like a shock.

However, no matter what, don't ever stop laughing. Nevertheless, don't ever stop making friends. Also, don't ever stop crying, because your tears are laughter kept in your heart.

You will have a child who will not want to keep moving. Right now, you think you won't want to be moving when you grow up.

However, there will be a time when you will want to keep moving. Just remember how it felt when you were a kid, so that your child will know how it feels to stay in one place for a long time. So that your child will also have more time laughing than crying. You will also have friends and loved ones that you will not want to leave behind or part with. Remember also, when you were a child, you grew up fast. Your child will also grow up fast, and Mama and Papa will grow old fast. Remember that there is not one day that can be repeated. Your family members are the only people whom it's possible to stay together with, if possible.

You will find a friend you will mutually be able to relate to more because they also moved around as a kid frequently. You will find so much joy if you have friends who know what moving frequently is like. You will always remember them because it is rare to find friends you can relate to this way. This type of friendship is deeper because you understand each other better and you don't have to explain everything.

In the future, when you have loved ones who will part, just remember that all your tears are laughter kept in your heart. Because of much laughter, there will likewise be many tears, but it is still a gift because they came from much laughter. Always remember to laugh as much as possible, nevertheless, because you won't have laughter to keep if you avoid happiness.

Love,
Myra

———

Myra Sheila Dumapias
Philippines; China; Malaysia; USA;
Germany; Romania; South Korea; Bahrain

Dear 15-year-old Tanya,

Congratulations! You've almost made it to the end of your family's time in the United States. I know you are counting down the days until you return to Australia. It's understandable you see your approaching departure as a 'finish line' given what a struggle these years have been.

I understand you recently realised that you won't have to take a science class ever again, which is very exciting for you. Might I suggest you let your Chemistry teacher down gently? She won't be quite as excited as you. And perhaps you could ceremoniously dump all your folders full of class materials in the bin at home rather than in front of your classmates a few weeks before midterms? It's a little hard for them to share your enthusiasm that since you're about to start a new school year, these grades mean nothing.

I love seeing your excitement and there really are things worth celebrating, yet since I have this opportunity, I want to share some information that could smooth the journey ahead of you in ways you can't imagine right now.

The first things you should know are that you are a Third Culture Kid (or TCK) and that you are about to go through 'repatriation'. A TCK has a cross-cultural childhood experience due to living in a country they are not a citizen of, and do not intend to become a citizen of—like you and your sisters these past two years. Repatriation is when you move to live in your country of citizenship—like you're about to do. Repatriation is just another international move, but also completely different. You're going to a city you used to live in, but it's different than it used to be—and so are you. Plus, there are completely different expectations! We expect it to feel like home and be easy, but it's not always that simple.

One thing you'll quickly notice is that while your sister does have a much stronger American accent, your whole family has adopted a sort of half-Australian, half-American accent. You can't tell yet, because to Americans you sound Australian. But in a few weeks, you will learn that to Australians you definitely sound American. I know this hurts to hear as you are so excited to 'be normal' and 'blend in' after two years of standing out every day. Be prepared for the nickname "Miss America". I'm sorry.

Your relationship with your accent is going to change many times over the next 28 years. You won't spend your whole life in Australia and your accent will shift many times. There will be a season in which sounding American angers you. In another season you will lose that 'international' twang and begin sounding more like a 'normal' Aussie, triggering a sense of loss. Mostly your accent will slide around. Eventually you won't really care anymore!

Your relationship with the US, where so many hard things have happened, is uncertain at best. There was the struggle to connect with peers and educators who are culturally different to you, and who struggled to have grace for your cultural differences. Cultural miscommunication (combined with neurodivergence you won't learn about for another 15 years) left you in a vulnerable position with an older boy, not knowing what to do. You were regularly belittled and misunderstood due to your nationality, leaving you the most patriotic you've ever felt! Plus, the lack of any academic assessment in the schools here means you will soon find yourself 18 months behind your Australian peers in mathematics.

It is very tempting to blame all these hard things on the country and its people rather than on the difficulties of cross-cultural communication, especially where the cross-cultural part goes unrecognised. You are going to want to make vows such as, "I will never live in America again" or "I will never date/marry an American". But this will never be about the US. It will always be about the ways you were hurt and misunderstood. One day you will meet sweet and kind US Americans who become your closest friends. You will start to acknowledge how much hurt you experienced during these years, process that grief, and be set free of it.

There has been a lot of unresolved hurt in these years, and a lot of difficult feelings you haven't fully understood. Hoping this will just go away isn't a wise solution. Changing countries won't change your brain. You need help to learn healthy coping strategies and to better understand yourself. What you've been feeling is called depression and anxiety. Lots of people feel this way! It will get better—but you can't do it alone by sheer willpower.

While it might be discouraging to know life will not always be smooth sailing, I hope it makes a difference to know that the difficult things you encounter are common. There is nothing wrong with you. Repatriation is hard for everyone. Wrestling with identity shifts is hard for everyone. Working out who you are and what matters to you is part of life for everyone. But now you know that this is part of your story, and you know that you are part of a community of TCKs and others around the world who have been through similar struggles. You are not alone. You can also talk to your parents and your sisters—you might be surprised to hear similarities in their stories, now and in the future!

I am excited to see where you go from here.

Love,
42-year-old Tanya

———

Tanya Crossman
Australia; Cambodia; China; USA

Dear Kezzie,

You are in Singkawang now—Singkawang of the rolling hills and valleys awash in lush verdure—the little town of Singkawang—your home.

Now you are six. What you understand of your life as a third-culture kid is that you have lived here for years, that this is the only place you remember living in, and that while you and your family will return to Singapore eventually, that time is far, far into the future.

But this is not the case. You will return to Singapore because of the virus you have faintly heard of Covid 19. And while you will hope to return once the virus is over—it will last a long, long time, longer than anyone imagined. You will not return to Singkawang for a long, long time—I have not been back, even as I write.

So, remember this, and treasure your time in Singkawang. What beautiful, rich, layered experiences you have had—of hosting trippers from Singapore, come to share the gospel—of learning Bahasa, trying to form its syllables on your little tongue, and adopting a slight accent—of homeschooling in a blackout. Your experiences are unlike so many of your peers' and of your friends'.

You are a third-culture kid, Kezzie. That means that you have your own unique set of joys and sorrows. There will be challenges that almost no one understands—of being asked well-meaning, prying questions of your time in that little town by former mission trippers: did you enjoy your time there? Was it enjoyable? Did you have a good time?

Such questions cause deep, rich memories to rise up—if I linger in that space too long I get buried in the sheer depth and joy and longing each one holds—that are too intimate to share. You can only nod your head, nod and answer a polite yes. Such an answer feels insufficient—brief—brusque, even—but what else can you say? Who would understand?

But I do not regret being a third-culture kid, even though there are challenges beyond what I have shared—those that cannot even be put into words but are keenly felt. What a beautiful thing it is to have such unique, vivid memories, to be able to recollect with fondness the years you have spent in Singkawang.

When you arrive back in Singapore, you will have new things to enjoy—and also new worries and sorrows. It will not be easy. But you have learnt eagerly and well; your experience as a third-culture kid will inform and guide you as you continue along this journey called life.

And that is my hope for every third-culture kid, and every cross-cultural kid—that they will hold dear their rich, deep, bittersweet memories of their experiences, overcoming the challenges they face along their journeys with resilience. I hope each memory they have will bring forth a depth of emotion—that they will sip the joy without forgetting the sorrow. I hope they will rise.

Kezzie, cherish these experiences, this time of learning and growing and being. You will never regret it.

Love the Lord; he will guide and lead you every step of the way. Love the people around you.

Keziah

———

Khoo Yue En Keziah
Singapore; East Asia; West Kalimantan,
Indonesia

sometimes worry that in our moving around I've created a huge problem in your life, by causing so much disruption and loss, that I haven't taught you how to make friends and how to keep relationships, that I've caused you to feel lonely

The ones you ran away from. The ones you left behind.

イチャ リバ チョ ーデー

Thank you for holding my hand listen it needed it most. If I could rewrite your childhood, would I?

Joskus yöllä, kun unici tule, ajattelen sinua.

Glad to see the top of the world with you! Happy Travels!

You gave me so much more than my first language lessons and a flag!

Section 3:
Letters to the Reader About Writing as a Therapy Technique

My two dearest toasted marshmallows

親愛的阿嬤 ca-má It's me, 阿 - Vi. I wish

Ma, three years ago, I came to live in Japan to establish my own relationship with your country so it would be my country too. That summer, I visited your hometown without you for the first time in my life.

Please Write
Lois J. Bushong; Retired Marriage and Family Therapist

Dear Reader,

I was born in Laredo, Texas, where my parents worked with Latin Americans. At the age of four, we moved to Honduras where I was raised alongside my Honduran friends and neighbors. I am completely bilingual, and I feel completely at ease in either Latin America or the United States. I attended boarding schools from the age of nine all the way through high school and college. There were very limited choices for the education of an expatriate during those early years. I thrived in boarding school in Honduras. My high school years were more difficult as I experienced the challenge of adjusting to U.S. culture. Upon my graduation from college, I worked with an international agency for about twenty years in Latin America and in the U.S.

Upon hitting midlife, I made a major pivot in my profession. I once again returned to graduate school and got my Master of Science in Community Counseling from Georgia State University in Atlanta, Georgia. After completing the necessary requirements, I was licensed as a Marriage and Family Therapist in the state of Indiana. My specialty and love have been to counsel expatriates, Adult Third Culture Kids, international families and marriages.

Near the end of my career in 2013, I wrote the only book on the market at that point, on how to counsel TCKs. "Belonging Everywhere & Nowhere: Insights in Counselling the Globally Mobile" which is still popular with therapists and coaches. After 35+ years in the counseling profession, I am now retired. I am currently doing some limited coaching of ATCKs or expatriates, consulting, speaking and writing through my own company, "Mango Tree Intercultural Services". I enjoy tapping into my experiences as a TCK in order to help the younger generation navigate their own major transitions.

April 22, 1956

Dear Mother and Daddy and Bobby,
We girls went camping last week. We went swimming at night and I jumped in the water with Mildred. We had a campfire and had roasted marshmallows. We

307

slept in the playhouse….We got cool aid and cookies.

We got to make our Easter baskets. We got some popcorn and candy eggs. The teachers hid the baskets. I found my basket on a chair.

Did you have a nice Easter? Tell me about your Easter. David found his basket in the place where you keep the games. One was in the car. Where were some of Bobby's eggs hidden?

I learned to swim on my back and jump in. I can swim all the way across the lake.

Love,
Lois Jean

Mondays, after recess, was the day we wrote letters home from our boarding school, Las Americas Academy in Siguatepeque, Honduras. Most of our letters were filled with what we did that week. My parents kept all of our letters that we wrote home. As I read through the stack of letters I wrote from the third grade through the eighth grade, I realized they were all similar in content. The format I followed was, "This is what I did this week... I had fun this week... This big event took place in the lives of my friends... A report on David (my younger brother that I was to watch over)... How is Bobby (my youngest brother)? How are my friends? Tell everyone to write to me." Our letters were our only way to communicate with our parents during this era between the late '50's to the '60's when we only went home after seven months away at school. Our letters were filled with the news of the week.

As I read through the stack of letters my parents saved, I noticed a slight difference in my "historical epistles" when I returned to the United States for high school at Toccoa Falls Academy in northern Georgia. TFA was a Christian boarding school and the students were mainly missionary kids, preacher's kids, wealthy kids, and kids placed in our school by the court system. In my letters I began to slowly share my opinion about what was taking place and how I felt about it.

I began to feel an internal burn forming. My letters were no longer just historical documents. This was the start of my quiet rebellion against always needing to be a good kid, take care of my younger brother, David, and not make waves.

I won't go into my letter writing to my various boyfriends. I don't have copies of those letters, and fortunately for me, my parents never

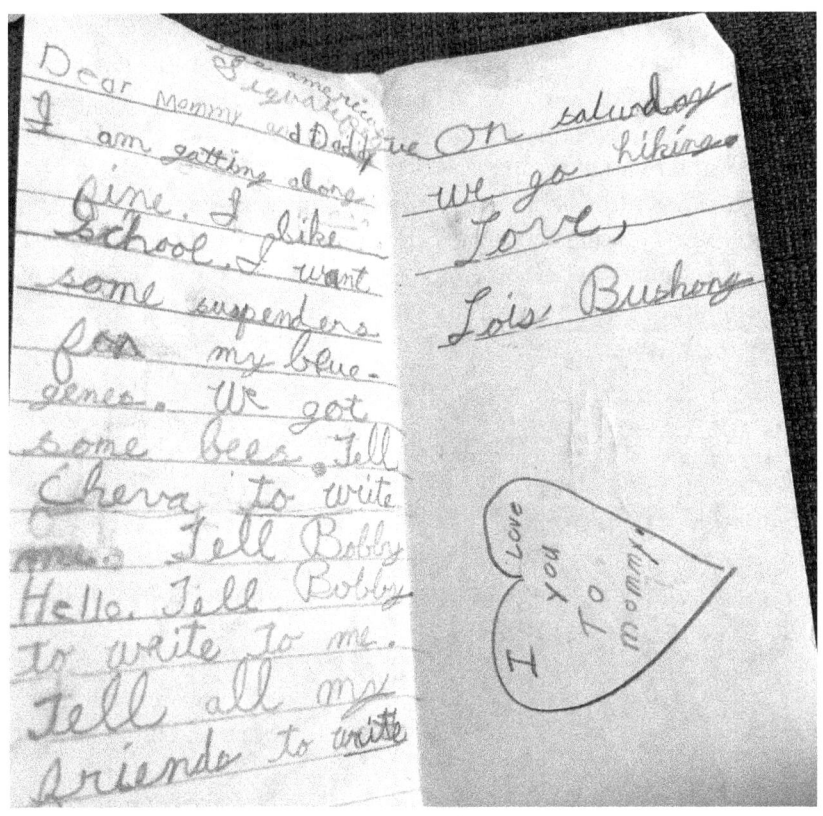

Handwritten letter from Lois to her parents from boarding school.

saw them or the boyfriends! Every breakup included the shredding of all cards and letters! No emotion there. Ha!

It was when I began to work as a marriage and family therapist that I realized the importance of letters filled with emotions and not just a communication of facts. Some of my clients flatly rejected the idea of writing in a journal, but they were good at writing letters. The letters written for our therapy sessions were not to be delivered to the person but only read in their therapy session with the client's consent. Then the clients chose whether to tear them up, put them away in a secure place or have me put them in their confidential file not to be read by anyone else.

For clients who struggle to talk about difficult events or feelings, writing is a mode of therapy that can access their emotions more easily than talking. Letter writing is one form of journaling. Some have problems journaling, but they can imagine they are writing to a loved one, or someone they despise, and thus journal more easily.

Ernest Hemingway said that writers should, "write hard and clear about what hurts." As you go through the process of writing whatever has happened it helps your mind organize the event in the brain. It also sends a message to your brain that you have it down on paper so you can stop ruminating on it so you don't forget any of the details. It might take writing about the event many times and from different perspectives—writing about the different individuals involved in the event, describing your thought process in detail, and flushing out all of your emotions and losses related to the event. Sometimes a different form of writing is helpful such as using a crayon or a dull pencil instead of a pen if you are talking about your childhood, drawing, or computerized drawings such as those in MineCraft. This facilitates the process of ultimately letting it go and bringing resolution.

Photo of Lois' diary.

There are letters that are written with the intention of actually mailing them to the recipient. In addition to communicating information, such as my letters to my parents from boarding school, they can share thoughts and feelings with someone else on a deeper level. This may result in the recipient feeling special such as the letters to my former boyfriends. They can be read over and over by the other person leading to emotional connection, understanding, and healing and thus providing long term emotional support. However, they can also destroy a relationship, whether intentionally or not. This is why it may be helpful to have someone else read your letter before you mail it to be sure it's on target with your goal and not sprinkled with "hot words" which would result in the reader getting defensive and thus missing the intention of your letter.

I mentioned my assignment of writing this piece to one of my clients, who was recently evacuated from her apartment in Los Angeles during the horrific fires a couple months ago. Her instant response was, "When I packed my little car, as I was escaping the fires, I jammed my to-go bag with all my important papers and my sixteen moleskine journals of the last 16 years of my life. I couldn't lose them; they are my life". I asked a second client why she journaled, and her initial response was, "My journaling saved me". This is why counselors assign letter writing or journaling to clients.

I want to conclude with a letter written after I arrived in the United States for high school at the boarding school in Georgia. Notice that I continue to share only facts, I find it interesting what facts I chose to share with my family. (Side note: we were not allowed to play rock and roll music in our home. But now, I was far away from home and under a new set of rules, figuring life out for myself. I had arrived in the U.S. at the height of the Beatles music).

Sept. 9, 1962

> *Dear Mommy, Daddy, David and Bobby,*
> *…..In 99% of the rooms on this campus they have either a radio or a record player. In our room there are two radios so there is always music in there. When you go out in the hall. Well you know how it sounds. There is a rule about playing rock and roll. Everyone plays it. If you do, you have to turn it way down.*
>
> *Lots of Love,*
> *Lois Jean*

A few days before, I had written in my own personal, little, blue diary with a lock on the cover about leaving for the United States for high school. I did not have a clue just how much my life would change then. Nor did I understand then how I would gradually learn to include an ever-wider range and depth of emotions on the pages of my journaling and letter writing over the years as I've lived throughout Latin America and the United States as an adult. This small beginning of sharing my emotions in my diary as a freshman in high school opened the door to this new pathway.

Photo of Lois' journal entry on August 22, 1962.

August 22, 1962

Left for the states with Susan and her mother. Had fun.
Stopped in BH [British Honduras now Belize]. Last
saw parents and David and Bobby for a long time.
Didn't cry.

Letter writing, whether the letters are sent or unsent, or in the form of journaling, is a significant tool for us Third Culture Kids that can travel with us wherever we go to bring understanding to our many changing worlds, experiences, stories and emotions. Maya Angelou stated, "There is no greater agony than bearing an untold story inside you." Please write.

Warmly,
Lois J. Bushong (aka Lois Jean)

Writing as a Tool for Embodiment: Integrating Complex Experiences and Feelings
Courtenay Irene Houk, MA, LMFT

Hello dear reader,

    My name is Courtenay Houk (she/they), and I am a trauma-informed somatic psychotherapist (LMFT) in the state of California, where I support adult individuals, couples, and relationships in the LGBTQIA+ and polyamorous communities. I grew up as a Third Culture Kid and Cross-Culture Kid hybrid: I was born in Pennsylvania, lived 1 year abroad in North-Eastern China in 1996-1997, 3 years on the Navajo Nation in New Mexico from 2000-2003, and finished out my childhood in the state of Vermont. Another layer of my intersectionality that feels important to mention is my status as a bisexual woman. Just like being a "Glocal" hybrid (Megan Norton, April 2024, Personal Correspondence), my queerness places me in a liminal space much of the time, where I experience myself as belonging in both/either community or culture. This is often a familiar experience to ATCKs, but feels particularly true for me, as I do not fit neatly into either ATCK or ACCK category. For many, the experience of the in-between or both/and is not a comfortable or a familiar one, but as a therapist, the experience of growing up as multiple hybrids has deeply informed how I work with people, how I see the world, and how I experience myself and my relationships. For many of my clients, writing or journaling has served as an entryway into deeper capacity for embodiment. I hope that my piece below on writing as a therapeutic tool for embodiment and the processing/integrating of difficult or stressful experiences can be supportive to you.

> *Language is not just a babbling in the dark, it can be a revelatory doorway into a reality that nobody's wanting to pay attention to.*
> —Don Hanlon Johnson (2022)

    Writing—a physical, emotional, and intellectual process—is also an embodied act. As an embodied act, writing can support and even facilitate the experience of strong sensations, feelings, imagery, and even elicit repressed traumatic memories, that the body has not yet processed. Robert Sapolsky (2004) in his book *Zebras Don't Get*

Ulcers discusses how animals are able to shake off the effects of trauma in the wild: their bodies and nervous systems do not hold onto stress and trauma the way human bodies do. Though it may be days, months, years, or even decades after the fact, writing could potentially serve as a uniquely human means of releasing or digesting a past traumatic or stressful experience. Additionally, as an embodied act, writing can serve as a therapeutic tool for processing and integrating difficult feelings and emotions. I found this to be the case for me, while I engaged myself with writing my Letters Now Sent to my child selves. The process of writing these letters also brought me back to a pivotal moment I recall from when I was in grad school.

I was sitting at home in my crammed three-bedroom apartment in the Mission District of San Francisco that I shared with two other roommates. Settling into the disheveled couch we had in the kitchen I tried to get comfortable as I prepared myself to journal for class. What started off as just a kernel of a memory, suddenly overtook my consciousness as the images whipped past me, much like how scenery appears while riding passengers in a moving car. I began scribbling furiously across the page as the images rushed through my mind like whiplash, bringing myself back to that precise moment in time that I was writing about.

I felt surprised by the intensity of my bodied response: my torso flooded with piercing adrenaline, hot rage washed across my skin, and an emotional pain that went so deep in my stomach that it felt like a sucker-punch in the gut, leaving me doubled-over in my seat. I recalled Pete Walker's (2013) description of an emotional flashback in his book *Complex PTSD: From Surviving to Thriving* and wondered, had I just facilitated my own flashback? Would I have recovered this memory if it hadn't been for this writing assignment?

That memory ultimately became an extremely formative moment in my personal development and is mentioned briefly in one of the letters I wrote to my child selves in this book. I had effectively repressed this memory from the time I was just eight years old, and in its place, a strong gut feeling emerged about my parents' dynamic that, at the time, I could not explain. On some level, my body had retained the traumatic experience but repressed the visual memory until I was ready to revisit and process it as an adult.

Similarly, the exercise of writing to my child selves as a contribution to this book brought up familiar albeit painful waves of feeling and sensation in my body. I had moments where tears were streaming down my face, and I needed to pause just so I could feel all that was being evoked for me through my writing. When I eventually felt complete with this exercise, my experience of myself was softer, kinder, and clearer, albeit a bit tender and raw, as if I had been unburdened of an enormous weight that I had been carrying with me ever since I was a child.

References
Hanlon Johnson, D. (2022). Final paper lecture. [Video]. Canvas.
Sapolsky, R. M. (2004). Why zebras don't get ulcers: The acclaimed guide to stress, stress-related diseases, and coping (3rd ed.). Holt.
Walker, P. (2013). Complex PTSD: From surviving to thriving. Azure Coyote.

Letter Writing Exercise: Now Write one to Yourself
Dr. Sally McGregor, Clinical Psychologist

Dear reader,

Hello! My name is Sally McGregor, and I am a U.S. licensed clinical psychologist and an ATCK who has spent a lot of time working on coming home to myself and helping many other ATCKs do the same. In the interstitial culture that is expat life, place identity and a sense of home can be nebulous. However, you don't have to be ungrounded and unmoored. Think of yourself as a patchwork quilt we are working on stitching together into a beautiful warm blanket that you cozy up with by a fire. Even if you don't have a home, you can be a home. Below I have created one exercise that I hope you find healing in terms of loving each and every part of you and your journey. I hope you will join me!

> *Someday, I would like to go home. The exact location of this place, I don't know, but someday I would like to go. There would be a pleasing feeling of familiarity and a sense of welcome in everything I saw. People would greet me warmly. They would remind me of the length of my absence and the thousands of miles I had travelled in those restless years, but mostly, they would tell me that I had been missed, and that things were better now I had returned. Autumn would come to this place of welcome, this place I would know to be home. Autumn would come and the air would grow cool, dry and magic, as it does that time of the year. At night, I would walk the streets but not feel lonely, for these are the streets of my hometown. These are the streets that I had thought about while far away, and now I was back, and all was as it should be. The trees and the falling leaves would welcome me. I would look up at the moon and remember seeing it in countries all over the world as I had restlessly journeyed for decades, never remembering it looking the same as when viewed from my hometown.*
> —Henry Rollins

Write so that you can come home to yourself.

There is still time to come home to yourself if you are willing to greet warmly, hug, and hold each version of you that has journeyed here.

Let's give it a try…

Close your eyes and picture a younger version of you. Maybe choose a younger you that is navigating a big transition or life change/obstacle. Open your eyes when that image feels solid.

- How old were you? 5? 10? 13?
- What was going on in your life at that time?
- What were your days like?
- What did you worry about?
- Who did you care about?
- What were your hopes and dreams for the future?

Now I want you to imagine your current self. Approach your younger self, in your mind's eye. Give that child a hug. Close your eyes. Imagine it.

- What would you tell younger you? What do you want this kid to know?
- What do you see in them? What strengths does this kid have, whether they know it not or yet, to make a beautiful life?
- What advice do you have for this kid?
- Take some more time to say it all. Write it out.
- What advice does this kid have for you?

Remember that this sweet kid lives inside of you, and you are still deserving of the love this kid needed, and the encouraging words you just bathed them in.

Pick some more ages you remember well. Perhaps even choose some earlier phases of your adult life. Write a letter to welcome each version of you home to yourself. Draw on their unique strength and wisdom when you need it. Especially welcome and hug the versions of you that struggled. Maybe there are versions of you that you hate and are not proud of. They need your letter the most and deserve to be welcomed home.

Save the Stamp:
Why Unsent Letters are Usually More Helpful
dr. fae frederick, ph.d.

Dear Reader,

My name is fae (she/her), and I'm a queer cisgender white woman from a working class American Deep South background. Both of my parents were trade workers and were unable to help me much financially or practically through my three college degrees (all in psychology), which stretched over 9 years, 4 states, 10 apartments, and 13 roommates. I struggled to fit in with people who came from higher socio-economic backgrounds and I did a lot of work in and out of my own therapy in finding all my identities and how they fit together—I'd say I'm still doing this work as like most humans, I keep growing and changing. After finishing my doctorate, I decided to do something crazy and leave the U.S.. The plan was to learn Spanish and return to the U.S. to practice bilingually.

It's been eight years since then and I've been to over 30 countries and I still don't speak Spanish very well. I now belong to and work with a unique group of people who are like cousins TCKs/ATCKs— people in the U.S. Foreign Service (FS). I defaulted into this group after meeting and marrying my husband overseas in Vietnam where we lived for 6ish years. Once we were married I was no longer allowed to work "on the local economy" which meant I had to start an online private practice, and working with other FS people seemed to make the most sense given (waves around wildly) everything.

FS people move every 1-4 years to a country that was on a list that they ranked, but they don't have control over what is on that list or where they finally end up. Sometimes the officer gets some language/culture training, most of the time family members do not, or get very little. As one can imagine, this can lead to a lot of the same feelings TCKs/ATCKs experience—not knowing where they fit in or feeling isolated from all cultures they have been a part of. All this along with the usual pressures of figuring out a new environment, new people, alongside the universal human experience of figuring out who they are and how all their identities constellate for them here and now. FS people have the safety of the U.S. embassy/consulate to help them navigate some of the most difficult parts of overseas life, but this bubble can also further isolate them from the place they are living. All this moving and changing can make for a lot of unfinished business and unprocessed grief. I have found letter writing to be a great way to help my clients connect with themselves and to create a more cohesive narrative in their patchwork lives. I'd like to share a bit about this practice with you in case you'd like to use it as well.

Letter writing is a difficult process, but it works. "Letters that aren't sent" are a common practice in Narrative Therapy, a psychological theory which emphasizes individuals create, or are taught stories about themselves, and those stories can be rewritten. Letter writing has been used for many emotion laden events outside of therapy (and long before modern therapy existed) across cultures: Dear John break up letters, letters of resignation, speeches, manifestos, wedding vows, and our last will and testaments.

Writing a letter (or even simply speaking out loud) helps translate our amorphous, tangential, emotion laden thoughts into structured sentences. Talking to someone—whether a friend or therapist—often works better than speaking to ourselves, since we're more likely to lose focus without an audience. Writing is often more effective than speaking because it forces us to slow down and reflect. Writing a letter is especially powerful, as it gives us a clear purpose, an audience (even if they're not reading), and a familiar format with a definite start and end.

Language has been likened to the "glue" that helps us bind together our sensations, emotions, and experiences.[1] Language (any language) helps us round out our experience of the world, which makes us more comfortable. When we better understand our experiences, we can share them with others, whether to strengthen relationships or end them with dignity and feedback. While humans struggle with holding contradictions, two opposing truths can coexist. Letter writing provides a unique and spacious place to express both love and anger, cherished memories and grievances. We can discuss our grief and how much we miss them as well as how their absence in our lives is a burden lifted. It allows us to acknowledge all aspects of a relationship, helping us find peace, closure, and a more nuanced, truthful narrative about the person involved.[2]

Modern technologies have contributed to fewer written letters to our loved ones (and enemies). However, a slower and more intentional connection may benefit our relationships. Think about how you feel after receiving a thoughtful birthday card or love letter—whether handwritten, via email, or a long text. These messages are so meaningful that many of us keep them for years. Similarly, difficult or painful letters can be just as valuable. They validate our feelings, honor our experiences, and give us space to defend ourselves and to express anger, grief, and hurt—especially when it is impossible to share these feelings due to death or when culturally it may not be appropriate to express these feelings to the one who caused them. We can also write letters to past/future you or to something abstract (e.g. cancer, a war, or the patriarchy).

Unfortunately, letters can't solve all of our problems. Difficult conversations are essential and shouldn't be avoided. Unspoken expectations lead to broken boundaries which can create emotional (and sometimes physical) distance. Too often, we let partners and friends drift away without expressing how they've hurt or disappointed us. Building a strong sense of self, can enable us to be vulnerable with loved ones and share our needs. If they meet us at our pain points, we can rebuild our connection together. But if someone repeatedly refuses to join us in that space, we must take responsibility for our own healing and create the emotional (and sometimes physical) distance needed to support that process. Writing a letter to someone who hurt you, whether you give it to them or not, helps to honor your truth, releasing the shame and guilt that can stick to us in ways we can't always see, but we can feel—these unhelpful feelings can drag us down for years. As one (very long) letter has told us, the truth will set you free.

We have all been harmed and we all deserve healing. I hope you are able to find healing and community in the letters enclosed within this book. The contributors are so brave to have committed their feelings to paper and to have shared them with the world. It is no small feat to hold all of the conflicting emotions of our relationships, and it can be even more difficult to write about them. I commend each and every contributor for their commitment to their truth and I'm grateful to Megan for bringing us all together in this space and for inviting me to share some of the truths I've learned as a healer. Should you feel inspired to write your own letter, here are some tips and best practices I share with my clients. May you find peace in your truth.

Tips for Letter Writing with Narrative Therapy
For letters you intend to share, I recommend two drafts: one for raw emotions, and another that balances those feelings with an understanding of their intent, your connection/commitment to a relationship with them, and clear communication of your needs. For letters that won't be sent, the first draft is enough.
- Be honest. Let it all out: the rage, the sadness, the disappointment, the dreams, the good memories, and the grief.
- Write the letter in the language you would speak to the person

the letter is about. We can hold different emotions, memories, and even personality traits in different languages. It's also okay to switch languages within the letter. Perhaps you learned some new things about that person or yourself in a different language.

- You do not need to write a perfect letter. You can have many drafts. It can be 1 page or 20 pages. If you find you have more to say after this letter is complete or after some time has passed, write another one. Our emotional process is long and ever changing.

What to Do with the Letter When You're Done
- Burn it, rip it up, throw it into a river, bury it, or otherwise dispose of it.
- Keep it in a safe place—or password protect it if it's digital
- Incorporate it into a grief ritual
- Write the response you'd like to receive
- You don't need to share this letter with the person it is to. In fact, it is usually NOT a good idea to share it. If you think you do want to share it with them, consider talking to trusted friends, elders, and healers about it. Be prepared—the person receiving the letter is usually not going to respond in the way you'd like, although it might be in the way you expect.
- If you do decide to share it, make sure you are sharing it for you. It should be something you need to say for you and it will be very helpful to not expect anything to change after you read the letter—at least not anything good. Sharing tough truths can create distance in relationships. What has been said cannot ever be taken back, and to take it back would likely feel invalidating to the version of you who needed to share their truth.
- It isn't absolutely necessary, but it can be very powerful to read your letter aloud to a therapist, healer, friend, or understanding family member. If reading to a friend or family member, be clear you only want them to listen, provide support, and to keep it between the two of you. You can also share the letter with strangers in an online format or in books like this one.
- Alternatively, you can read it while imagining the person the letter is to is in front of you. If you choose this route you can use this process:
    ◊ Call them into the room and imagine them sitting in front of them.
    ◊ Remember, they can't talk back to you. They are only there to listen.

◊ When you are done reading, ask them to leave the room and imagine them walking out.
◊ Give yourself time to feel and reflect once they are gone.

Below are some letter prompts. You can pick and choose whatever feels right or helpful.

- This letter is difficult to write because…
- I wish I could have told you…
- I'm so angry/sad that you…
- What I learned from you is…
- My favorite memory of you is…
- Now that you're gone I feel…
- I'm thankful that…
- When I think about (event) I feel…
- I used to think…and now I know…
- I'm going to miss…
- My wish for you is…
- I'm ready to let go of…
- Now and in the future I will…

References
1. Lindquist KA, MacCormack JK, Shablack H. The role of language in emotion: predictions from psychological constructionism. Front Psychol. 2015 Apr 14;6:444. doi: 10.3389/fpsyg.2015.00444.
2. Larsen, L. H. (2024). Letter Writing as a Clinical Tool in Grief Psychotherapy. OMEGA—Journal of Death and Dying, 89(1), 222-246. https://doi.org/10.1177/00302228211070155.

In a different place

お母さん.

: 数年 辛かったね。

「辛かったね」と書くだけで

涙が ：ぼれる.

You will look like an American, mostly speak like an American, but something in the back of your mind will always make you feel like a foreigner.

The endless goodbyes followed swiftly by hesitant hellos...

Section 4:
Invitation to Write
Your Own Letter

Know that the memory you create for yourself with these repeated new-kid day, kid-new-kid keep you to build your sense of self, your ability to blend well and reconnect.

You are living proof that home isn't just a place - it's a feeling, a collection of memories, and a tapestry of experiences.

There's so much left unsaid.

Hey beautiful!
Just a note saying I think of you often.
Hope life is treating you like the treasure you are! ♡ you

I never meant for it to be so hard...

I encourage you to anchor yourself in supportive relationships that provide rhythm, consistency

Taprooted to the Source with you,

Dear Reader,

I close with an image of a postcard I never sent. It was addressed to my grandmother-in-law, whom I came to know through my marriage to Bryce. Right before our wedding in June 2024, I went on a global trek with my brother, revisiting some of our heart homes. It was a "passage" I intentionally went on before marriage to say farewell to my unmarried life. (I am drafting a book about that experience!)

After the wedding in June, I relocated to a new US state with my

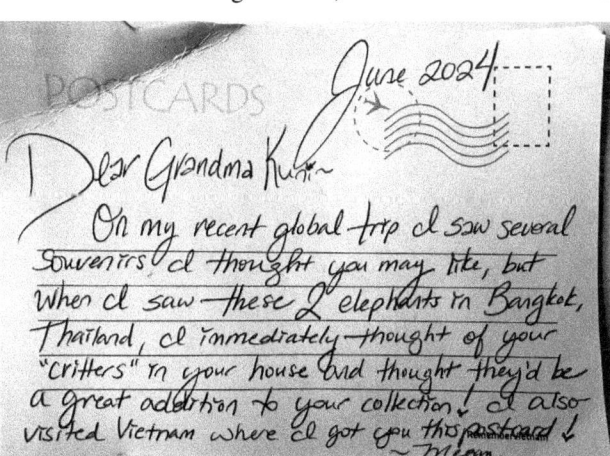

husband. Amid the whirlwind of packing— and now still unpacking in April 2025— I came across this postcard, along with the small elephant figurines it mentions.

I never had the chance to give it to Grandma Kuni, as she passed away in December 2024. And so, I include it here—for you, Grandma Kuni. I've placed the elephant figurines I meant to give you beside the one I inherited from you. One of your beloved "critters" now sits next to the ones I had hoped would join your collection.

How I cried when I found this in a box. I never sent it. I never gave it. I wasn't able to communicate that I had thought of her in my travels. It had been a joy to write a postcard and get a gift for her, as I would have done for my own grandparents if they were still alive.

So this is my invitation to you, dear reader: Write the letter. Say the words. Reconcile. Affirm. Say the "I love yous" and the "I miss yous." Speak your gratitude.

In the pages that follow, you'll find space to write a letter to someone you love. I encourage you to use it. And send it.

Love you all.

curiosity is the key to staying
interested. Plenty inquiry into
finding ones about if new idea
or perspective can help you open
soon try I don't know and
then find out more, and
repeat this practice every
single day

But then we extended our stay and I had two names,
one in English and one in German, one for home, the other for School

Section 5:
List of Contributors to
Letters Now Sent,
Volume 1

Ik ben ongeloofelijk trots op je
En kan niet wachten om e zien
h   jouw pad min volwassenheid
vervolgd En sooref   weer!

becoming is an action in the present tense.
im still, and will always be, becoming me.

I LOVE YOU,

TAKE CARE.

STAY THE COURSE.

If I could go back, I would ask you
without fear, "How are you?"
... I confused the duty I felt to take
care of you with setting boundaries to
your freedom to be said.

What a beautiful thing it is
to have such unique vivid
memories.
to be able to recollect with fond
the years you have spent in
Singkawang.

So my own daughter,
This card spoke
volumes to me - such
happy memories!
Thae you, but know
you're where you're
supposed to live.
Lots of love g love

I can imagine that someday everyone
will live as can the bud and the out
Gossip bodies as our journeys take us
will without being added to shaw our papers

Be kind to yourself, too.
Offer yourself compassion.
Keep your self talk encourag
+ be your best champion.
In the face of so many
challenges it can be easy to
fall into frustration just
because things don't flow as
well as they did before.

Many blessings to you both.

ABOUT MEGAN

Megan C. Norton-Newbanks, MA, MS, is an author, Cross-Cultural Kid/Third Culture Kid (CCK/TCK) consultant, intercultural trainer, host of the podcast *A Culture Story*, and writer at adultthirdculturekid.com. Megan's research and writing have been featured in various magazines and online platforms.

As a U.S. diplomat dependent, Megan grew up in six countries and has since lived in four more as an Adult Third Culture Kid, in addition to six U.S. states. Her cross-cultural upbringing deeply informs her work with globally mobile individuals and communities.

Her debut book, *Belonging Beyond Borders: How Adult Third Culture Kids Can Cultivate a Sense of Belonging*, equips and empowers globally mobile youth to recognize their cultural competencies and apply them in various contexts.

Combining her expertise in intercultural training with a strong background in international education, Megan designs socio-emotional and educational programming tailored to the needs of TCKs, CCKs, and globally mobile families. She regularly facilitates in-person and virtual workshops, university student retreats, and intercultural dialogue groups across sectors and international organizations.

Megan is actively involved with organizations that support expatriates and TCKs/CCKs, including Expat Valley, NAFSA, MuKappa International, the Foreign Service Youth Foundation, Families in Global Transition, and a number of Christian faith-based nonprofits and missionary organizations.

Passionate about hearing and honoring TCK/CCK stories, Megan is dedicated to supporting individuals as they navigate their sense of home, identity, and belonging.

In 2022, she launched Beyond Borders Publishing, a platform committed to amplifying cross-cultural voices and stories.

CONNECT

Connect with Us on Our Website
www.beyondborderspublishing.com

Visit our website to find out when submission forms
open for your letter to the next volume of
Letters Now Sent.

Connect with us on Social Media Platforms
@beyondborderspublishing

We'd love to hear from you!
We welcome you to reach out to us via social media
or through our website. If you have a comment or a
thoughtful response to one of the letter writers featured
in this book, we encourage you to share it. Submissions
will be reviewed, and selected messages may be
published on our platforms, allowing the authors to see
and engage with your reflections.

Belonging Beyond Borders, LLC